The Philip Johnson Tapes

THE PHILIP JOHNSON TAPES

INTERVIEWS BY
ROBERT A.M. STERN

Edited by Kazys Varnelis

The Monacelli Press
A Buell Center / Columbia Book of Architecture

Published in the United States by The Monacelli Press,
a division of Random House, Inc., New York.

The Monacelli Press and colophon are trademarks of Random House, Inc.

Library of Congress Cataloging-in-Publication Data

Johnson, Philip, 1906–2005.
The Philip Johnson tapes : interviews by Robert A. M. Stern.
p. cm.

Includes bibliographical references and index.
ISBN 978-1-58093-214-1 (hardcover : alk. paper)

1. Johnson, Philip, 1906–2005--Interviews. 2. Architects--United States--Interviews.
3. Architecture--United States--20th century. I. Stern, Robert A. M. II. Title.

NA737.J6A35 2008
720.92'2--dc22
2008022929

Printed in China

10 9 8 7 6 5 4 3 2 1
First edition

Design by Pentagram

www.monacellipress.com

Contents

8   Encounters with Philip Johnson:
A Partial Memoir
Robert A. M. Stern

16   Upbringing

37   MoMA and the International Style

62   The Right

76   Architecture School and Military Service

102   Philip Johnson, Architect

116   MoMA and the Practice in the 1950s

136   Seagram

151   Lincoln Center

165   The Institutional Commissions

182   Patronage, Competition, and the New Generation

191   Afterword: Johnson's Rolodex
Kazys Varnelis

196   Index

206   Illustration Credits

Acknowledgments

This book is based on a series of ten interviews of Philip Johnson conducted by Robert A. M. Stern in 1985. The preparation of this material for publication and the selection of the accompanying photographs have been a collaboration between Kazys Varnelis, guest editor at the Temple Hoyne Buell Center for American Architecture at Columbia University, and David Fishman and Jacob Tilove at Robert A. M. Stern Architects.

For contributions to the editorial process, we are grateful to Kurt W. Forster, Mark Jarzombek, Denise Bratton, Leah Meisterlin, Patrick Ciccone, and Sarah Acheson.

We are particularly indebted to Philip J. Dempsey, who generously allowed us access to family photo albums and provided invaluable information on Philip Johnson's family history. Christy MacLear, Jeri Coppola, and Irene Shum Allen of the Glass House facilitated the search for new photography. We would also like to thank the staff at the Getty Research Institute, including Wim de Wit, Virginia Mokslaveskas, and Emmabeth Nanol.

It has been a pleasure to work with the creative group that has given the book its form: Michael Bierut and Yve Ludwig at Pentagram and Elizabeth White and Stacee Lawrence at The Monacelli Press.

Encounters with Philip Johnson:
A Partial Memoir

Robert A. M. Stern

Philip Johnson was a great friend to me. I first encountered him as a beginning architecture student at Yale. He was in New Haven, serving on a special jury convened to decide between two candidates tied for the Winchester Prize, the school's top honor carrying with it funds for travel abroad. We did not meet, but I saw him in action as I sat with other students. I was dazzled by Philip's brilliant critical assessments of the student work he was evaluating. He talked circles around the other critics.

Like most of my fellow students, I knew about Philip's work from publications, especially his Glass House and about his role assisting Mies van der Rohe in the design of the Seagram Building. Most of us had also read his and Henry-Russell Hitchcock's book *The International Style: Architecture Since 1922* (1932), and we knew that he was an important "king-maker" because of his long and intimate connection with the Museum of Modern Art, then still regarded by students as a powerful showcase for new ideas in the arts and the only important exhibition venue for architecture.

Some of us also knew that Johnson's work was taking a new direction, that he was breaking away from Mies's austere vocabulary of gridded structural frames and entering a more playful phase. From Vincent Scully's classes, from articles in the

1. Judith Anderson (b. 1938) and Robert A. M. Stern (b. 1939) on their first visit to the Glass House, 1961.

2. Vincent J. Scully, *Louis I. Kahn* (New York: George Braziller, 1962).

3. Robert A. M. Stern, *George Howe: Toward a Modern American Architecture* (New Haven, Conn.: Yale University Press, 1975).

professional journals, and from gossip—the sometimes quite bitchy gossip of petty and jealous studio teachers—we knew of his 1930s flirtation with extreme right-wing politics, and of his homosexuality. Despite all this, or perhaps because of it, my class of first years, which included, for then virtually all-male Yale, an unprecedented number of women—six in a class of thirty-two, two of whom had studied under Russell Hitchcock at Smith College—were fascinated by this smartly dressed, highly articulate man. In his presence many of us felt more connected to the wider world of architecture than with any other architect-teacher or visitor to the school.

In the fall term of our second year a few of us got to chatting, and someone piped up that he or she—I can't remember which—would love to visit the Glass House. I was delegated to get on the phone and call Philip to ask if such a visit were possible. As I recall, I called on a Saturday morning—his telephone number was listed in the phone book!—and Philip's reply was "Sure. Bring the boys down." So a date was set—but it was "boys and girls" who arrived. I still have a photo of Judith Anderson[1] and me crossing the threshold on that first visit.

From the first Philip and I hit it off. We liked the same things. History. Professional gossip. And, as I began to help Vincent Scully with the research on his Louis Kahn book,[2] and at the same time got interested in the architect George Howe about whom I much later published a book,[3] Philip and I had lots to say to each other. With a few others, including my classmate John Hagmann, who had a car and with whom I would later form a professional partnership, I visited the Glass House two, three, maybe four times a year, sometimes on a Saturday but more typically a Sunday afternoon. As evening fell John and I would ferry Philip to the Stamford train station for his return trip to New York.

Ours was by no means the only group of Yale students to visit Philip at the Glass House. Over the years since its completion in 1949, at which time he was teaching at Yale,[4] Philip had welcomed Yale students and faculty—most notably Paul Rudolph and Vincent Scully—to what was in effect an ongoing seminar on architecture. I was thrilled

4. Philip Johnson (1906–2005) teaching at Yale, c. 1955 (above), and in 1960 (right), standing in front of a thesis project.

to be part of that informal study group, which frequently also included established architects, critics, and journalists whom Johnson would invite to lunch, as well as museum figures and artists. Johnson was age-blind: young and old were equal to him, provided they amused.

David Whitney,[5] who first met Johnson in 1960 while still a student at the Rhode Island School of Design, was a regular at these Glass House seminars; soon he would become a partner in Johnson's personal life. David was smart as a whip, capable of quick "takes" on people, with a great gift for gossip. He also had a great eye for contemporary art.

When Johnson had taught at Yale in the early 1950s, a number of students shared a loft-like space above some shops on Chapel Street. Known as The Studio, it was the setting for informal architectural discussions involving faculty and visitors (excerpts from some of these were collaged into a conversation and published as "On the Responsibility of the Architect" in *Perspecta* 2 [1953]). When, in the late 1950s, Phyllis Lambert, fresh from her triumph as director of planning for the Seagram Building, decided to study architecture she chose Yale. Probably she made that choice at Johnson's recommendation. While a student in New Haven, Phyllis restored a brownstone house a block from the school. When she transferred to the Illinois Institute of Technology, the house was rented by a recent graduate who, married with a young child, found it difficult to manage. Phyllis then asked Philip to help find a new tenant, and he approached me, stressing that its double parlor would be a great setting for parties and discussions like those which had taken place in The Studio ten years before. I took over the house until Phyllis sold it a year or two later and, as Philip predicted, it proved a wonderful place for parties, particularly after public lectures in the school.

At one party I vividly remember from 1963, Philip came to the house after giving

6. In addition to Johnson, the recording also includes interviews conducted by John Peter and Edward A. Hamilton with Ludwig Mies van der Rohe, Walter Gropius, Richard J. Neutra, Eero Saarinen, and Gordon Bunshaft.

5. David Whitney (1939–2005), c. 1975.

a lecture on his recent projects. As drinks were served, he asked me what I wanted him to do. I said, "Talk." And so he did, brilliantly, as always. This time, he began—and remember these were the early days of international jet plane travel—by saying "Yesterday in Cairo" and going on to describe a tour, I believe with Hassan Fathy, the Egyptian architect then unknown to most of us, of traditional Cairo houses, leading enthralled party guests through the spatial sequence of the plans, the play of light and shadow in the courtyards, the rooftops, and other aspects of their design I can no longer recall, in such a way as to make each of us in that room feel, at least as he spoke, that we had been with him, seeing what he saw. I emphasize this for a number of reasons. Philip was a master interpreter of architecture—one can sense this in many of his writings and in his recorded descriptions of buildings, most notably of Frank Lloyd Wright's Fallingwater, to be found on a phonograph record issued in 1956 by the Reynolds Metals Company entitled *Conversations Regarding the Future of Architecture*.[6] But I draw attention to this for another reason. At the time of this party, very many student architects at Yale were increasingly disenchanted with Johnson's work and with the man himself, whom they saw as a self-important power-broker. But even the naysayers in that party crowd had to admit the brilliance of Johnson's discourse on Cairo.

In the spring term of 1965, as my classmates and I were busily at work on center stage in the double-height drafting studio of Paul Rudolph's recently completed Art and Architecture Building,[7] finishing our thesis projects prior to graduation,[8] the telephone rang. As was the custom, whoever was nearby answered, shouting out both the name of the person being called and that of the person calling. On this occasion it was Philip calling for me, causing everyone to turn in my direction as I strode to the phone. Philip had a proposition: I would become the Architectural League of New York's first J. Clawson Mills Fellow, developing programs. The League, then a faltering institution,

 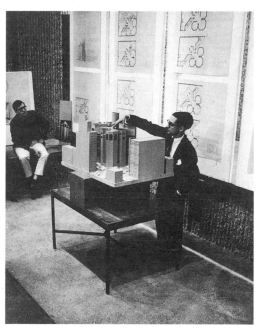

7. Drafting studio, Art and Architecture Building, Yale University. Paul Rudolph (1918–1997), 1963.

8. Robert A. M. Stern, thesis presentation, Yale School of Architecture, 1965.

had wanted to elect Philip its president but had settled for his agreeing to take on the responsibility for its programming as part of a three-man committee that also included Skidmore, Owings & Merrill partner Robert W. Cutler and Robert Allan Jacobs of the firm Kahn & Jacobs. As we discussed this tempting and flattering offer, I said to Philip that I had planned on getting a job in an architectural office to which he replied, "Why would you want to do that? I never did." Philip was very persuasive, and I took the Mills fellowship on, working for a year under his direct supervision—Cutler and Jacobs were infrequently consulted.

My year at the Architectural League cemented our friendship and our architectural co-conspiracy:[9] we would regularly meet to discuss the rising talents he admired— the Austrian Hans Hollein, especially, and for a nanosecond the Australian-born John Andrews, and those I favored, especially Robert Venturi and Charles Moore. Over many lunches he would tell me about the evolution of his practice, about his problems with his partner Richard Foster, about his misgivings over his successor at the Museum of Modern Art, Arthur Drexler, and much more. We would also talk about the history of modernist architecture—he clung to the term "modern," although he was increasingly coming to regard modernism as just a style within the larger category of modern architecture. He never took seriously the claims that modernism was an ethical or moral crusade.

The visits to the Glass House continued, through years of marriage, then divorce.[10] But they were not so frequent after the 1970s. As Philip grew older, he increasingly cherished the privacy of his New Canaan weekends as a time to relax and to do some serious architectural thinking. That brings me to the oral history project that forms the basis of this book. In 1967, when he was sixty-one years old and out of favor with critics and younger architects and experiencing considerable self-doubt, Philip entered into partnership with John Burgee. The partnership proved to be extraordinarily fruitful,

9. 1965 Architectural League dinner honoring Kenzo Tange
(1913–2005). Left to right: Paul Rudolph, Robert A. M. Stern,
Tange, Johnson, and Takeo Kamiya (b. 1946).

enabling Philip to reinvent himself as a corporate architect. But in the 1980s when professional plans were formulated on an assumption of Philip's eventual retirement, the relationship began to sour.[11] Ironically, at an age when most of us prepare to depart the stage, Philip had become more than ever a principal player. Johnson's reputation

10. Left to right, Andy Warhol (1928–1987), David Whitney, Johnson, Dr. John Dalton, and Robert A. M. Stern at the Glass House, 1964.

11. For this story, see Suzanne Stephens, "Architect Abuse/When Partnerships Are Dissolved," *Oculus* 54 (June 1992): 8–9; Mitchell Pacelle, "Noted Architects' Firm Falls Apart in Fight Over Control, Clients," *Wall Street Journal* (September 2, 1992), A: 1, 9.

12. Photograph taken at the occasion of Johnson receiving the AIA Gold Medal, 1978. Back row, left to right: Michael Graves (b. 1934), Cesar Pelli (b. 1926), Charles Gwathmey (b. 1938), and Peter Eisenman (b. 1932). Front row, left to right: Frank Gehry (b. 1929), Charles Moore (1925–1993), Johnson, Stanley Tigerman (b. 1930), and Robert A. M. Stern.

rebounded to an extraordinary extent, especially among the younger generation whom he called the "kids."[12] Consequently, tensions rose up between Johnson and Burgee as the "kids" were independently establishing themselves as design professionals and, after all, lionizing Philip—and being lionized by him.

The resurrection of Philip's reputation among the young can be said to have begun in 1975 when he held an audience of Columbia students spellbound as he delivered a lecture, "What Makes Me Tick."[13] Soon afterward, he was the focus of a weekend-long gathering of younger architects that Jaquelin Robertson and Peter Eisenman assembled in 1982, published as *The Charlottesville Tapes*.[14]

In 1982, Eisenman conducted a series of interviews with Johnson, which both of them were very excited about. Reportedly, they were exceptionally candid; but for various reasons these were never transcribed and are now only partially archived.[15] With the Eisenman tapes as background, I set out to interview Johnson at greater length with the explicit understanding that the contents of the talks would remain private during his lifetime and that the greater but not exclusive emphasis would be on professional rather than personal matters. The tapes were undertaken during my term (1984–1988) as inaugural director of the Temple Hoyne Buell Center for the Study of American Architecture at Columbia University, when I charted a program of research and outreach that included publications and public colloquia as well as a projected series of oral histories of architects undertaken in conjunction with Columbia's long-established Oral History program. During my time at the Buell Center, I was only able to conduct one series of interviews, resulting in ten tapes of approximately two hours each with Philip Johnson, recorded in his apartment at Museum Tower, 15 West

----

13. Philip Johnson, "What Makes Me Tick," in *Philip Johnson: Writings*, eds. Peter Eisenman and Robert A. M. Stern (New York: Oxford University Press, 1979), 258–65.

14. *The Charlottesville Tapes* (New York: Rizzoli International Publications, 1985).

15. Philip Johnson Papers, Box 61, 5 cassettes, Getty Research Institute.

16. Johnson apartment, Museum Tower, 15 West Fifty-third Street, New York. Philip Johnson, 1985.

Fifty-third Street,[16] between January and October 1985. These tapes form the basis of this book. The interviews offer new information concerning familiar aspects of the architect's life and career, and also introduce fresh material. The full transcriptions of the tapes, *Reminiscences of Philip Cortelyou Johnson: Oral History, 1985* are at Columbia. For this book Kazys Varnelis has masterfully edited them to restructure the discussion in accord with broad themes. To complement the text, we have included photographs of Johnson and the colleagues and projects he discusses, a significant number of which have never been published.

1. Upbringing

RS: I thought, Philip, that we should simply start at the beginning.[1] Why don't you talk about your birth, your family, Cleveland, and then just go on. You were one of three children. You had an older sister and a younger sister.[2]

PJ: I was born in Cleveland in a hospital. My mother[3] was a very strange woman. She didn't like children and so we were brought up by nannies—in my case, by a German woman. My earliest memories are of the portrait of the Kaiser in the closet that she didn't think she ought to bring out because it was near the War.

We were brought up outside the family. As soon as any of us children were born, Mother would go off to Europe with our father and leave us with a nurse. She just didn't like children.

Father[4] was an extraordinarily outgoing, lovely person, as my sisters Jeannette[5] and Theo[6] are today. I'm much more like my mother, introverted and solitary in my reactions. But I have got some of my father's superficial get-along-with-people-ism that makes me an easy speaker like Father was. He could speak on any subject and never made much sense, but didn't have to because his spirit was so strong and so pleasant and so outgoing that he was a very effective man. When he died he was called "Mr. Cleveland" because he was so popular. He was extraordinarily proud of that kind of honor in Cleveland.

1. Philip Johnson, 1910.

2. Philip with sister Jeannette, cousin Virginia, and nurse, 1910.

3. Louise Pope Johnson, 1869–1957.

But they told me in the firm—he was a lawyer—that he made no sense at all as a lawyer, that he was just a talker and the real work was done by somebody in the back room. He made a great deal of money for the family; so the money we lived on was from the back room.

My father was a gentleman. He had a few phobias and he hated blacks—no, he loved blacks and hated Catholics. I knew there was something funny. But all Middle Westerners had these kinds of prejudices so I was brought up with the usual prejudices, anti-Semitic as well as anti-, well, mostly anti-Catholic. Father thought the Pope was going to take over the country. There was a great influx of Slavs at that time, Poles and Italians.

We lived in Cleveland and, amusingly enough, just like in all Middle Western cities in all Middle Western novels, we lived on the hill, and just over the edge of the hill was Little Italy. Whenever they climbed up the hill, we'd shoo them back down again.

RS: Would you say that your family—was it a cultured background?

PJ: I would say cultured because of my mother. My father was just a farmer from outside Cleveland and to send him through law school—his father had ambitions for his son—he cut down the family forests, they had to, to sell the wood and send him to law school. But that was his only schooling; it was a pretty narrow schooling. He had no outside interests in music, art, or anything else.

Whereas my mother came from a cultured family. Her first cousin was Theo Pope Riddle[7] and her father was a cultured but impecunious businessman who kept failing in his jobs and kept getting bailed out by Uncle Alfred, Theo's father. So Mother[8] came from a failing family. All her brothers were failures, business failures, which in that world meant failure. To us, of another generation, failure in business means nothing. It may mean you were a good artist or something. But then there was only one kind of failure and that was in business. They all took minor jobs when they thought they should be doing better.

Mother was a teacher and a collector. She had stereopticons, she had lantern slides, but mostly she had sepias, mounted sepias, that in my memory were two or three feet across. There were enormous cases in the living room and you'd lift them out and

---

4. Homer Hosea Johnson, 1862–1960, pictured c. 1918.

5. Jeannette Johnson, 1902–2005.

6. Theodate Johnson, 1907–2002.

7. Theodate Pope Riddle, 1867–1946, one of the first American women architects.

there was Michelangelo's ceiling and there was Raphael and there were all the great sixteenth-century painters.

She had seen them on her travels and she was especially interested in Sienese painting of the late medieval and early Renaissance periods, Duccio to Masaccio. When we went to Europe, we were carried from museum to museum and we lived on museums and were taken on university tours. We were given culture.

RS: Did she endeavor to introduce you to the arts in a methodical way?

PJ: Not in a methodical way, but she would show us her slides all the time and she liked to lecture, and she did lecture to the Pinehurst culture group. It was pretty bad, pretty boring, and Father used to try to have her stop at forty minutes and she wouldn't. You know, all those lectures went on and on and on. She would say, "I had to make that point, Homer."

Our house was very large and full. It was done over in 1914 by a man named Dyer.[9] Louis Rorimer[10] was the architect of Mother's bedroom. This room was done in 1914 in purest Art Nouveau, ivory and mahogany swirls with special imported tiles and appliqués in German silver, whatever that was, amid a blue and cream or ivory paneling. It was a paneled room and it was an extraordinary thing for those times in Cleveland. Mother was always way out.

RS: The house, itself, had no—

PJ: No interest. It was a Tudor house, belonged to Father. Mother added a wing and made it look big, but it wasn't large.

Then in the winters Father liked to play golf and, since he wasn't much help around the office, I don't suppose it hurt anything. We went to Pinehurst, North Carolina, where we had a house. Mother would spend the winters there and Father would come down. We all imagined that he had little lady friends at home; I hope he did because mother was a rather forbidding character.

They didn't like each other very much, really.[11] Mother died first—she got to the age of eighty. My father was ninety-six when he died. He lived on after her and was terribly, terribly lonely. In other words, they had got to be very good friends.

He used to complain that she would never let people in the house. He loved to see

----

9. J. Milton Dyer, 1870–1957, Cleveland architect.

10. Louis Rorimer, 1872–1939, Cleveland painter, sculptor, and interior designer.

8. Philip with his mother, Jeannette (standing), and Theodate, c. 1917.

11. Philip with his parents and Theodate, c. 1917.

people. People mattered to the roots of his hair. Hale fellow. He was very, very popular. But he couldn't bring his friends home. In the first place, there was the problem of liquor. It couldn't be allowed in our house, not even beer or wine. All of his drinking friends couldn't come unless they got drunk before they came. They hated it in our house. There was dead silence.

So I was brought up as a loner because of my mother's antisocial attitude, which stayed with me all my life.[12] I had lots of psychosomatic troubles as a young man. I don't think I was dyslexic, but I couldn't write papers.

RS: You just couldn't finish them?

PJ: No, I was blocked, but to a degree that would indicate a dyslexia, usually, except that I don't seem to have any trouble reading. So I would not write and I'd have hysterics instead. It got so bad that they'd take me out of school, all that kind of stuff. It isn't unusual, I guess, but it was horrifying at the time. So that made me shrink even more from playing fields.

I remember when I was first sent to public school. My mother was a great believer in public education. I was sent out of our district, carried by the chauffeur in our big limousine to this public school. Of course, all of us kids tried to make the chauffeur drop us off several blocks away so we wouldn't be seen stepping out of a limousine at a public school. Then we had our own lunches with us, much fancier than anyone else's, of course, and I used to take mine out the front door of the school, which no one used, and sit alone and eat on the steps. I didn't mix with people. So I had a lonely early childhood.

In summers, we went out to New London, Ohio, where we weren't allowed to mix with the locals.[13] The farm boys were not exactly frowned on but you couldn't let them in the back door, could you? Or the front door, in their bare feet. So we were discouraged and we were alone again.

Mother would teach us. For instance, when she knew I was going away to boarding school, she started me a year ahead on Greek. And biology—she had a teacher one summer to teach us biology, pinning up frogs and things like that.

The only thing my father ever was, was violently Republican. So we were all violent liberals.

RS: So he was a liberal?

PJ: Oh, yes! He did the unforgivable—he was a good Republican, of course, until

12. Philip, c. 1918.

13. Philip, c. 1920.

Woodrow Wilson came along and he voted for Woodrow Wilson and was read out of the Republican Party. He was an Independent ever after. But he believed in justice across a green-baize table, that all the things in the world could be settled by lawyers sitting around a green table. Just like Woodrow Wilson. If you've read Woodrow Wilson, my father's mind was in perfect accord. It's the most old-fashioned thing imaginable now, but he believed in something that's just so funny that it's hard to believe that anything could be named this: the League to Enforce Peace.

RS: Like the League of Nations?

PJ: Oh, the League of Nations! Father was passionate about it. He took us to the Versailles Treaty confabulations in Paris. We lived in Paris. Father was a commissioner there for Poland, appointed by Wilson.[14] So we lived in Paris. The summers I spent learning French in Geneva. All those things were perfectly easy, but again, I went all alone. To see architecture, I learned the great way, I learned the map of the Métro. The Métro was as well-run then as it is now, and with a perfect map. At the age of twelve, I learned the whole system. Of course, none of the rest of my family could talk as good French as I could.

RS: Nor would they be seen on the Métro.

PJ: They wouldn't bother with the Métro. But everyone was surprised that they'd let a twelve-year-old boy wander around. So I found the Buttes Chaumont. The Buttes Chaumont is still the greatest romantic park in the world. It has totally artificial mountains and bridges and lakes, right in the middle of Paris.

RS: How did you happen to find it?

PJ: I just saw it on the map—it was a romantic name.

RS: So did you go to look at Les Barrières then in any systematic way?

PJ: No. You see, at that age, there was no way I could know of my future interest in the Barrières. The Barrières I saw and I appreciated, but I wouldn't have known that a gate to Paris was a monument to look at. No, I didn't really like Paris much architecturally. I still don't. French architecture doesn't give me much of a kick.

RS: When you went to Europe, do you remember seeing anything architecturally interesting?

PJ: Not architecturally. I did notice that I loved architecture and that was the only part where I seemed to depart from my mother, much to my surprise. Because I was a pure mama's boy, I had no inkling that there was any knowledge in the world worth having except what she could tell me. So when I first liked a building—I guess it was the Parthenon, naturally—I burst into tears and she didn't know why.

That she didn't see what I saw there was as annoying to me as it was to her when I didn't appreciate a Simone Martini that she liked in the Siena museum. But we wouldn't be disagreeable to each other, and I loved all of the museums with her, but couldn't partake of her particular passion. Although later I did—my rooms at Harvard had nothing but Simone Martini.

RS: So that was her passion originally?

PJ: Yes, I got that from her. And then I got interested in music through Theo, my sister, who wanted to be a singer. So I decided that I wanted to be a singer. Well, it

---

14. Together with Henry Morgenthau and General Edgar Jadwin, Homer Johnson was appointed to a committee to investigate wartime massacres of Jews in Poland.

couldn't have been a stupider idea. But we all have crazy ambitions and all of mine were cultural. I never wanted to be in business. I couldn't see the sense in making money.

We must have disgusted Father. I didn't want to be a lawyer, I showed no interest in it at all.

RS: Did you play the piano also?

PJ: I played the piano extremely badly.[15] I used to play dual pianos with my mother, who really was quite good. I played in public once, God help me.

RS: When you say extremely badly, you only mean by comparison with a professional. You were competent, more than competent.

PJ: No, I wasn't. I could play one or two pieces by the time I got through. No, it really was a disgrace. But I knew that finally and got out of it.

RS: So you went to Hackley[16] and you obviously learned how to write a paper somewhere along the way.

PJ: No, I never did. My writing was always crabbed. If I couldn't say it in a few words, I didn't say it at all. I never was a writer. I always had trouble with my papers.

At Hackley, I was first in the class, except that I got beat out by a chap who was a harder worker, more consistent, more logical. I was always fog-minded. He could work harder and more logically than I could. So he became first in the class and we both went on to Harvard, same year. All without exams in those days. They were so anxious to take the bright kids from each school.

RS: What happened to that poor fellow?

PJ: He is still in Worcester. Dim, grim, and . . . nothing. He was nothing at the time. I couldn't understand why he got better marks than I did, it was obvious that I was the brighter kid. I was voted the most likely to succeed, which wasn't very hard. [Laughter.]

RS: Well, I think you've done it.

PJ: As it happened, yes. That part went all right.

I was still completely alone. It was an all-boys school. There was no such thing in those days as coeducation. I was in love with a—no, I had a crush on, that was the word in those days—one of the older boys. But I hadn't become in any way active sexually at that time. And then the teachers, several of whom were homosexuals, were very kind to me, but we never became friends. But I knew the teachers better than I knew the students, always.

In fact, the next year I took "Daddy Bogues,"[17] one of the best and most popular

---

16. Hackley School, Tarrytown, New York.

17. Frank Ellis Bogues, 1878–1970.

15. Philip playing piano at the Hackley School, 1922.

teachers there, on a motor trip through England to see the English cathedrals. But all he wanted to see was where Samuel Johnson wrote his *Dictionary*, or something, and I went off to look at Winchester Cathedral. I spent my entire summer looking at cathedrals and couldn't understand why he didn't. You see, I never could understand why everybody didn't adore architecture.

It seemed to me it was a contrariness that should be slapped out of them.

RS: But by this time your own architectural interests were defined.

PJ: Yes, but not out loud. I mean, I was just going to Europe. To me, going to Europe meant going to look at cathedrals. Of course, I couldn't express it that way. Nobody asked me, "What do you want to see a cathedral for?" So we sort of parted company by the end of the summer in spite of the fact that I was responsible for taking him, and that was the end of that. At the same time, in summers, I was sent out to camp in Montana, which is the other love I've never forgotten, of the mountains and horses.[18]

RS: This was to toughen you up?

PJ: And become a man? Nothing like that. This was a cultural camp. This was a camp—

RS: Oh, my word, I never knew there were such things.

PJ: Yes, we had a biologist as the head of the camp. The *sportif* types couldn't understand why we went there and pinned little firs to pieces of paper. But I, on the contrary, wanted to know the name of every goddamned little grass, you see.

RS: Which you're still interested in?

PJ: I become interested in anything I'm working at, don't you? What's the point of me sitting out there and not learning something?

Harvard Undergraduate

RS: So, you graduated from Hackley when?

PJ: 1923.

RS: What did you think you would do with yourself when you got to Harvard?

PJ: Music. I lived at Symphony Hall. That was as a freshman. And since I was so lonely, I didn't really do much except music, listen to music. But it was more that than any real passion, because I haven't got a good ear. Oh, I joined the Harvard Glee Club,

18. Philip, third from rear, vacationing at the Grand Canyon, 1923.

but I can't keep a tune very well. You know, maybe it's better to be a lonely person because you do then start looking and being intellectually curious, inquisitive.[19]

My first kick in architecture was, of course, Greece.

RS: This was a trip with your mother?

PJ: Yes, that was in 1928.

RS: 1928!

PJ: Yes. Very late. We did Egypt and Greece and Italy and the Flemish countries, all that one trip.[20]

RS: With your parents?

PJ: No. My father wouldn't go.

RS: With your mother? Still, you were that old—

PJ: Very old, twenty-two. Still a virgin and still hadn't gotten off on my own in any way.

RS: Intellectually?

PJ: Or physically or psychologically.

RS: What did you do at Harvard? There were all those interesting people, some of whom became your friends.

PJ: Well, they were, again, teachers. When I took a beginning philosophy course, I became a friend with the chief teacher, Raphael Demos.[21] He became a lifelong friend, even if he had troubles. We ate together almost every night at either the Harvard Club in town or a Greek restaurant; he was Greek. But none of the others—well, one or two students, nothing that ever lasted; I never knew anybody.

RS: What about Kirstein and people like that?

19. Philip, 1925.

20. Philip in Egypt (top) and in Sicily, 1928.

21. Raphael Demos, 1892–1968.

PJ: Lincoln was there. Lincoln Kirstein[22] was a very powerful figure around the campus and the art world. I would shyly say, "I'd like to join," but he doesn't remember me then.

RS: And Eddie Warburg.

PJ: Eddie Warburg[23] was a class ahead—neither of them were quite classmates. I was held up by psychological troubles I was having at the time.

RS: Did you have a nervous breakdown?

PJ: A nervous breakdown—those are just words, perhaps, but what I had was what my nerve doctor—in those days we didn't have psychiatrists—called psychothymia, that is, manic depression.

I couldn't write; I couldn't read. I couldn't do the work in school. In none of my courses could I work. I had just a total block on my life. So he said, "Why don't you go home for a year? And when you get to where you feel better, you come back." He was a very, very good doctor, a real healer, like a priest. And I said, "What can I do?" He said, "There's nothing you can do. Just forget it." I went home and used to call him monthly, "Doc, you've got to do something! I'm in agony." He said, "I told you I wouldn't see you. Now, you just stay there."

So I cried all day long. I read detective stories every day—started piling them up in the corners. And he said, "You'll get over it. You don't think you will, but you're going to get over it. It's just like pneumonia or a broken leg or anything else. Don't be silly." But it had been caused, of course, by my homosexuality. And not understanding it and not knowing how to express it. This was his analysis. It never crossed his mind, as it would since then, to try to do anything about it. It never crossed his mind that I should express it in any way.

But he found out who I was soon enough, after all the interviews. He kept catching me looking at the art on his walls. So he said, "Well, that's very unusual. You're interested in art." I said, "Oh, am I?" It seemed to me perfectly natural to study a work of art on the wall. That's when he said, "Well, there've been an awful lot of people who've led very successful lives as homosexuals: Tchaikovsky and Shakespeare." I said, "Oh, that's interesting. I never knew that."

RS: You just had very little self-awareness.

PJ: I thought I was the only one who had these feelings. He said, "Oh, heavens! You can make a perfectly good life." That was the beginning of my saying, "You can."

I thought I was going to die a total failure at the age of twenty. That feeling kept

22. Lincoln Kirstein, 1907–1996, publisher, ballet impresario, c. 1927.

23. Edward M. M. Warburg, 1908–1992, philanthropist, c. 1930.

recurring. I'd go back to Harvard for six months, or half a term, and then break down again.

During one of those summers, I went to Heidelberg. It was the summer of 1929. I was fascinated by the German language, which, of course, I'd learned as a child, but I didn't know that I had. It made learning German quite easy. I lived with a family that couldn't talk a word of English, which is the only proper way to learn.

RS: How did you justify the trip to Heidelberg?

PJ: Well, it was summer vacation. You were supposed to travel.

RS: Why Heidelberg as opposed to Berlin?

PJ: Heidelberg was culture, you see. It sounded more cultural. Then too my sister Jeannette was sent to Berlin in 1913 and was there when war broke out and she had to run and scramble back the way Theo had to scramble back from Paris with the next war. So I went to Heidelberg and promptly fell in love with the first kid that walked down the street. I mean fell in love—no physical problems, but I became attached to him. Of course, it was a very good way to learn a language. The horizontal method is always the best way. So I learned to speak German. Speak it but not write it. I can't read great literature. I can read the newspaper, but I can't read Goethe. Nobody believes this, of course, because I sound just like a German. But I don't really know the language. I was always getting by on things.

At the time the architecture part was not so important. More important was that I had a car. Of course this was most unusual; we're talking 1929 and a car in Germany.[24] But I had to have my local car—of course in those days it was a Cord, a front-wheel-drive Cord.

RS: You had one shipped over from the States?

PJ: Oh, yes. I always brought my cars from the States. Another summer I went with mother and we had the car and chauffeur and drove around Europe.

RS: That sounds like Edith Wharton.

PJ: Yes, like Edith Wharton. And yet it didn't seem funny. It really didn't. Mother wasn't that type at all. She was a very earnest art looker-ater. By then, of course, I was looking at every church in southern Bavaria. We visited Vierzehnheiligen and all the famous churches.

RS: Well, when you looked at them, you obviously had an appreciation.

PJ: Yes, although I didn't know I was going to be an architect or a historian. That didn't ever cross my mind. I was just enjoying it. I didn't know what I was going to do. I don't think anybody does [know] unless they're pushed, at that age, into what they're

---

24. Philip's note on clipping from German newspaper, 1929: "How would you like me to call on you in this? The best car I have seen yet."

going to do. So when the question came along as to what I should major in at Harvard, I was getting along very well with this professor of 101 Philosophy [Demos], so there was nothing more natural than to go into the philosophy department, where I got along better with the teacher than with the material.

25. Alfred North Whitehead, 1861–1947, philosopher.

HARVARD UNIVERSITY
CAMBRIDGE, MASS.

Jan. 19

Dear mother,

Last night I went to Prof. Whitehead's house with Demos. I actually had a few words with the great man all to myself. He is a wonderful person. His wife is a peach and all the others there were intelligent. I was a most successful evening from all points of view.

Peter and I went over the Sermon on the Mount the other night and tried to interpret it to our own satisfaction, he reading the German and I the English. We are ashamed of our helplessness, and I am ashamed of his ignorance. I thought most people were abysmally ignorant, but I did not know there was anyone who thought that Jesus had written the four Gospels. But after a page or so we got branched off on the subject of the existence and the relation of good and evil and never got back to the Bible.

Last night I was telling a friend in Demos' presence that I had changed my field of concentration to Philosophy thanks to Mr. Demos. Whereupon Demos speaks up," Just now he is concentrating in Demos, next year in something else I suppose." To have him express is was too funny. Thank good ness his sense of humor is wider than philosophy. Mr. Whitehead's mind is superior to any subject or subjects. He is human first.

I like to think that I am not narrow enough to get all A's in my courses. Warren Farr gets A 's but what does he know. He knows he knows much less than I do. I say I like to think so but I reality realize that all it is is a laziness to do the extra amount of work between mediocre and excellent work. That extra amount is considerable and it is the dross of the labor. I can get the point of the course and, what is more and bears no relation to marks, of the subject. But our system of education is so rotten that any way of grading is bound to be poor. Boys like Warren Farr live in an uninteresting world so that since they have a modicum of intelligence and curiosity they can throw themselves into their work. But Warren, for instance, is absolutely incapable of abstract thought or of interest in it. He knows a lot about his work, but seldom correlates it to his own experience. Conundrum; Why is a steam engine like our educational system? Ans: Because it is 6% efficient.

If it is any warmer in Pinehurst than it is here tonight I am sorry for you. Your summer clothes will stifle you. We have all our windows open and go out of doors in our shirt sleeves. The snow has all disappeared in a day. Strange winter.   Love, Philip

26. Letter from Philip to his mother, January 19, 1926.

Whitehead[25] and then especially Mrs. Whitehead and I became great friends. She collected weak, young, attractive students who'd gather around on a Sunday evening and listen to the great man.[26] But she would have another group that she'd talk to too. We used to take rides in the country. Lots of fun.

But I was absolutely no good as a philosopher. I could do the regular work. If you had to do the history of Aristotle's thought, I could bone up on it. I was very interested in Aristotle. So that was easy. But the metaphysics or any abstract thought wasn't my dish, and this finally all came out. It was at the time of my so-called nervous breakdown. Whitehead, who was trying to be kind, said, "Philip, I always give only A's and B's in my class because I don't like marking. It doesn't make any sense to me. And you got a B." I flunked, obviously. I knew it. I went off and never saw him again.

And I realized that that wasn't the world for me. Well, then, what was? Was there a world at all?

RS: That's what sent you back home.

PJ: That sent me back home several times. I was determined to become a writer at one time and a professional musician at another. Different things happened. One time I had to leave because I couldn't do a term paper. I had the block again. Of course, that was a good excuse. One invents excuses for oneself.

I couldn't draw—I still can't—but I knew that lots of other people couldn't either, so that didn't bother me too much. But it never crossed my mind to go to architectural school, because all you were taught were washes. Washes were very much like trying to fix this [tape recording] machine, as far as I'm concerned, hopeless.

The entrance to Harvard Architectural School required a manual dexterity in handling washes and the outlines of the orders. Well, that struck me as not the way. But then I was beginning to get more and more interested in architecture. And in 1928 I picked up—of course, the famous story's been told many times—I picked up a copy of *The Arts*.[27]

See, Mother must have sent me subscriptions to these magazines. Why would I have ever seen *The Arts*? There was an article by a man named Hitchcock[28] on an architect named J. J. P. Oud.[29] Just one picture—the Hook of Holland—and I said, "My future's in architecture." As simple as that. A Saul-to-Paul conversion.

THE ARTS

H. R. HITCHCOCK ON THE ARCHITECTURE OF
J. J. P. OUD—J. G. FLETCHER ON THE SCULP-
TURE OF ERIC GILL — VIRGIL BARKER ON
THE PAINTINGS OF ALLEN TUCKER

50 cents a copy   FEBRUARY, 1928   *$5.00 a year*

27. Henry-Russell Hitchcock, "The Architectural Work of J. J. P. Oud," *The Arts* 13 (February 1928).

28. Henry-Russell Hitchcock, 1903–1987, historian of architecture, coauthor with Johnson of *The International Style: Architecture Since 1922* and co-organizer of the exhibition *Modern Architecture — International Exhibition.*

29. Jacobus Johannes Pieter Oud, 1890–1963.

European Travels with Hitchcock

RS: So you didn't know Russell—

PJ: I didn't know Russell.

RS: —who was presumably still at Harvard?

PJ: He was three years ahead of me. Well, by then he had finished. I was in one of my extra years in 1928. But my mother was head of the alumnae at Wellesley and knew there was a man who was teaching there named Alfred Barr.[30] She said, "You ought to meet that man. He's interested in modern architecture." She couldn't understand why the hell I wanted to look at these funny-looking buildings. So then I split with my mother's eyes. My eyes, while sympathetic, were not of the same channel. Then, with this in mind, I met Alfred Barr. At the third meeting, Barr said, "Would you like to start a Museum of Modern Art? I'm founding one in New York next year, with Mrs. Rockefeller[31] and I want somebody to do architecture."

So I said, "Of course."

RS: Did you pay your own way when you got there?

PJ: I had about a million dollars, which in these days is nothing but in those days was comfortable. So I could pay my own salary. That was the big thing. I charged into the Museum in 1929 and I founded the department because I was so immensely wealthy that I could pay my own salary and pay my assistant's salary.

RS: What was Barr like in those days?

PJ: Well, you talk about private people! But you see, we were both private people and we hit it off enormously. We both had the ridiculous Puritan idea of reform, for instance, which went along with the International Style, long before we knew about the International Style in architecture. We both had the reformist zeal, he in museology, and me naturally in architecture. So he said, "I know Hitchcock. Don't you want to meet him?" I said, "I'd do anything to meet him. I mean, this is the future of the world." To me, it was! So in the spring of 1930, we met in Paris.

RS: Not at Harvard?

PJ: No, he wasn't at Harvard. He was teaching at Wesleyan. We said, let's take a trip around and look at all the architecture, the modern architecture, of which there is very little. So I bought a car and we started out.

RS: The three of you?

PJ: Two of us.

30. Alfred H. Barr Jr., 1902–1981, art historian, first director of the Museum of Modern Art.

31. Abby Aldrich Rockefeller, 1874–1948, socialite and philanthropist.

32. Henry-Russell Hitchcock, *Modern Architecture: Romanticism and Reintegration* (New York: Payson & Clarke, 1929).

33. Robert A. M. Stern, *George Howe: Toward a Modern American Architecture* (New Haven, Conn.: Yale University Press, 1975).

34. The last line of text in *The International Style: Architecture Since 1922* reads: "We have an architecture still." Published in New York by W. W. Norton and Company, 1932.

RS: Just you and Russell? What was Russell like in those days?

PJ: Much the same as he is now. He was very excitable but extremely knowledgeable. His book *Modern Architecture: Romanticism and Reintegration* was already published and, of course, it was my bible at that time.[32] He'd written that as a graduate student, the way you wrote your seminal George Howe book when you were a graduate student.[33] Of course, that appalled me because I didn't have that kind of a brain or knowledge of history, ever. But just the sheer excitement of seeing all these things! For him, it was a great chance to see things that he wouldn't get to see.

RS: Because you had the car.

PJ: I had the car and the money. So we made a perfect team and we went around. In the middle of it we decided: why not make it into a book? Because we felt so strongly that this was "an architecture still" and that we had to preach it to the world.[34] I was more excitable and excited than he was and I influenced him slightly.

RS: Yes, you must have, because you say that he was excitable and, you know, Russell is not to me an excitable person.

PJ: Well, yes, he is, in an entirely different way. I mean, there was his "stop the car!" business. We spent one summer—was it 1930 or 1931 or 1932 or 1933—in Chicago. He was studying the Chicago School; I was pulled along. We stopped the car in the damnedest west side slums. He would say, "There's a building by [Louis] Sullivan." I would say, "Well, it certainly isn't." And it was, and it wasn't in Morrison.[35] It didn't exist when you looked it up.

Hitchcock just knew from driving by. And it was early Sullivan, which doesn't look like Sullivan, as anybody knows now. But Russell knew that when he was just a kid. I mean, he just knew those things.

He could steer me off my bad enthusiasms in modern architecture, when I would like a building and he wouldn't. But mostly we liked the same things. We split when we came to the top, though. He was a Corbusier man—although he didn't know it—completely, and I was a Mies van der Rohe enthusiast. But Hitchcock used to say about Mies that he was too decoratory for him. He [Mies] liked the pattern of the marble; he liked silk; he liked Macassar ebony. None of this was Corbusier's dish. He was really a Purist painter.

RS: Corbusier was a moralist and Mies was not a moralist.

PJ: Mies was an anti-moralist, but Russell wasn't a moralist either.

RS: If you didn't get them from Mies, where did you get your morals?

PJ: I cannot imagine where except in the air. I mean, the whole German movement, you see—Russell's German wasn't as good as mine—and the whole German movement was a moralist thing. Of course, they became more English than the English through Muthesius,[36] who got it from Morris[37] and Ruskin.[38] I didn't realize how much that morality was influencing me. When we started to write the book [*The International Style*] it was perfectly clear that we were going to write it as an anti-moralist moral lecture in the end. But showing through that text is my moral fervor for reforming the world.

Of course, Corbusier was both. Don't forget, there was a historical admiration

---

35. Hugh Morrison, *Louis Sullivan, Prophet of Modern Architecture* (New York: The Museum of Modern Art and W. W. Norton, 1935).

36. Hermann Muthesius, 1861–1927, German architect who was a leader of the Werkbund and an expert on English architecture.

37. William Morris, 1834–1896, leader of the British Arts and Crafts Movement.

38. John Ruskin, 1819–1900, British art and architecture critic.

of ancient times, as in his Mediterranean studies, and then his contradictory urbanism and moralization.

RS: Urbanism was academic French at the core.

PJ: Ridiculous. And his morals—like, you'd be a better man if you lived in a glass house kind of thing—well, it was in the air.

The only sensible man was Oud and I don't think his modern architecture book has been translated to this day, has it?

RS: No. First of all, he made the sad mistake of not producing.

PJ: On the contrary, he had written the best of the Bauhaus books, but that book has not even yet been translated.[39] He was the one who attacked Corbusier: "I do not see what is so great architecturally about a steamboat." I myself think it is a very beautiful object. But, you see, *Vers une architecture* was his great enemy. It was and still is a very contradictory book.[40]

RS: Absolutely.

PJ: Oud was much more sensible. So Oud and I became much better friends than Oud and Russell or Russell and I.

RS: Although Oud was the first of Russell's researches.

PJ: Yes, it was Oud's articles in French magazines and then later in American magazines that got me interested in architecture. So that's the first thing we did. We got into the car and drove to Rotterdam.

Oud[41] was a charming, outgoing, sensible, good designer in the most down-to-earth fashion, unlike Corbusier, whom I never—you couldn't—like. Corbusier would never know whether you were there or not. It was brilliant talk and we enjoyed it. But there was no rapport, any more than there was with Mies, really, ever. But with Oud you could become friends. I did and we corresponded and I helped him out through the war with CARE packages.

RS: You commissioned a house with Oud.[42]

PJ: Well, I didn't commission it. But he said, "When I work on a building, it has to be specific. Now, it isn't that you're giving me enough money to build a house, but you've got to give me a project. I'm not a fantasist." In other words, he was distancing himself from Taut[43] and from Corbusier's ideal plan. He didn't approve of that. Mies would too. He was more like Gropius, I suppose—I hate to say that about anybody. But I'm the same way. I like to have a client—you do too. I want to know that it might be built. Otherwise, I can't take it seriously and get my mind on it. Whether that's

---

39. J. J. P. Oud, *Holländische Architektur*, Bauhausbücher 10 (Munich: A. Langen, 1926).

40. Le Corbusier, *Vers une architecture* (Paris: Éditions Vincent, Fréal & Cie., 1923) translated by Frederick Etchells as *Towards a New Architecture* (New York: Putnam & Warren, 1927). See also the critical translation by John Goodman, *Toward an Architecture*, introduction by Jean-Louis Cohen (Los Angeles: Getty Research Institute, 2007).

41. J. J. P. Oud (center), with his wife and László Moholy-Nagy, 1894–1946, in Kijkduin, Netherlands, c. 1926.

good or bad, we don't have to discuss right now. But anyhow, he felt that so strongly that I said, "Mother, you don't have to pay for it, but why don't we design a house for Pinehurst?" She thought it was an absolutely glorious idea: "Where shall we put it?" So we picked a lot and sent him a topo and he said, "Well, how many bedrooms?" Mother made it up—she had no trouble. She loved to build houses. She'd always wanted a Frank Lloyd Wright house, all her life, from way back before I was born, 1906. Father wouldn't ever build houses. We were always redoing houses.

RS: In the 1920s, to go back to that, did she redo houses again?

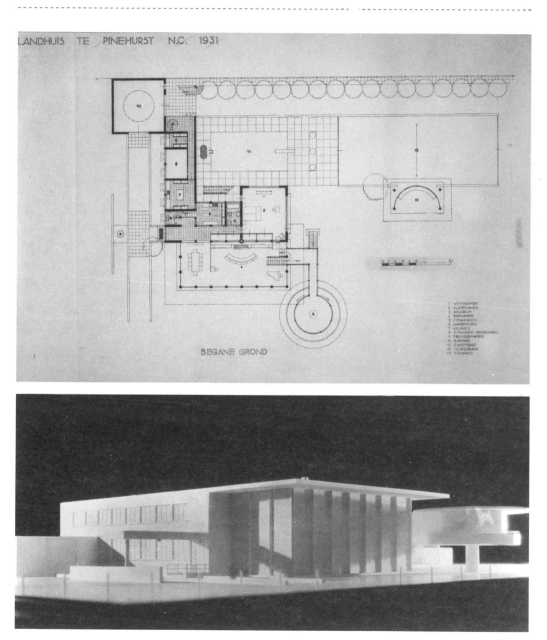

42. Project for Johnson family house at Pinehurst, North Carolina. J. J. P. Oud, 1931. Plan and model.

43. Bruno Taut, 1880–1938, German architect who founded the Glass Chain, a group of young architects who exchanged utopian fantasy drawings, after World War I.

PJ: Yes, she used Donald Deskey[44] in Pinehurst. That was at the time of my break-down in the 1920s. He did modern architecture, Art Deco, post–Art Deco, sympathetic. There weren't any neo-Art Deco garlands or angles like Kahn's[45] lobbies or anything fancy, but he was a modern interior designer. Alfred Clauss[46] also worked for my mother. I commissioned Clauss to do the dining-room table. And Donald Deskey did the chandelier, I remember, which was a series of tubes that hung down from the ceiling making a horrible light. But it was all very modern. He did some chairs for Mother. Mother was always up with the latest modern.

RS: That explains why she sent you the Hitchcock article.

PJ: Oh, she didn't send me that. It was a subscription. No, I found that article by myself and was just knocked over by it. Funny, I remember the day. I spent the day in a fog. And of course, that was our first stop, the Hook of Holland.

RS: What were those places like then?

PJ: Well, as I recall them now through the fog of history, all I know is that my excitement was so great that I could not understand the rest of the world, you see. Why, if you'd seen the Hook of Holland,[47] why wouldn't you give this man a country to build? I just didn't understand.

Of course, my greatest enemy, intellectually, was the Amsterdam School, de Klerk,[48] which I rejected completely. Russell didn't.

RS: Even then?

PJ: Even then. Russell said, "You're making a great mistake. Don't just cut things off this way." It wasn't called the Amsterdam School then. It was called Dutch modern architecture. Russell said, "Amsterdam is terrific. You mustn't say that Hilversum, Dudok,[49] or the Zonnestraal"—what was the name of the architect? Bijvoet[50] and Duiker,[51] "or the Van Nelle Factory are the only things to see in Holland." There was this fantastic craftsmanship that was in the expressionist—whatever the Amsterdam School was called. And we went to look at it. I said, "Oh, Russell, let's go on and get back to the real stuff." But Russell was always broadminded.

RS: He was the historian and you were the —

PJ: Well, he was much more. I mean, he was never a Scully.[52] He wasn't an enthusiast in different directions. He was always that strange balance.

RS: And Russell was trained as an architect, to some extent.

PJ: Russell went to architectural school and left after a month because he simply had no hand, any more than I do. Handling those washes—they just went all over the

---

44. Donald Deskey, 1894–1989, interior and industrial designer.

45. Ely Jacques Kahn, 1884–1972, prominent New York architect specializing in office buildings.

46. Alfred Clauss, 1906–1998, architect.

47. Hook of Holland housing project. J. J. P. Oud, 1924–31. View under construction with Oud and probably his son.

place. They said, "You don't belong here, young man." He, of course, was equally livid with what you had to do with the orders. To this day, his only feeling that I remember as not being completely objective was his dislike of the orders. If he saw a pedimented order or a Georgian projecting porch, he wouldn't like the building. Palladio wouldn't interest him in any way. It's his one, if you want to say, prejudice.

RS: So going back to Harvard. You're traveling around Europe during these three years and obviously you're looking forward. The whole political situation that you get involved in later, was this anything to you at this point?

PJ: Nothing, absolutely nothing. But I later got interested in that in a funny way. A great friend of ours was an art dealer here in town, a woman, Mrs. Read.[53]

RS: She was an art critic, wasn't she, for the *Brooklyn Eagle*?

PJ: Art critic, that's right. But then later her sister worked at the Whitney Museum as a desk lady for twenty or thirty years. But she was the art critic on the *Brooklyn Eagle*. Heavens, how would you know that? She was a perfectly lovely lady and she was a Germanophile. I have no idea why. A spinster lady, who later became head of Portraits, Inc. She lived in one of those old Brooklyn houses up on the Heights. It was wonderful. I don't know how we became friends; it had nothing to do with politics. But once we ran into her in Germany. Mother was with us; we had the limousine, 1931 or 1932. 1932, probably. She was a friend or an acquaintance of Putzi Hanfstaengl,[54] who was the propaganda chief for Hitler. She said, "Wouldn't you be amused to go and see one of these rallies?" It was out in the fields in those days. It was long before they were great organized affairs, so maybe it was 1931. It was febrilely exciting.

At that time, you see, what it appealed to was, believe it or not, the socialist side, the moral side. I mean, Germany was being run down by the rich. The German Workers Party was the only solution.

He [Hitler] was a magnetic, shall we say, speaker. It was how he did it.

RS: Of course.

PJ: Mrs. Read influenced us a great deal to listen to what was going on in the German Workers Party. So then I started reading the *Völkischer Beobachter*. Their paper was better written than the liberal papers and more pungent. It was more like what the *Daily News* was in its great day, and easy reading. That was pretty good for a foreigner. And the brilliant *Tageblatt*. All those people who were Manchesterian

---

48. Michel de Klerk, 1884–1934, Dutch architect.

49. Willem Dudok, 1884–1974, Dutch architect.

50. Bernard Bijvoet, 1889–1979, Dutch architect.

51. Johannes Duiker, 1890–1935, Dutch architect.

52. Vincent Scully, b. 1920, architectural historian and critic.

53. Helen Appleton Read, 1887–1974.

54. Ernst Putzi Hanfstaengl, 1887–1975, Harvard-educated German-American, later Nazi enthusiast, publisher, head of the Foreign Press Bureau in Berlin.

and long-winded and liberal said, "This is all wrong, what these people want." To any idealist, you either became as Isherwood did—who was there at the same time—a communist, or you didn't. And I didn't. Of course, having money may have helped. But I think it was a matter of temperament more than anything. The days in Berlin were exactly as he describes.

RS: Isherwood? It was as he recorded it?[55]

PJ: It was as he reported. Exactly! It's fantastic! I walked almost the same streets as he did—with the one exception that he lived in the communist district—with German boys. I was picking up the same boys, because I was awakening in Germany, which was the logical place to awaken. . .

And that added excitement to go back to Germany in the summers.

RS: What about the literary situation in Berlin?

PJ: In Berlin it was sin, mainly, as it was for Auden and Isherwood, that attracted us there. And the life that went with the sin. The incredible music and dance, the plays. Writers I didn't know so much. But of course there were the art exhibitions with Flechtheim.[56] He was a leader; he just makes Castelli[57] look like a joke. Flechtheim was a very great man who started the beautiful magazine *Der Querschnitt*.[58] Berlin was great for magazines, for feuilletons, in the way that Vienna had been.

We had photographers like Lerski,[59] who did my portrait. You know, the photograph of me with just sort of a half face and a hat on.

RS: I forget. Oh, yes, yes, yes.

PJ: And somehow or other life was kept busy. Of course, there were the great museums of ancient art. It was an enormous center. There is no way of telling—though Isherwood does it best in his *Berlin Stories*—the feel of the town. Just driving around Sundays down to the Schinkel works and back was an incredible experience.

RS: How about your mother?

PJ: That was the last trip with Mother, 1931 or 1932, whenever the chauffeur was along. Then I got excited, I suppose through Russell, although he was never as excited as I was, about Persius,[60] the architect who I thought was the only good Schinkelschüler. I thought that the Gärtnerei in the Sanssouci Gardens, the garden pavilion there, which may be the greatest work of the romantic side of Schinkel, was a good Persius.[61] But Russell knew perfectly well that it was Schinkel, and, of course, Russell did not err.

---

55. Christopher Isherwood, 1904–1986, English author of *Last of Mr. Norris* (New York: W. Morrow and Company, 1935) and *Goodbye to Berlin* (London: The Hogarth Press, 1939), published jointly as *The Berlin Stories* (New York: New Directions, 1946).

56. Alfred Flechtheim, 1877–1937, German art dealer.

57. Leo Castelli, 1907–1999, American art dealer specializing in neo-avant-garde works during the 1960s and 1970s.

58. *Der Querschnitt* (The Cross-Section) was a journal of literature and culture that published many of the leading thinkers and artists of the day such as Walter Benjamin, Richard Huelsenbeck, Michel Leiris, Carl Einstein, George Grosz, László Moholy-Nagy, and Ludwig Mies van der Rohe, while also publishing articles and images on Americanism, sports, nudism, and other aspects of contemporary life.

59. Portrait of Philip, c. 1930, by Helmar Lerski, 1871–1956.

So I said, "Well, here's a gap. Maybe I want to be an architectural historian, even if second rate. But let's just try." I had a camera made, if you please, a big mahogany thing that took up a lot of space.[62] A most elaborate thing. I wish I hadn't thrown it away. It was the most beautiful German instrument-making. You see, nobody had any work until 1932, and I could get the most fantastically detailed things. For instance, the plates that came down over the thing—they were big plates that we were using—were done in hundreds of little strips of wood that were made together like a curtain.

RS: You mean like a tambour?

PJ: Tambour! That's the word. It was a real pleasure just to close that tambour. Each one of those strips, all highly polished wood. I'd have James get out and set up the tripod for me.

Poor Mother would have to sit in the car and wait for me to go and set up my camera so that I got my collection of Persius pictures.[63]

RS: I can't even imagine you taking a photograph with an Instamatic, no less this. Just to have the patience for it. What happened to those pictures?

PJ: I don't know. Isn't it appalling! I have a few lying around. Yes. Jeannette may have some left.

Anyhow, I took pictures and that was my first inkling that I was going to be connected definitely with architecture.

RS: That summer.

PJ: That summer of 1930 or 1931 or 1932. The years get mixed up in my mind. Theo would know the exact summer. But my passion in those days was Persius, not Hitler.

Then the next year I must have gone over. I wasn't there in '33, so in '32 I was there and I did go to Nuremberg.

---

60. Friedrich Ludwig Persius, 1803–1845, architect, disciple of Karl Friedrich Schinkel, 1781–1841, painter and architect.

61. Johnson is referring to Schinkel's Gardener's House at the Sanssouci Gardens, Potsdam, 1829–1833. A *Gärtnerei* is where the plants are raised and the tools are kept, and, in this instance, where the gardener lived. Architectural historian Kurt Forster suggests that in its dainty proportions, modest scale, and refined details, it does look somewhat like a Persius. Since Persius was in Schinkel's office at the time, he may indeed have had a hand in it.

62. Philip, with custom-made camera and chauffeur James, Potsdam, Germany, 1932.

RS: Now, 1932 would have been after the opening of the modern architecture show at the Museum of Modern Art.

PJ: Yes, that's right. 1932 it opened. So my passion and work were all involved in that. But afterward, as sort of a vacation, I went to a Parteitag in Nuremberg and, of course, got very, very excited. Then I continued to work at the Museum until 1934.

63. Philip's photographs, 1932, of Orangery (top) and Wirtschaftsgebäude (farm building), Schloss Glienicke, Berlin-Zehlendorf, by Ludwig Persius, c. 1839.

2. MoMA and the International Style

RS: Well, let's go back a bit. You finally finished Harvard when?

PJ: 1930. I was Class of 1927, but I lost a half a year here and a half a year there and then took the other half a year in Berlin to work on the book.

RS: You mean *The International Style*?

PJ: Yes. And I had a secretary because I was doing all the dirty work.

Russell was nice enough to list my name, but it wasn't an equal collaboration by any means. I did the dirty work gladly. I wrote to all the people. It was very hard to collect pictures. It was hard then because there weren't very many good pictures and they weren't publicity minded, these architects. So I had to sometimes go and get them directly.

RS: Did you see everything that was in the book?

PJ: Everything, but I remember one we did not see, the de Mandrot House. I didn't see Mathes either.[1]

RS: But you went to the Tugendhat House?

PJ: Tugendhat I went to twice.[2] All the Czechoslovak houses and all the German and all the Dutch.

RS: And the Tugendhats were, as I imagine, the great bourgeois heavy, unimaginative family?

---

1. Le Corbusier's de Mandrot house, Le Pradet, France (1930–31). Johnson could not have seen Le Corbusier's Villa at Mathes, France, as it was not completed until 1935.

2. Tugendhat House, Brno, Czechoslovakia. Ludwig Mies van der Rohe, 1930. Children's room (left) and garden facade.

PJ: Very heavy. They were unfortunately, Jewish, and had some interest in worldly things, but not a bit of interest in architecture. I didn't see them when they were here last; Arthur[3] did.

RS: Do they still exist?

PJ: Yes, they went to Venezuela, into exile in Venezuela.[4] I visited the house. It was pretty gruesome, because Mies used only industrial lighting, of course, and I went at night the first time.

RS: I know the lights are practically just bare bulbs.

PJ: They weren't bare; they were very pretty things, neo-Behrens. I mean, descended from Behrens's[5] work. Concentric shapes. Very pretty to look at, but the lighting was just appalling. But the only defeat that Mies felt was the Oriental rug in the library.

RS: And the great sliding glass doors did work?

PJ: They worked perfectly. There was no problem. You see, German technology during the Depression was entirely at the disposal of Mies — as it was for George Howe's time at PSFS. George said, "You just can't believe it. We could go to Cartier's and say, 'Make us a clock.'" And the clock was made by Cartier's.[6]

Today you have to take what's in the catalog. Nothing had to be taken out of the catalog in those days. Mies had everything made too. There was no trouble getting his chairs made.

I asked him, "How do you get this craftsmanship?"

"What craftsmanship?"

He just drew the outline of the chairs. Lilly Reich[7] took care of all the art part.

RS: And he had young men in the office who were very gifted, I assume, at carrying out his designs.

PJ: He had one or two, but the one great gifted person was Lilly Reich. Oh, oh, what a woman! A really great woman. But mean. And perhaps she should be.

Let's keep to the subject.

---

3. Arthur Drexler, 1925–1987, architectural curator, director of Department of Architecture, MoMA, 1956–1985.

4. The Tugendhat family: Grete Tugendhat, 1903–1970; Fritz Tugendhat, 1895–1958; Hanna Lambek, née Weiss, 1924–1991; Ernst Tugendhat, b. 1930; Herbert Tugendhat, 1933–1980; Ruth Guggenheim-Tugendhat, b. 1942; Daniela Hammer-Tugendhat, b. 1946.

5. Peter Behrens, 1868–1940, German architect and industrial designer.

7. Lilly Reich, 1885–1947, interior designer romantically involved with Mies, pictured with him on an excursion boat on the Wannsee, near Berlin, 1933.

8. Josef Hoffmann, 1870–1956, Austrian architect and designer.

9. Josef Frank, 1885–1967, Austrian architect and designer.

6. Clock, Philadelphia Saving Fund Society Building, Philadelphia. Howe & Lescaze, 1929–31.

We were maundering around getting the book ready. We went to Vienna, but nothing.

RS: Did you see Hoffmann[8] or any of the older figures when you were in Vienna?

PJ: Not that time—I saw him later—because we were looking for a certain specific modern architecture building. I'm trying to think what architect we visited. Josef Frank![9] He wasn't very good. We didn't feel him sympathetic toward International Style. The minute you crossed the Czech border it was a brand new state, you see. They were more gung-ho for modern.

RS: Did you go to the fair in Stockholm?

PJ: We certainly did. In 1930, I was there at the fair.[10] I met Asplund[11] and Åhrén.[12] We thought then that Asplund was pre-modern or half-modern or whichever word we're using these days. We didn't study him in depth or we would have been more appreciative, I'm sure. But it was the library[13] which I rather liked and I liked the town hall.[14] Russell, of course, spurned that as romantic nonsense. The fair was pure International Style by Asplund. And we saw Åhrén's Theater and things of that kind. But we didn't go to Finland, so we didn't see Aalto.

RS: Was it a conscious decision not to?

PJ: No, it was just awfully far, at that time. We should have gone. We knew we should have gone.

11. Erik Gunnar Asplund, 1885–1940, highly-regarded Swedish architect whose work evolved from classicism to International Style modernism to a widely emulated synthesis of the two in his last project, the Woodland Crematorium (1935–40) in Stockholm.

12. Uno Åhrén, 1897–1977, Swedish architect and critic.

13. Stockholm Public Library. Erik Gunnar Asplund, 1918–28.

10. Stockholm Exhibition, Stockholm, Sweden. Paradise Restaurant. Erik Gunnar Asplund and Nils Einar Eriksson (1899–1978), 1930 (top); Advertising mast and press gallery. Sigurd Lewerentz, 1930.

14. Town Hall, Stockholm. Ragnar Östberg (1866–1945), 1923.

RS: What about the whole split in the show between a European or international perspective and an American perspective? And then your and Russell Hitchcock's discovery of Wright?[15]

PJ: That was the most difficult thing and the most delicate. I, of course, being a propagandist, wanted to make it pure.

Alfred and Russell quite rightly believed that if we could get more Americans in, it would make a more complete and not so European-looking show. So by stretching and pushing and shoving, over our own better judgments, we got in Ray Hood,[16] who we at that time believed to be the best architect of the decade. But we felt that he wasn't very sympathetic with our moral point of view and, indeed, he wasn't. That was the only real battle we had with Ray.

Russell actually called him one day and said, "Mr. Hood, would you mind taking off the ornament on that building that you handed in for the show because it doesn't really fit in with our policy of the show?"

The obscenities that came back on the phone should have been recorded. He said, "Look, if I put decoration on a building, it's because I like decoration on a building." He was, of course, right, but it didn't fit our definition, and Russell felt that it wasn't such a terrible tower but that the ornament was really disgusting, which it was.

RS: He had to have the ornament on the top of McGraw-Hill, presumably.

PJ: I never liked the McGraw-Hill, but we were discussing his tower.

RS: Oh, the Dobbs Ferry—

PJ: The Dobbs Ferry tower[17] that he handed in for the show. See, we had it in front of us and were getting the catalog ready and here was his only building in the show.

RS: Did he make that building up for the show?

PJ: He made that building up for the show, not that he didn't have a prospective client. He probably did. In fact, I remember reading about it. But it was always his idea that one should live in tall buildings. What his relation was to Corbusier's living in tall buildings, I don't know, because he always pretended not to know who Corbusier was.

---

15. Frank Lloyd Wright, 1867–1959.

16. Raymond Hood, 1881–1934, architect specializing in skyscrapers.

17. Project for an Apartment Tower in the Country, Dobbs Ferry, New York. Raymond Hood, 1932.

18. Telegram from Frank Lloyd Wright to Philip Johnson, January 18, 1932.

19. Joseph Lyman Silsbee, 1848–1913, architect; Wright's first employer.

Anyhow, he felt that we were insulting his architectural integrity, which, of course, we were. Then the other great battles, of course, were with Frank Lloyd Wright.[18] But it's interesting that he did a more modern building for the International Style show than he'd ever done in real life.

RS: And in researching for the book you also went to visit Wright?

PJ: We visited Wright.

RS: It is apocryphally stated that Russell told you you should go see Wright, and you said, "I thought he was dead."

PJ: Not in connection with this. But I did think once that he was dead. Then the other famous remark I made was that he was an architect of the nineteenth century. But we had been fighting a good deal around the time I said this. Some of our exchanges are in that book of Wright's letters, but not the bad ones.

We went to see Wright in 1930 in Taliesin East. I stayed overnight in the part that's now all closed in and ruined, in the upper terrace there, just above the big room. We visited and had a great time and we realized that he was a very, very great man. But he and I didn't get along. It was a love-hate relationship from the beginning.

Russell, not being as dogmatic as I was, was very interested in Silsbee[19] and in the Hillside Home School,[20] which was a total wreck at the time. We enjoyed seeing that very much, although it was very romantic, I felt. Rigid, very good old stuff.

We did realize this, and that's why we put him in the show. But we wanted very much to have the absolutely latest modern thing. I'm surprised he accepted.

RS: Who paid for Wright's Mesa project in the show? Did you advance money for it?

PJ: We advanced money to each of the architects in the show, whether they had money or not.

RS: Was that your money?

PJ: No. Well, some was my father's. It sounds funny now, but all the architects jumped at the chance.

RS: Well, it was the Depression.

PJ: $2,000. It was the Depression. This would be near $50,000 now. Anyhow there wasn't a single architect who didn't drop everything. Mies put his money in his model; he sent a beautiful model—I mean, well constructed. Corbusier sent the dump that we have.[21] Frank Lloyd Wright had the kids put up some matchsticks.[22] Of course, it fell apart right away. Hood had a decent model made. See, that sum was to include everything.

20. Hillside Home School, Spring Green, Wisconsin.
Frank Lloyd Wright, 1903. Photograph c.1932.

RS: The model, the photographs.

PJ: Whatever they wanted. They could spend it on the model if they wanted to. We had the photographs made.

RS: Then there were the Bowman brothers.[23]

PJ: That was Philip Johnson's little contribution. They made a very slick rendering of those houses and it was published in the *New York Times*, by accident. You know the Sunday *Times* does an odd article when you least expect it. And they were very horizontal, International Style–looking.

I wasn't able at that time to make judgments about quality. I felt that a ribbon window was a ribbon window was a ribbon window. That was the characteristic that made modern architecture what it was. I think Russell was a little doubtful, but we needed Americans so badly that we took them in.

Then we made a really bad mistake, which I think I should take the blame for myself, which was to leave out Schindler.[24] Although Schindler always was more de Stijl than modern, International, nevertheless, he was an architect of, even at that time, greatness. I liked his later work, his juicier work, better, but at least he had done his own house. I had visited it.

RS: Oh, you had been there. Had you seen Schindler's Lovell Beach House[25] or, for that matter, the Lovell House by Richard Neutra[26] in Los Angeles?

PJ: I had not seen the Lovell Beach House or the Lovell House.

RS: Because Russell had. He had written about them before.

PJ: Yes, I know. He had seen Neutra's Lovell House. But maybe that's why I didn't see it. How I got to Schindler's Kings Road House,[27] I don't remember. It was right across from the Dodge House[28] and so we wanted to see that.

But Schindler, you see, refused to agree to the term International Style, and he was at that time estranged from our American leader, Richard Neutra. So Neutra got all our friendship and love in return for his smartness and pushiness. Neutra was a publicist of the worst kind and later on proved not to be a very good architect, whereas Schindler was exactly the opposite. And I've been looking at it today in Gebhard's book on Los Angeles—it is a marvelous guide.[29] Of course, he liked Schindler. Schindler got better and better in the 1930s, something I didn't know.

RS: Did you go out to California to see the Neutra?

21. Le Corbusier exhibit, *Modern Architecture — International Exhibition*, The Museum of Modern Art, New York, 1932. At center: Model of the Villa Savoye, Poissy-sur-Seine, France, 1930.

22. Frank Lloyd Wright exhibit, *Modern Architecture— International Exhibition*, The Museum of Modern Art, New York, 1932. At right: Model of Project for a House on the Mesa, Denver, 1932.

PJ: No, but I think Russell did. I never saw the Lovell House. I still haven't seen it.

RS: Now that you must see! You know what I think of Neutra, but it's still—

PJ: I know. It's still the best.

RS: If you have to do one building, you might as well get it right, and that's it. He did get it right.

PJ: Yes, that's the one. But I remember arguing with him about it. I said, "Why do you have these spandrels here in metal and these spandrels in stucco?" His answer was not the truth, which was it was better-looking that way. His answer was, "I like to experiment with materials and wanted to see what the metal looked like." He always would use the wrong reasons to justify sometimes perfectly right decisions.

But Schindler, I missed on entirely. I should have known better. But his work wasn't strict enough to the goddamn rules that I invented. Those little strange quirks kept showing up. His original house, being cut in two and being cramped and crabbed and difficult, really was horrible. The later things that had freedom of massing were much more interesting.

RS: What about Bucky Fuller in relationship to these?

PJ: Bucky Fuller[30] and I always disliked each other because I told him he wasn't an architect. I gave the A. I. A. in public—written—form hell for giving a medal to a non-architect, whereupon Bucky, of course, took a year off and became an architect.

RS: Oh, really? I didn't know that.

PJ: Yes. He went to school and passed all his state exams. Of course, he was a very quick learner.

RS: A very bright man, but impossible.

PJ: Impossible. Oh, you did know him?

RS: I did know him, yes.

PJ: You see, I had known him at Harvard in 1927 or 1926, when he first showed the Dymaxion House, and then we had a show of him at the Modern. But we didn't think he was an architect. So we didn't put him in the show.

----

23. Irving Bowman, 1906–1990, and Monroe Bowman, 1901–1994.

24. Rudolph Schindler, 1887–1953, Austrian-born architect living in Los Angeles.

26. Richard Neutra, 1892–1970, Austrian-born architect living in Los Angeles; his Lovell House dates from 1928–29.

27. Kings Road House, West Hollywood, California. Rudolph Schindler, 1922.

28. Dodge House, West Hollywood, California. Irving Gill (1879–1936), 1914–16.

29. David Gebhard and Robert Winter, *Architecture in Los Angeles: A Compleat Guide* (Salt Lake City: Peregrine Smith, 1985).

30. Richard Buckminster Fuller, 1895–1983, inventor and technologist, initially known for his Dymaxion house (1927) and three-wheeled Dymaxion car (1933).

25. Lovell Beach House, Newport Beach, California. Rudolph Schindler, 1922–26.

From Harvard to New York

RS: Before we go back to what you saw in Europe, I'd like to hear about how you went from Harvard in 1930 to New York. You had Barr's invitation to help put together the museum.

Presumably every day you went to the office, or what?

PJ: No, there was no room in the Heckscher Building.[31] There were no places to sit down, so my secretary would come to my apartment at 424 East Fifty-second Street.[32]

RS: And that's where the Mies room was installed?

PJ: That's where the Mies room was installed and Lilly Reich—let's say it—did all the work. Just one amusing change there: of course, my piano was part of my life. Mies said, "Do you have to have that piano in that room?" I said, "No." Thank God, because of course he made room. There wouldn't have been room enough at all.[33]

RS: Was that the only room in your apartment? Was it a one-room apartment?

PJ: No. It was one bedroom. Mies was a great admirer of the American apartment house plan because it was so extremely logical, with closets and everything. In Germany, there was no place for closets; you just put cupboards up against the wall. He thought our planning by Candela[34] and those people was far superior.

RS: If the study looked as it did in the book, what did the rest of the apartment look like? Did you take a flight of design in the other part of it, in the bedroom?

PJ: No, he did the bedroom.

RS: Oh, he did. I've never seen a photo.

PJ: Oh, yes, you have, but you didn't know it was a bedroom, because it had that cabinet that I now have in the country at the end of the bed and then the silk with the squared patterns came down to the floor. It looked like a couch. And the bookcase—the books all fell down. I mean, it wasn't made practically, so I had to redesign some things to hold the posts back against the wall. He had the posts out in front of the books.

RS: So with no lateral support.[35]

---

31. Heckscher Building (Warren & Wetmore, 1922), 730 Fifth Avenue, where MoMA had its first galleries, 1929–32.

33. Johnson may have been mistaken. The plans show a piano in the living room.

34. Rosario Candela, 1890–1953, architect specializing in apartment houses; later, during World War II, cryptographer.

32. Philip Johnson apartment, 424 East Fifty-second Street, New York. Ludwig Mies van der Rohe and Lilly Reich, 1930. Study.

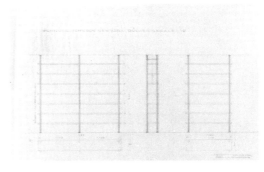

35. Elevations and plans for bookshelf in Johnson apartment. Ludwig Mies van der Rohe, 1930–31.

PJ: It was a post from floor to ceiling, so of course the weight pushed out the little things and then they crashed.

RS: This was all made in Germany and sent to the U. S.?

PJ: All made in Germany; all itemized and calculated. There wasn't a mistake of any kind and there wasn't a test. We didn't say, well, did we like this or did we like that; It was done.

RS: So you were here in New York setting up this department of architecture and you also undertook to design a few apartments. I know you did one for Warburg.[36]

PJ: Eddie Warburg. You couldn't sit in the chairs. They were quite handsome, but impossible to sit in.

RS: Oh, you designed chairs for him, the furniture?

PJ: We designed the furniture, except the Mies furniture and the table. Of course, Poppa[37] sat on the edge and fell in the classic way that you do on a Mies chair. Before they were taken over by Knoll[38] those chairs used to tip. In fact, the ones I have do. But no one in the last forty years has done that.

RS: One learns to suffer adversity for art.

PJ: One does. It's funny. You want to change chairs? Those chairs are much more comfortable.

RS: No, no. I'm fine. I'll suffer for art.

PJ: You suffer for art.

36. Edward M. M. Warburg apartment, 37 Beekman Place, New York. Philip Johnson, 1933. Living room.

37. Felix Warburg, 1871–1937, banker and philanthropist.

38. Knoll International, producer of workplace furnishings designed by major International Style architects.

RS: So you did Warburg's apartment.

PJ: That's the only one I did.

RS: What was New York like? How were you maneuvering in the scene? An Ohio boy from Harvard who had a little trouble getting through college arrives in New York.

PJ: I said to my family I was moving to New York.[39] They didn't say anything. Now, Theo[40] came with me and lived in the apartment there at the—what's that called, the gardens where Katherine Hepburn still lives.[41]

RS: Were you then making friends with Lincoln Kirstein and people like that?

PJ: Yes, it could have been the beginning of that. I was also on my search for other architects. Alfred Clauss came from Germany with Daub,[42] an American.

Then Ray Hood.[43] I was a great admirer of him, but he was a tough nut.

RS: What was he like?

PJ: Very rough, very bristly. Well, he was a bristly man and he had this bristly hair. He felt like a hairbrush. Very quick and snappy and impatient.

I was mean. I said to him, "Why did you put that front on the Daily News Building? The Daily News Building was beautiful. They just applied that stuff; they didn't connect it." He was so mad. He said, "If you had a client come to you and you had to design in six weeks, you'd have put a grille like that up there too." In other words, he knew it. The famous apocryphal story about the top, I don't know if it's true. Hood said to Frank Lloyd Wright, "I don't know how to end it," and Wright said, "Why don't you leave it alone?" It doesn't sound like either one of them.

RS: No. Well, it sounds like Wright, but it doesn't sound like Ray Hood.

PJ: No, but of course before that he had had tops on them—on the Radiator Building. I tried to get him further work, but he was too busy on skyscrapers.

RS: Did you get him that Dobbs Ferry job?

PJ: No, no, I never got him a job, dammit. Mrs. Sullivan[44] wanted to develop the

40. Johnson and Theodate in the apartment they shared at 241 East Forty-ninth Street, 1934.

41. Turtle Bay Gardens. This is the apartment at 241 East Forty-ninth Street.

42. George Daub, 1901–1966.

39. Philip Johnson apartment, 241 East Forty-ninth Street. Philip Johnson, 1934.

point that stuck out into the river up there where she lived, just north of the big Pennsylvania Railroad bridge.

RS: Hell Gate.

PJ: Hell Gate is a big thing. It comes out into the Salt Run now, but it was all woods then. She said, "Let's develop it all." So I said, "Ray, come out to Mrs. Sullivan's and we'll do something about it." He said, "Another Christ-awful lunch. I don't want to do that." He was quite right, of course, but I didn't know at the time that if you're a busy man the last thing you want to hear about is a fly-by-night development somewhere.

Who else? Lescaze[45] I knew very well, of course, through Howe,[46] but why did I know Howe? I knew Howe because of Sheldon,[47] but why did I know Sheldon? Through Daub? Through Clauss? Possible.

But George Howe, of course, was the greatest gentleman we've ever had in architecture. He had thorough sympathy, but no knowledge at all about what went into putting a piece of design together in this field, as marvelous as he was with those early stone houses. He didn't know how good they were. He was such a modest man. I think I met him [Lescaze] through Howe and even then they didn't like each other very much. He and I were very suspicious of each other. Of course, he was working on spec for the Museum of Modern Art tower.

RS: Did you bring him in on that?

PJ: No. He just appeared. Both he and George were in on that and did several schemes.[48]

RS: Very interesting ones.

PJ: Very interesting, yes. They had nothing to do with the museum. They weren't very practicable, but that wasn't the point. The point was that they pointed in good directions. So I got to know him and his wife very well.

RS: What about Hugh Ferriss?[49]

PJ: Hugh, of course, I knew, but, again, the skyscraper school was an aberration to me at that time. Everything had to look like the PSFS[50] or nothing.

RS: So it was oil and water.

PJ: Yes, oil and water. I was so narrow-minded.

RS: Let's talk about the museum some more. Barr was there and working away at his museum. What was your relationship to Mrs. [Abby Aldrich] Rockefeller?

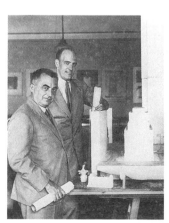

43. Raymond Hood (left) and Wallace K. Harrison, 1895–1981, with model of Rockefeller Center, c. 1931.

44. Mrs. Cornelius J. Sullivan, née Mary Josephine Quinn, 1877–1939. She lived at 1801 Wolcott Avenue (now 21st Avenue) in the Astoria section of Queens.

45. William Lescaze, 1896–1969, Swiss-born architect living in New York.

46. George Howe, 1886–1955, Philadelphia-based architect who adopted the International Style in 1927; later, 1950–54, chairman, Department of Architecture, Yale University.

47. Sheldon Cheney, 1886–1980, architectural writer.

PJ: Mrs. Rockefeller Jr., was of course very close. She was a great patron of ours, of Alfred's, and a very strong woman indeed. Blanchette[51] tries to copy that strength. Of course, she's not the same woman. She [Abby Rockefeller] never had any money; that was the catch. Mr. Rockefeller wasn't sympathetic to the museum idea.

RS: At all?

PJ: Not at all. So he grudgingly went along—to keep her happy.

RS: And the other cofounders?

PJ: Well, then I became closest with Nelson[52] and we became friends for the rest of our lives. He was away when the Museum was founded.

RS: Probably just out of college.

PJ: Yes, and he was sent around the world for the usual broadening tour. But she kept saying, "Wait until Nelson gets back. Wait until Nelson gets back." And indeed it was, of course, a revelation. Then Wally,[53] who was close to Nelson personally, took over the closest relationship and I became lower down the line for Nelson.

RS: Wally was married, of course, to a Rockefeller and also didn't have your political tastes.

PJ: No. You see, my political tastes were particularly anathema about that time, and quite rightly. That was about 1934.

RS: Were you just allowed to play at architecture and design because it was a subject nobody knew anything about or—

PJ: I was allowed to play because I had Alfred Barr's backing and I paid no attention to budgets. I paid no attention to dates. I could interrupt the dates and put on my own shows whenever I wanted.

RS: Did you pay for the shows at the Museum of Modern Art yourself?

PJ: I paid for the shows. They didn't amount to much. I had my own secretary, which I paid for. So there was no expense to the Museum, which was the only way we

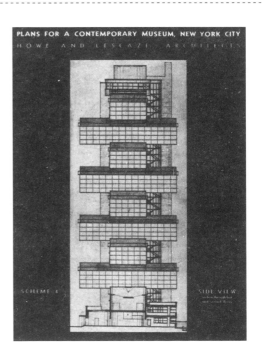

48. Proposals for The Museum of Modern Art, prototypical site. Howe & Lescaze, 1930.

got the department started because the trustees didn't like it at all. I came a cropper the night that I tried to explain the thing to the trustees. They were horrified and Mrs. Rockefeller tried to defend it to her brother who was on the board, a very great architect named Nelson Aldrich.[54]

RS: Not the same Nelson Aldrich—

PJ: The father.

RS: Oh, the father was an architect as well?

PJ: Yes. But I don't think he was Nelson—something Aldrich. It could have been Nelson Aldrich. But he hated the idea of modern architecture, you see.

RS: Modern is all right for painting, if you must.

PJ: That's right.

RS: So you really made yourself a job.

PJ: Yes, I created the job. And without Alfred, they'd have thrown me out lots of times because I was a goddamn nuisance around the place.

RS: You're still not very popular there.

PJ: Really?

RS: That's what you hear outside. Troublemaker.

PJ: Troublemaker. Well, that, of course, is a thing that never bothered me much.

RS: But when you took off from the Museum, the Museum continued to have architecture. How do you explain that?

PJ: Well, by then the department was established, you see, and Alfred could call upon my successor [Kaufmann] and John McAndrew.[55]

PJ: He [McAndrew] and I, strange to say, had started talking in front of the Manet in the Mannheim museum, the great *Execution of Maximilian.*

He was an architect and I was an architect and I said, "I'm just wandering around alone. Shall we go look at some architecture?" So in 1929 he and I drove all over

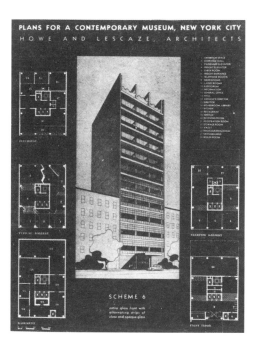

49. Hugh Ferriss, 1889–1962, architectural illustrator.

50. Philadelphia Saving Fund Society Building, 1929–31, Howe & Lescaze's pioneering skyscraper in Philadelphia.

51. Mrs. John D. Rockefeller 3rd, née Blanchette Hooker, 1909–1992.

52. Nelson A. Rockefeller, 1908–1979, second son of Mr. and Mrs. John D. Rockefeller, Jr.

53. Wallace K. Harrison, architect.

54. Johnson is referring to William T. Aldrich, 1880–1966, father of Nelson W. Aldrich, 1911–1986. Both were Boston architects.

Europe looking at architecture. It was the year before I met Hitchcock. And we were in Prague when the Crash came and I came home. I wanted to support my family. But there was no reason to; I wasn't hurt, and it was a lot of trouble.

RS: Your family survived the Crash easily enough.

PJ: Well, lawyers are not bad off.

RS: They get to preside over the doom and the gloom.

PJ: They learn better every time. My nephew[56] says every time they change a law in Washington, they add another hundred men, especially a tax law. They are in clover. If they were in clover before, think of this year.

So John McAndrew and I became good friends and went around looking. He wasn't as enthusiastic about the International Style type of work as I was. Of course, Prague to us was a baroque city and that was what we looked at. In Berlin, I guess it was mostly sex. Isherwood period.

RS: Did you go out to the Bauhaus, the actual building?

PJ: Oh, yes, I went out to the Bauhaus.

RS: With McAndrew or with Russell?

PJ: I think both. That was very impressive indeed, and that's when I met Paul Klee.[57] I bought my first little Klee for seventy-five dollars. I was afraid to tell my mother because it was too much to spend.

RS: It's worth more than seventy-five today.

PJ: Oh, I know it would be worth $750 or $7,500.

RS: $7,500, maybe.

PJ: About ten times. But then he was unknown, of course. It was one of his early shows in Munich, and I went and bought it from him.

I was only twenty,[58] so collecting was a small part of my life. That influence came through Alfred Barr. You see, we all know where these strains come from.

Now, I had met Gropius,[59] but I think Hannes Meyer[60] was already at the Bauhaus, you see.

55. Edgar Kaufmann Jr., 1910–1989, design curator and historian; John McAndrew, 1904–1978, pictured above, architect and curator.

56. John Dempsey, 1888–1963, lawyer.

57. Paul Klee, 1879–1940, Swiss-born artist.

58. Johnson was actually twenty-three years old.

59. Walter Gropius, 1883-1969, architect, founder of Bauhaus; later, 1937–52, chairman, Department of Architecture, Harvard University.

60. Hannes Meyer, 1889–1954, architect, director of Bauhaus from 1928 to 1930.

I think it was the first time I met Mies, too, in 1929. That's why I already knew Mies before I met Oud and Hitchcock. Hitchcock never could see Mies as a great—

RS: Person?

PJ: No, as an architect. Nobody saw him as a person. He didn't talk any English and whatever language he talked was rather slow and rather uninteresting unless we had many martinis.

RS: But he was revered as a guru, at least at the end.

PJ: Oh, my God! Yes! Well, Russell would never dare say a word against him, but he wasn't his enthusiast. You really can't tell with Russell. It's almost subcutaneous, his enthusiasms, because he's so objective-seeming.

RS: But Mies wasn't a person to have a meal with.

PJ: He was only for me.

RS: You could?

PJ: Well, he was lonely and I loved to talk German.

You know what it's like to play with a new toy. I never could talk German; I can't talk now at all. But he and I never talked English. That loosened him up. But the two martinis! In Europe, it was schnapps, of course, straight.

RS: Did you, when you went to Paris, go to the Villa Savoye?

PJ: Yes, I did, in the spring of 1930.

RS: What were your impressions of it?

PJ: I was flabbergasted. I'd been well prepared, don't forget, having seen all the pictures by then, and being totally excited by Oud. I still found it willful—not "lifted-finger," but arbitrary in a way that I didn't find Oud. I was surprised by the painting influences of the decoration of the roof, for instance, and the colors. To me the colors weren't necessary for the architecture, and they could mar the architecture. Although, of course, I was a functionalist still.

RS: Still!

PJ: Well, I hadn't begun to be one yet, but I mean, that came with the package. And the ramp, which I can perfectly well see from an artistic point of view—you need it—made a hash of the usefulness of the house. So I was a little disappointed in certain ways, and very, very excited in other ways. But the idea of lifting the house up on those pillars sent a thrill through me that I had hardly had before, never had before. It was one of the great moments.[61]

61. Villa Savoye, Poissy-sur-Seine, France. Le Corbusier and Pierre Jeanneret, 1929–31.

RS: Was the family in residence? What was it like? Who were they?

PJ: Yes. They were very bourgeois, very non-spoken and didn't know why we were there. They had built a famous monument so they couldn't keep people out, but they wished we weren't there.

It was underfurnished; it remained that way, of course. Another thing that disappointed me was the approach: you came in from the ass-end, you see.

RS: Past that little gatehouse.

PJ: Well, the gatehouse was the most charming thing of all.[62] I mean, never has a gatehouse been such a piece of perfection. The posts are exactly the right distance in, and the windows are exactly the right proportion between the top and the bottom. That was a jewel. But you came in at the back of the building, almost flat. The flat side made two dog's legs out of the elevation.

62. Villa Savoye. Poissy-sur-Seine, France. Le Corbusier and
Pierre Jeanneret, 1929–31. Gatehouse.

63. Michael Stein, 1865–1938, older brother of Gertrude Stein,
1874–1946, and his wife, Sarah Samuels Stein, 1870–1953,
American expatriates.

64. Villa Stein, Garches, France. Le Corbusier, 1926–27.
Entrance facade with gatehouse on right.

RS: That's right. It's in and out almost like a drive-in.

PJ: What do you mean almost? It is. Then you go in and drop off. That is not a fitting entrance.

RS: Did you go with Le Corbusier?

PJ: No, no I didn't. I went with Russell and Alfred, maybe not with Russell, but certainly with Alfred. Alfred was just as excited about modern architecture, of course, as we were.

RS: Did you go to the Villa Stein as well?

PJ: I went to the Villa Stein. I remember there was a great reception. They were there. The Michael Steins.[63] The house, of course, was a great favorite of Russell's because of the connection with people he knew. But not to me. To me, it was a disappointment. To me, it was a house that had a double entrance, again a problem—the servants' entrance and the main entrance.

RS: It had a nice gatehouse also.[64]

PJ: The gatehouse I don't even remember. It had the one-story gatehouse, not the two-story gatehouse.

RS: Right.

PJ: But then we came around to the greatest space, and that's the back,[65] the great terraces, the double terrace, and through the double terrace to two single terraces. I still find it hard to imagine how it worked so incredibly well. Then you got up to the middle-sized terrace, and up to the roof of the lower terrace and down to the lower terrace, framed. And that was the excitement! I really felt that the master had outdone himself. I prefer that to any single effect at the Savoye House.

RS: But what about the twisting circulation from the entrance hall?

PJ: That part I just didn't like. I didn't like the double curve of the stairs. It didn't send me, let's put it that way. But then his finishes never did. The house, you know, is just stucco, just thrown together. He obviously was an artist who thought in spatial terms and color but not in materials, and not in comfort, and not in functionalist terms—no place to sit. He never sat down.

RS: Well, it was stuffed with furniture, that house.

PJ: My memory is not "stuffed."

RS: The photographs I've seen are just filled with rather heavy Spanish chests.

PJ: I know. And that's what I always think of in the pictures. But my memory of the house is that it was empty, practically empty.

65. Villa Stein, Garches, France. Le Corbusier, 1926–27.
Rear façade (left) and living room.

RS: And color on the walls?

PJ: Color, color, but nothing like Savoye. Nothing as beautiful as the pink and chocolate and blue of Savoye.

RS: Going back to Savoye, what did the family use that top roof deck for when you were there?

PJ: Nothing.

RS: Nothing.

PJ: Absolutely empty. Of course, it was an experience if you wanted to walk way up there for no reason. It was just tacked on there to make the curves. Then, you see, since Le Corbusier didn't particularly care about building, the top part had to be held up with pilasters.

RS: That's right, yes.

PJ: And they were very out of keeping. What you're supposed to do is to see the house from the fields and from the outside, where it's always photographed from, but we never saw that. And on the inside all these pilasters and beams, retaining beams, were very awkward. It seems to me, well, post-Monday morning, it would have been very easy just to tell them to make it a thick wall. It wouldn't have made any difference.

RS: The ideology of it—

PJ: Yes, the ideology was very important to him. And then the back corridors of the Savoye were about 5′ 6″, more like a Frank Lloyd Wright corridor.

All these feelings were answered when I got to the approach to a Mies villa, the big entrance. All his corridors were eight feet. All his ceilings were high. All finishes were perfect, no color. Standard.

RS: Mies never used any color.

PJ: No color on the walls, no artificial color. The walls were sacred to him. So all of his things appeared just in one house, the Tugendhat.

Bauhaus

RS: How many times did you see the Bauhaus?

PJ: Many times, five or six times. The Germans had airlines then, when no one else did. Dessau was only an hour's drive from Berlin, but I took an airplane. I was the only passenger usually, and I was so amazed by having an air service with a regular timetable. Mainly I went to visit Klee. I didn't visit the director who was still there at that time, Hannes Meyer. I failed to realize how good he was.

RS: You never met him at all?

PJ: Never met him. And Mies didn't much hold with him because he was a communist. He was very obviously not there for long. And I visited Kandinsky.[66] Klee and I stayed with him for half a day, just going through pictures, and that was a thrill of a different kind.

The Bauhaus building, I loved. I didn't like what Russell and I always called even in our book, the fake banding—that is, the painting of the space in between the windows in gray, to pretend they weren't there. We always thought that didn't work. Gropius was always trying to pretend there was a window where there wasn't. Well, no one does that anymore. But the Bauhaus was great, of course, from the glass side, in the front, and then the little windows in the back, the little balconies —

RS: Where Herbert Bayer[67] took those photographs . . .

PJ: Famous photographs, Bayer photographs, wonderful.

RS: Did you talk to Bayer and Moholy?[68]

PJ: I talked to Bayer when he was already back in Berlin. Breuer[69] too was in Berlin. They had left because of Hannes Meyer, I suppose.

RS: Did you know the Americans who studied at the Bauhaus [70] in those days?

PJ: Yes, I think I did. I think I got them there, a lot of them. I didn't get Dearstyne[71] there, but I think Michael van Beuren[72] went there because of me.

RS: I don't know that name at all.

PJ: Michael van Beuren? Oh, he's in all the books. He's living in Mexico City now. He's lived there ever since. And Dearstyne, of course, is dead.

RS: And then, Bertrand Goldberg[73] is said to have gone there.

PJ: I must have missed him entirely, but I used to see Michael when he was studying there. It was all very heady for him. But he never amounted to anything.

RS: And Gropius was in Berlin?

PJ: Gropius was in Berlin. I was there when he appointed Mies,[74] and I asked him why he appointed Mies because I knew how Mies would feel. The Bauhaus wasn't exactly his way of doing things. He said, "Because there was no one else. Who else would you possibly think of? He was the obvious man."

RS: And did you have conversations with Gropius? I mean, socially?

PJ: No. He and I, we just had one of those relationships where the chemistry didn't work. Well, he knew I was a good friend of Mies already. But there was a total split [between Gropius and Mies] before that, before I'd ever arrived. Then I went down to visit Mies at the Bauhaus when he was in charge. I didn't know him well, but we always liked to talk. He'd talk about the school and how he'd gotten rid of the communists and how he'd changed the curriculum. I think Kandinsky stayed, and Klee stayed.

RS: Did you visit those small houses that were built around the Bauhaus area?

---

66. Wassily Kandinsky, 1866–1944, Russian-born artist.

67. Herbert Bayer, 1900–1985, German-born photographer and graphic designer.

68. László Moholy-Nagy, Hungarian-born photographer, filmmaker, and painter.

69. Marcel Breuer, 1902–1981, Hungarian-born architect.

71. Howard Dearstyne, 1903–1979, Chicago architect.

72. Michael van Beuren, 1911–2005.

73. Bertrand Goldberg, 1913–1997, Chicago architect.

74. Gropius appointed Ludwig Mies van der Rohe director of the Bauhaus in 1930.

70. Bauhaus Building, Dessau, Germany. Walter Gropius, 1925–26. Workshop wing.

PJ: I did indeed. I visited Törten. Dessau Törten was the best. It was excellent. The only catch was, of course, the Existenzminimum. That meant that the ceilings were about 6′ 2″. They didn't have our laws in this country. It was very, very depressing with those ceilings, but the design was excellent. And the taller building there that formed the town square at Törten was good. The thing we liked best in Dessau was the—I mean, one of the best—was the Arbeitsamt.

RS: Employment office.[75]

PJ: Yes, of brick, yellow brick.

RS: But that didn't fit into your theory of skin.

PJ: That's right, but we somehow blinked. All of a sudden brick became skin.

75. City Employment Office, Dessau, Germany.
Walter Gropius, 1928.

76. Bauhaus Masters Houses, Dessau, Germany.
Walter Gropius, 1925–26.

RS: It's a thin brick.

PJ: Very, very thin brick.

RS: Did you go into any of the houses Gropius had designed for the masters, the individual houses?[76]

PJ: Yes, surely.

RS: What were they like?

PJ: They were messes, as plans. But that whole Bauhaus group never went in for interesting plans. That was left to Mies. At the Weissenhof,[77] the Gropius house didn't have an interesting plan. See, by tightening up so much on his functionalism, the space got lost. There wasn't even as much space as there was in the famous house designed by the philosopher Wittgenstein,[78] which I saw later in Vienna. It was Gropius-esque in a strange way.

RS: What was Gropius-esque? That it lacked any detailed architecture?

PJ: No detail, no architecture, as far as I can see. As our dear friend,[79] the classical architect here in town, says,

"Architecture begins when modern architecture is over." Mies, of course, couldn't help doing architecture.

RS: When you were in Berlin, did you look at the housing? How about the housing in Frankfurt by May?[80]

PJ: I went to May's house in Frankfurt because that was the most famous thing there. Of course, his magazine was the best known of the magazines, *Die Neue Frankfurt,* and der Römerstadt[81] was laid out in a very nice curve in the valley. That part of it was quite good. Although the more housing I visited, the more I appreciated Otto Haesler.[82]

RS: Oh, yes. His works were quite nice.

PJ: Haesler did *zeilenbau*—row housing—better than Gropius, I felt. He was cleaner and more careful in his proportions, and with equal success on cost, it seems. His housing was just more interesting, but he was a minor artist, really. Oh, Stam.[83] Stam was an artist whom, again, I had under-appreciated, especially at Dessau, after the Weissenhof, but he was marvelous. I remember the big project of his that Russell liked even better than I did, and Russell was right, and that's the Altersheim, the old people's home in the Frankfurt suburbs. That had a fine staircase. But the Bauhaus people—

---

77. Weissenhofsiedlung, housing exhibition, Stuttgart, Germany, 1927.

78. Wittgenstein house, 19 Kundmanngasse, Vienna, Austria. Designed by Ludwig Wittgenstein, 1889–1951, and Paul Engelmann, 1891–1965, in 1926–28 for Wittgenstein's sister, Margarethe Stonborough, 1882–1958.

79. Allan Greenberg, b. 1938.

80. Ernst May, 1886–1970, German architect and city planner.

81. Planned suburb by Ernst May.

82. Otto Haesler, 1880–1962, German architect.

83. Mart Stam, 1899–1986, Dutch architect.

I mean the modern architects in Germany—weren't really interested in staircases because staircases mean space unless you just put them up between two walls.

RS: Except that the Bauhaus has quite a beautiful staircase.

PJ: The Bauhaus has stairs, and the Altersheim has beautiful stairs.[84] And the Bauhaus is not as good at stairs as you think, from its pictures, but it was pretty. Whereas the Altersheim stair has a sweeping central portion and double-width stairs.

RS: Probably would have been judged *retardataire*.

PJ: No, no Russell liked it, and I said, "Well, not *retardataire*." Not quite. That was my feeling, and he said, "It's a successful piece of art." Then, of course, we found Stam's original chair, which was the beginning, it seems, of all front-legged chairs. But I missed meeting him, too, personally. Mies thought highly of Stam.

RS: But Stam was a communist also, wasn't he?

PJ: Yes, yes. So what?

RS: But Mies didn't mind that?

PJ: Mies never minded communists. He just didn't think Meyer was running a good school, and I don't think he liked his architecture as much as I do now. But Mies never was political in any way. It was the damnedest thing. You know, he did the monument for Rosa Luxemburg and Karl Liebknecht.[85]

RS: Did you see that?

PJ: No, it was gone already. No, it wasn't. I didn't visit it. Damned fool. Because that's when we would have found out that it was just a little wall.

RS: Isn't it a huge—

PJ: No, it's very, very thin. It's just a wall.

RS: So no one has ever tried to count the bricks.

PJ: I had only seen the picture. But if you saw the real thing, it was very strange. The people who saw it said it was quite a shock. And then Mies did a house,[86] which is in our book, for Karl Lemke, the editor of *Rote Fahne* or the *Red Flag*. An "L" house.

RS: You've seen that?

PJ: No, no. Mies tended not to think much of the house. It was modest, shall we say. And I only visited what he wanted me to see. That wasn't one of them. In those days, it was only interiors and the exhibition house, of course, at the Berlin Building Exposition of 1931.

RS: Where was the Building Exposition?

PJ: In the halls there, near Poelzig's[87] radio tower. There were some halls near it. Big halls, big spans. And Mies built a house, with Lilly Reich, in there. And Breuer and Gropius's contributions were there.

RS: You wrote about that for the *New York Times?*

PJ: Yes. No. Did I? For the *New York Times* but also for Lincoln Kirstein's *Hound and Horn.*

RS: In Germany, did you go and look at older things? We talked a bit about Schinkel and Persius, but what about [Peter] Behrens and that period?

PJ: I missed Behrens. Behrens was a very stupid gap. I always very much disliked the corner of the Turbinenhalle, and so I didn't go to see that. I deliberately tried to see Mies's housing in Wedding on Afrikanische Strasse,[88] but never could find it. I went back a couple years ago with Kleihues,[89] and we couldn't find it. And it was right up near Gropiusstadt.

RS: Having organized the Museum of Modern Art show in 1932, what did you envision yourself going on to do?

PJ: Being a director of the department, which I did through 1934, Christmas Day 1934. And what I did after that was the Machine Art show.

RS: You did that after you were the director?

PJ: Yes, I became director at the Modern.

84. Old People's Home for the Henry and Emma Budge Foundation, Frankfurt am Main, Germany. Mart Stam and Werner Moser (1896–1970), 1928–30.

85. Rosa Luxemburg, 1871–1919, and Karl Liebknecht, 1871–1919, were cofounders of Germany's Communist Party. Above: Monument to the November Revolution, Berlin-Lichtenberg, Germany. Ludwig Mies van der Rohe, 1926.

86. Mr. and Mrs. Karl Lemke house, Berlin, Germany. Ludwig Mies van der Rohe, 1932.

87. Hans Poelziq, 1869–1936, German architect.

RS: The Machine Art show was the first one. You also did one comparing 1900 to —

PJ: That was a show of a smaller size than this room we're sitting in.[90] It was very small. Alfred [Barr] was away, one of his illnesses, and got furious with me for not—I should have done a catalog of some kind. There is a typewritten thing on it somewhere, but no pictures or anything. That was a smart-ass show all right.

RS: Was pretty clever?

PJ: Very clever. It was too clever, perhaps. I mean, nobody got the point except those who were in the know already. But that's who you do shows for. You don't do shows for the public. The public will look in the room and walk right on. I watched their faces. You know, they couldn't understand the points. No, it was much cleverer than I realized at the time.

RS: Well, what about the Machine Art show?[91]

PJ: The show was a great *succès de scandale*. I mean, why would you want to show pots and pans? It was called "Pots and Pans" by the staff and everybody. It was mainly an exercise in installation. We took big copper bowls and gradated them down to little ones, and showed them all on their own. You couldn't go wrong. Then we took another row of stainless steel bowls and gradated them the other way. Then you put them on two shelves. In other words, it was an installation passion of mine that was fulfilled. Then we had Amelia Earhart[92] as a judge, and we managed to succeed in making her pick the propeller for the prize. It was very beautiful.

RS: Well, that was one of your first impulses toward actually designing things, wouldn't you say?

PJ: Yes, I would, and I didn't even know what it was. It was all an instinct. That's what I wanted to do. I didn't know any different. I thought everybody designed exhibitions.[93] I designed a watch, you know, made by Cartier, for my sister. She still has it.

RS: Oh, you did? I didn't know that.

PJ: I had it hand made, specially designed. The watch is small. The ladies' watch was then one hundred and twenty-five dollars.

88. Afrikanischestrasse Municipal Housing, Berlin-Wedding.
Ludwig Mies van der Rohe, 1925–27.

89. Josef Paul Kleihues, 1933–2004, German architect.

RS: A hundred and twenty-five dollars was worth a bit more than it is today.

PJ: Well, yes. Ten times the amount. But a thousand dollars wouldn't get you a hand-designed Cartier watch.

Now, it was the same period, don't forget, as George Howe's [PSFS] skyscraper, for which all the clocks were made by Cartier. In other words, you could get specialties then that you can't get now.

90. MoMA Exhibition #27: *Objects 1900 and Today*, April 10–25, 1933.

93. Johnson at MoMA Exhibition #25a: *Typography Competition*, March 27–April 6, 1933.

91. MoMA Exhibition #34: *Machine Art,* March 6–April 30, 1934.

92. Amelia Earhart, 1897–1937, aviatrix. The propeller was awarded second prize. First prize went to a section of a spring made by the American Steel and Wire Company. Judging the *Machine Art* exhibition: Amelia Earhart, John Dewey, 1859–1952, and Charles R. Richards, 1865–1936, holding the first, second, and third prize winners, respectively.

3. The Right

RS: Next comes your growing political—

PJ: Interest.

RS: Interest.

PJ: That came with the Depression. All of my friends were becoming communists, which I understood. And the only thing I could see around that was comparable was Huey Long, which I preferred to that eternal talk which my leftist friends would indulge in.

RS: Well, certainly Eddie Warburg was not a communist, was he?

PJ: Oh, my Lord, no. I didn't get it from him.

RS: Or Lincoln Kirstein.

PJ: Lincoln Kirstein was "never nuttin'." I should have stayed never nuttin'.

RS: Well, you would have been in less trouble. Right. And Alfred Barr . . .

PJ: Alfred Barr wasn't.

RS: Well, then who were all your friends who were communists?

PJ: The ones I ran into in college. Varian Fry.[1] When I say friends, I think it was more my invention than anything.

RS: People didn't invite you to communist cell meetings?

PJ: No. I never went to a cell meeting [in the 1930s]. I wasn't sympathetic with the functionalists [in architecture], you see. There was the trouble. And what I knew of the communists in Germany—they were so earnest and so anti-art, you see, that it struck

1. Varian Fry,1907–1967, Harvard-trained classicist turned social activist, known for rescuing French Jews during World War II.

2. Catherine Bauer, later Catherine Bauer Wurster, 1905–1965, housing activist.

3. Lewis Mumford, 1895–1990, architectural critic who prepared the housing section of the Museum of Modern Art's *Modern Architecture—International Exhibition* (1932).

me as the wrong way to go about reform. Although I was perfectly willing to see that being hungry in this land of plenty was asinine. And I felt so strongly about it that that became a ruling passion.

RS: Did Catherine Bauer[2] play a role in this?

PJ: Catherine Bauer. We didn't talk much. I knew her opinions, of course, and Mumford's.[3] She was Mumford's mistress, I guess, at the time, and her articles and everything would—well, remember, his speech to the trustees, after all. It was published, I think. He said, "So conduct yourselves as if you belong in a communist country." And that jarred me because it had nothing do with architecture, or with housing, really, except that housing was so connected with leftism. Let's not use the word communist. Let's just talk about the leftist approach, for which leftism somehow would be the promised land. I thought the promised land was something a lot more direct than that.

RS: You had no impulse to run off to FDR in Washington and be a bright young man of that stripe?

PJ: Oh, yes, I did. But I felt it was ineffectual compared to Huey Long's[4] more direct way. Don't forget, Franklin was a weasler. That's why he was President four times. Because he wasn't much of a leftist.

RS: A good accommodator.

PJ: The one who was much clearer was his wife, you see. She had principles. Now, I admired her enormously. I thought she was great because she had the courage of her own conviction, which was: Let's do something about it. But Franklin would go along with whatever would get him reelected. I knew that Huey was a self-promoter, of course, but what I liked about him was his taking on Standard Oil. No one had ever done it, just put a tax on it. If you want to leave the state, go ahead, but there's your plant.

RS: Even though your father had been a—

PJ: Well, that didn't please my father too much. And you know Cleveland. They've never forgiven him. But it was that side of Huey that I saw. He could be very smart. But he took it out on Roosevelt, who wasn't so far from his own position as Huey said he was. But he had to be against someone.

RS: Did you go down and see him?

PJ: I went down and saw him and realized that there was nothing really in politics. I went down with Alan Blackburn from the Museum.[5]

4. Huey Long, 1893–1935, Louisiana right-wing populist politician.

5. Alan Blackburn, 1907–1999, was at this time assistant treasurer of the Museum of Modern Art. Pictured kneeling, with (left to right) John Dempsey, Jeannette, Johnson, and Theodate, c. 1933.

RS: Now, what was Alan Blackburn's connection to—

PJ: His connection? He was the business head of the Museum at the time. I recommended him to Alfred. Dick Abbott[6] later had his job, on the business side. The Modern was so small that there were only six of us then. He agreed with me on the philosophy of Huey Longism, so we took off.

RS: How did he get into this?

PJ: He got into it because he was the John Burgee[7]—I've always had a John Burgee, invented one if not—to keep things on the straight and narrow.

And he had more sense than I did. But I had the ideas and the flair. It's always the same combination. I connect myself with able, straight people. I mean straight in all senses. Alan Blackburn was a competent manager. Richard Foster[8] was a competent manager. Of course, Burgee is a great deal more than a competent manager. Somehow I seem to need that to complement my personality, to make sense out of the world.

RS: But in the case of Blackburn, he's never been heard of since.

PJ: No. He later became manager of a hospital in Cleveland, married a local girl from New London, and settled down there. He is a manager—I think he's a consultant on hospital management. No, I seem to have a sort of charisma that I don't understand at all. It isn't due to ability.

RS: But you and he went off—

PJ: We went off to see Huey Long on Christmas Day 1934 in a Packard 12.

RS: Your Packard 12?

PJ: My Packard 12. Oh, yes. The money all came from me.

RS: He doesn't sound like he had as much sense as you ascribe to him.

PJ: No, probably not. I suppose my gurus, my sensible people, never do. But they do the job very well for me. Then there was Foster. I guess he was extraordinarily sensible, and still is. But, of course, he didn't want to be around Burgee, and Burgee would never speak to him. So I could never combine my skillful people.

No, it's a peculiar characteristic of mine. I'm not a strong—I'm a weak person. I remember Russell pointing out that I was a weak architect and designer.

Of course, the big thing was Joe Alsop's[9] part in this.

RS: I don't know anything about that.

PJ: Joe was a reporter on the *Tribune*[10] and as fat as this table and could hardly move. He was—just as he is now—very witty, jolly, and perceptive. He wrote about our quitting here, leaving Christmas morning for Huey Long. That was a fantastic story. And the *Tribune* was a little more free than the *Times* and put it on the front page. And that, of course, cooked it.

RS: You were celebrities before you got to Louisiana.

PJ: I should say.

RS: And everybody—

PJ: One person approved—A. Conger Goodyear,[11] the president of the Museum.

RS: Just on the theory that boys should be boys?

PJ: Boys should be boys. This was great. "Why don't you go and do something, if

---

6. John E. Abbott, executive vice president of the Museum of Modern Art.

7. John Burgee, b. 1933, Johnson's architectural partner from 1967 to 1991.

8. Richard Foster, 1919–2002, architect and Johnson's partner from 1964 to 1967.

9. Joseph Alsop, 1910–1989, journalist and political columnist.

you feel that way?" And he had a kind of closet admiration for our crazinesses. Nobody listened. And Alfred always was a friend and understood. "You're off to the world, aren't you?"

Long was very smart indeed, and he was an extremely attractive man, and well, he wanted us as ideologists, but he didn't really need us around because how many votes did we have? How many votes does the Pope have? So we weren't any use to him.

RS: So you went down there and—

PJ: Hung around because we were too ashamed to come high-tailing it back again. We went to Washington, and we tried helping him with speeches, and things like that, but we weren't any use, because he had much better ideas. A couple of Harvard undergraduates would be very much in the way, which we were. And we liked him all right. But, especially his staff, they hated our guts. They were all rednecks and action people, not gun-toting in those days, of course, but toughies. And see, what the hell were fancy pants from Harvard doing around? And Huey was pretty disgusted with us, and he didn't see us. So we came back [to New York].

RS: Then what did you do?

PJ: Nothing. It was the worst period in my life. I lived at Hidden House, as Theo called it later when she lived there, on Third Avenue, 747 Third Avenue.[12] You went through a hole in a brownstone, under the "el" and came out in a courtyard ten feet wide. So the house was twenty-five minus ten, about fifteen feet. Two-story house.

10. Front page article by Joseph Alsop in the *New York Herald Tribune*, December 18, 1934.

11. A. Conger Goodyear, 1877–1964, industrialist, art collector, and first president of the Museum of Modern Art (1929–39).

Of course, it was absolutely charming, very quiet, and right in the middle of New York, where we lived. Then we entertained more or less talkers rather than fascists.

RS: Theo shared this house?

PJ: Theo shared the house. No, I lived there at that time. I guess I'm skipping a little, but that was when we came back. Before that, Theo and I lived together in Turtle Bay. After that, I lived in Hidden House, and she lived there when I went to war. And I saw then mostly talkers. That is, people like Lawrence Dennis,[13] author of *The Coming American Fascism*. He was the leading theorist, and he didn't mind using the word "fascism" because he felt that there had to be some kind of [government] controls if we were going to get out of the Depression. Of course, the war did exactly that. See, what people don't really understand is that we didn't get out of the Depression until 1939, when the war scare started making us make destroyers [ships] for England. Extraordinary. I mean, we didn't mind war any more than Reagan does, for the same reason—it makes things work. And Roosevelt didn't mind because he wanted to make the destroyers and he felt people were excited by the war. Indeed we were, and so we came out of that extremity. But, at that time, during the 1930s, we were still in the Depression and it was a great talking period, with all the theories, the crazinesses that could be imagined. And my best friend was Lawrence Dennis. He wrote several books.

I once got brash and was going to buy the *Mercury*.[14]

RS: From Mencken?

PJ: Not from Mencken. It was from the next purchaser, a young gentleman. He wanted to sell it and had sense enough not to let me buy it. I was no more able to do that than anything else. It's funny how little one knows one's capabilities. Being a late bloomer by instinct, thank God, I didn't make an ass of myself as I might have. And

12. The address of "Hidden House," named by Theodate, was actually 751 Third Avenue. It was a small "back" house renovated and occupied by Philip Johnson in 1940.

so I did my own good talk and had lunches with similarly minded people.

RS: So that must have been 1935. It couldn't have been later, could it?

PJ: Couldn't have been later. It must have been 1935. I had a long period in the hospital with rheumatic fever. That's right. I had a hard winter. In fact, 1935, I must have taken that house. From 1935 to 1940, I must have lived in Third Avenue.[15] And then I decided that I was—you get to the bottle the way drunks do. As ex-drunks always tell me, the only way you can recover is to get in the gutter. When you really can't stand it anymore, then it's not such a hard problem getting back.

RS: But people have told me over the years that you were this outrageous person who would come to these fashionable dinner parties and say outrageous things, things about politics and so forth. Is that apocryphal or true?

PJ: That's apocryphal. I was a diner-outer later. At that time, I was anathema to the dowager crowd.

My only friend was Alfred Barr,[16] who never, never deserted me. Never wouldn't see me. Always was fascinated by the intellectual reasoning behind my standpoints and always made me defend them, as best I could, and argue. That, of course, kept me alive.

I was with Marga[17] the other night and she said that to his last conscious moments I was the only person that he completely trusted, no matter what I did.

Now she said, "He did hate what you were doing" about my Nazi period. But he never, never stopped loving me, nor did he break off our friendship. He followed me along and asked me, "What am I doing right on this facade?" He fought to get Mies, as you know, to do the facade [of the new museum building MoMA was planning to build] after he lost that battle with the Rockefellers to do the building. Then I would come to town and criticize the facade, making Stone[18] absolutely livid, and would leave again. Then, of course, a young influence over Alfred came in, my successor, John McAndrew, who put the cheese holes in.[19]

13. Lawrence Dennis, 1893–1977.

14. *The American Mercury*, a literary journal known for its satiric take on American life and politics, was founded in 1924 by journalist and editor H. L. Mencken, 1880–1956, and drama critic George Jean Nathan, 1882–1958.

15. Johnson is mistaken. From 1934 to 1940 he lived just off Third Avenue at 241 East Forty-ninth Street.

16. Alfred Barr, right, with Johnson on Lake Maggiore, Italy, April 1933.

17. Margaret Scolari Barr, 1901–1987.

18. Edward Durell Stone, 1902–1978, architect; co-architect and a principal designer, with Philip L. Goodwin, 1885–1958, of the Museum of Modern Art's first permanent home, 1939.

RS: The cheese holes were among the most interesting features, I thought.

PJ: Those were put on by McAndrew as was the other thing that you appreciate.

RS: The S-curve.

PJ: Yes, at the entrance.

RS: Which I think we should restore.[20]

PJ: Well, it would look awfully funny on the present building. That was McAndrew, whom I couldn't get rid of. In a way I didn't have much to do [with things]; I had a negative influence for a few minutes, but I never had any connection until after the war. Then I went back.

RS: And Lincoln Kirstein in this?

PJ: Lincoln and Russell were always best of friends. It was Lincoln who, whenever I got into a problem—Lincoln thought I had a problem during the war. He wrote a

19. Museum of Modern Art, 11 West Fifty-third Street. Philip L. Goodwin and Edward Durell Stone, 1939.

20. The entire facade, including the S-curve entrance, was restored in 2004.

letter to the War Department on my loyalty and non-anti-Semitism. A very steaming, very loyal, lovely letter. Lincoln and Eddie [Warburg], they stayed friends.

But I didn't want to see them, because I wanted to know more about the revolutionary, radical movements. They were later called, everything was called fascist, of course, by the communists. That wasn't the point. And there were hangers-on-ers that I saw. I can't remember the names. They were unimportant.

RS: Would you say these were strictly intellectual?

PJ: Of course they were. They were younger, feckless hangers-on-ers. They were also friends of Lawrence Dennis. See, he was a real intellectual. His books were regarded even by the leftists then as being very, very good. He had great friends among liberals, and Jewish New York intellectuals.

So I was in a much higher rung of people intellectually than Huey [Long], you see. That had its compensations, but it wasn't enough, and I felt useless. I mean, I wasn't an intellectual in the sense that Dennis was, and I felt that.

RS: You did write for Father Coughlin's[21] *Social Justice*.[22]

PJ: That was when I went back to the farm and sat in the earth. You know, one gets those feelings. Now you would never have that feeling, I guess. City boy.

RS: Well, no. But I go to the garden and read. I read about it.

PJ: You read about the feeling of the good earth and connection with the people on the earth. I felt it and I ran a milk strike program for the milk farmers.

RS: This is out in New London, Ohio?

PJ: New London, Ohio. And then I ran on the Democratic ticket for the state legislature, which I would have won, but the thought of living in Columbus, Ohio, was too boring. So I didn't. Instead, we went up to visit Coughlin. He was Catholic and funny, and didn't really fit with our direct needs, but he was the nearest thing around. [His movement] had lots of excitement to it, and so we did things for him, odd jobs. And he thought we were hot stuff, because we were really reasonably intellectually organized. But it wasn't satisfactory. So then that must have been when I said, oh, let's lay off it, and came back here.

RS: But you wrote for him?

PJ: We, both of us [Johnson and Blackburn], wrote for that magazine, and again in the war. Now we'll jump to the opening of the war in 1939. I was in Berlin when war

21. Father Charles Edward Coughlin, 1891–1979, Detroit Roman Catholic radio priest, held extreme right-wing opinions and was outspokenly anti-Semitic. Pictured at a rally in Cleveland, May 10, 1936.

broke out, in Munich, and left for Switzerland to be sure I could get out. And I then went back, thinking: Goddamn, you're so near a war, you gotta watch what's going on. And I went back to Berlin, leaving Theo, whom I was traveling with that summer of 1939, in Zurich. I had no means of getting around and seeing things, so I said, Well, I guess I'm a correspondent for *Social Justice*[23] so I told the Germans that I was a journalist. And that's where Shirer[24] came in and thought I was a spy for the Germans, and what I was doing was amusing myself. So to keep my *bonas fides* I wrote a couple of articles for them, which Mr. Eisenman[25] has kept with increasing delight.

RS: They were political articles?

PJ: Yes, unfortunately.

RS: And they were—you want to say anything about them now?

PJ: I wish I could. I can't remember. I block out that time.

RS: And Peter [Eisenman] did not show them to you?

PJ: Peter says they're slightly anti-Semitic. I suppose I was. You see, that part I block out, too.

RS: I mean, but how can you—

PJ: I couldn't have gotten that far.

RS: How could you have been an anti—

PJ: How could I be?

RS: Well, you must have been, or you weren't. How did Lincoln Kirstein deal with it?

PJ: Oh, well, Lincoln said I wasn't, and that it was just put on and I was just making a joke and it was silly. But, I must have been, or what was I doing there [in Germany]? You

22. Front page of *Social Justice*, November 6, 1939. Johnson's article, "This Sit-Down War," is advertised at bottom.

23. Johnson's article in *Social Justice*, September 11, 1939.

see, I mean, a violent philo-Semite, the way I am today, simply wouldn't be near these things, would he? It stands to reason. But I don't remember the development of the ideas.

See, actually, the only thing I do remember very well is trying to save a Jewish friend of mine. I didn't know he was Jewish. [Otto] Haesler, the architect, very good architect in Brno, whom I visited in 1939. The Nazis had him arrested just because he was Jewish. And so I wrote to J. J. P. Oud and I said, "Aren't there any funds we can get for architects, perhaps, or something?" And that letter we still have somewhere. Haesler was a very nice man. Oh, tragic. So you see, that's what I remember. Now that isn't actually—that couldn't have been all that happened.

RS: It is an untold chapter. The whole, say, 1935 to 1940 period. There's got to be more than that.

PJ: No.

RS: You couldn't just have lunch with a cadre of intellectuals, unless you were in a kind of semi-intellectual stupor yourself.

PJ: Yes, I was. I must have been. I remember the lunches, and where we ate around the corner, five or six of us. I remember seeing Alfred Barr. I mainly remember seeing Lawrence Dennis and his wife—his family lived in Teaneck—and going out there a great deal. But it wasn't a life. And I couldn't write the way Dennis could. Dennis gave me book reviews to write in that same magazine, *The American Mercury*, which was slightly rightist, shall we say.

RS: And you did write book reviews there?

PJ: I did, but they didn't print any, ever. And I realized that I wasn't cut out as a writer and theorist, and that infuriated me. One doesn't like not to be good. You must have run into some parts of your professional—

RS: Yes. I've given up tap dancing and piano playing and many other things.

PJ: I had to give up piano playing. I had to give up philosophy after Whitehead. One has to give up certain things to get, perhaps, other things.

RS: Yes. One recognizes one's inclinations are not always in line with one's talents.

PJ: Not at the same time. But the ambitions were there. The piano was really a very strong impulse.

RS: At this point, or back in the 1920s?

PJ: No, no, no, no. A long time before.

RS: We talked about that.

PJ: We talked about it, yes. But at this time I just felt lost, and the farm hadn't given me enough sustenance in managing it to make me want to go on being a farmer. I realized that wasn't my *métier*. And the life in New London was, shall we say, stifling.

RS: Cleveland was out?

PJ: Cleveland was out because of family. I didn't like my family enough to want to be near them. That's natural too, I mean. In fact, everything seemed perfectly natural, but I couldn't go back to the Modern, having thumbed my nose at them in that egregious way. So that never even came up.

RS: You had no role at the Modern, during this period, in influencing your successor or anything like that?

----

24. William Shirer, 1904–1993, newspaperman, pioneering radio journalist, and author of *Berlin Diary: The Journal of a Foreign Correspondent, 1934–1941* (New York: Alfred A. Knopf, 1941).

25. Peter D. Eisenman, b. 1932, architect.

PJ: No. My successor, John McAndrew, was a great friend of Alfred's, but didn't like me. He thought I never appreciated him, although I had toured Central Europe with him in 1929, at the time of the Crash. But he wasn't liked by Stephen Clark[26] who really ran the Museum. So they tossed him out. Then I came back after the war.

RS: Were you involved at all in the commissioning of the museum's building, the first building by Goodwin and [Edward Durell] Stone?

PJ: Yes.

Just how I got to be *persona grata* again is very amusing. And my companion, Mr. Blackburn, was always blackballed, although he was able.

RS: Now, what about Russell? Were you keeping in touch with Russell on matters of architecture in this period?

PJ: Yes, yes. He was teaching at Wesleyan and I would stop in but very, very seldom. Of course, he wouldn't acknowledge that I had any other life. He's very good at that, you know. What he was interested in was architecture. So I'd keep up [appearances] a little bit that way.

RS: Russell, of course, was working with [Frank Lloyd] Wright in these years.

PJ: I didn't know that. That's how I know I lost track of Russell, because he was working on *In the Nature of Materials*[27] and I didn't even know it.

RS: Did you keep up with architectural magazines? Can you remember any of that?

PJ: No, I don't think I did. I think I deliberately said, "Look, I'm interested in this political thing and that's what I do."

RS: Did you have anything to do with bringing Mies here?

PJ: No. That was all done through Holabird.[28] I wasn't around; I wasn't interested. That wasn't my thing at the time.

RS: And did you go to Germany or Europe in those years?

PJ: No. Wait a minute. I must have gone to Germany. 1932 was the last year I remember well going to Germany because we had the car. And everybody thought we were Hitler because there were no cars in Germany in 1932, and we had a limousine.

RS: You went to see some of the big rallies, didn't you?

PJ: Oh, yes. We went to Nuremberg, which was very exciting no matter how much an enemy [of Hitler] you were. That many people screaming out loud was a very emotional sight. I was astonished by—what's his name?

RS: Speer?[29]

PJ: No, not Speer. No, my big enemy of the moment.

RS: Oh, Shirer.

PJ: Shirer was also very excited. You couldn't help it. I was not there at the Olympics. That was 1936. Possibly I went in 1935, but if so I never saw anybody. Oh, I must have gone one year in between, because I met a woman who had worked for the Party and who liked me and drove me around to the German housing of the Nazi period, which was excellent, of course, being done in Heimatstil.

---

26. Stephen C. Clark, 1882–1960, prominent art collector.

27. Henry-Russell Hitchcock, *In the Nature of Materials 1887–1941: The Buildings of Frank Lloyd Wright* (New York: Duell, Sloan, and Pearce, 1942).

28. John A. Holabird, 1886–1945, prominent Chicago architect.

29. Albert Speer, 1905–1981, architect and Hitler's close confidant.

30. Heinrich Tessenow, 1876–1950, leading advocate of an architecture of simplified forms expressive of national culture, teacher of Albert Speer.

31. Hermann Göring, 1893–1946, top Nazi official.

32. Ordensburgen, originally fortresses built in Germany by crusading military orders, were elite military schools in Nazi Germany.

RS: Tessenow-inspired.[30]

PJ: Nowhere near as good as Tessenow, but clean and bearable. Of course, Nazi architecture is all over the place. I mean, Göring's[31] architecture is just like any other International Style, it tells what's going on. I rather liked the Ordensburgen,[32] which were very romantic, and hated the public buildings of Speer, especially.

RS: You did hate Speer.

PJ: Oh! Well, I didn't like those buildings.

RS: But how could you not come to terms with that intellectually? I mean, there you were, interested in National Socialism.

PJ: Hated the architecture. The most infuriating were filling stations. Filling stations still come out modern, you see, to me.

RS: You commissioned one.

PJ: Yes. Clauss & Daub.[33] That was in 1930. It was published in the book [*The International Style*]. But the filling stations in Germany were all built with enormous straw roofs, and a big straw roof like this looks awfully silly on pilotis, which you had to have in order to drive up to get the gasoline. So the particular contradiction between function and form was so awfully imposed by the officials. I remember being shown through a modern house by a silly young Party member, who said, "You see, it was the Jews that didn't like windows. And notice we now put in big windows." So much for history writing.

RS: Did you see Mies when you went to Germany on that trip?

PJ: Yes. I saw Mies in, must have been, 1935. And he said, "It's getting harder and

33. Filling Station for the Standard Oil Company of Ohio, Cleveland, Ohio. Clauss & Daub, 1931.

harder." He was working on the silk factory still. He said, "I can still do that because they don't mind flat roofs on factories." But he said, "The minute they told me that I had to build pitched roofs on my houses, I knew it was all over. That's against my conscience as an artist. But," he said, "I'm still German, and I'm going to stay." But he didn't. I said goodbye to him and never saw him again until after the war.

But yes, we did. I remember I used to take him out for trips, him and Lilly Reich, even then. I remember it only because we went within five miles of a camp.

RS: Really?

PJ: Yes. Just the thought of that. I never saw anything, of course. That sure is a memory down one's spine.

RS: And she eventually was incarcerated?

PJ: No, I don't think so. Mies said, "I had only one regret. That I didn't help Lilly get out of Germany." I don't know whether she's Jewish or not. Now that I think back, I suppose she was.[34]

RS: Reich as a name tends to be —

PJ: Tends to be. But those things never came up in Mies's mind. But she was still there. I gave them food, which they liked. Went to very good restaurants that wouldn't cost us anything. It's like going over now.

But we just talked — well, Mies talked — architecture, principally, and visited more churches. We talked more about Schinkel. He wasn't interested in politics until it interfered with his direct activities. Then, when Holabird sent for him, he accepted. I never knew the story of the battle to get him to Harvard, or at the Museum of Modern Art.

Alfred [Barr] asked him to do the facade on MoMA. You can imagine how much it must have pleased Philip Goodwin.

----

34. Lilly Reich survived the war.

35. Oswald Mosely, 1896–1980, founder of British Union of Fascists.

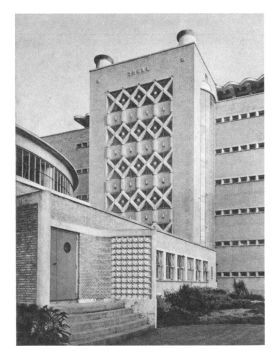

36. Shell Building, The Hague, J. J. P. Oud, 1937–42.

RS: And when you were in Europe, do you remember going to Paris or to London in those days?

PJ: Yes. I went to London. I thought it would be amusing to meet Mosely.[35] But I never did.

RS: The architecture, of course, was not interesting for you.

PJ: Not interesting.

RS: We never talked much of Holland.

PJ: Oh, Holland. In this period, I didn't visit it anymore because — no, it wasn't till Oud built the Shell building,[36] was it? It annoyed me so much that we lost track of each other. Except for the war thing. I sent him CARE packages, and we never lost our personal friendship. I'm still like his son and all that, but it sort of cooled. You know, Shell wasn't even good postmodern.

4. Architecture School and Military Service

RS: : So there you were, in 1939, going to observe the German invasion of Poland. How did you decide to go back to Harvard to become an architect?

PJ: Well, it didn't happen that fast. I came home realizing: what the hell was I doing over there? That's the winter when I became more and more self—I mean, I would never want to commit suicide, but I realized that I was a total failure. I felt that I wasn't that dumb, but that something had to be done.

So more and more as that winter wore on, I just sat and talked with Lawrence Dennis and any hangers-on that we could find, mostly at lunches. You know, you can take up a whole lifetime, if you want to, having lunches and dinners. It's what most society ladies do all the time. It's not that hard. So I did manage to piss away a whole lot of time. I did read, but I didn't do anything. It sounds as if I must have been hiding something. I simply wasn't; there simply wasn't any hiding to do.

I remember one unpleasant incident. I'd built a lamp at that time, not a very good one, and the manufacturer of it became sort of friendly with me. I didn't have anything else to do anyhow. He said, "You ought not to leave your letters lying around." I said, "What are you talking about?" He said, "Oh, don't you know?"

He was the man who let the F.B.I. into my house.

RS: The man from whom—

PJ: I had ordered the lamps. The search was so totally illegal, of course. They were looking for evidence that I wasn't a good American.

RS: This is before the war.

PJ: Oh, yes. We weren't even in the war.

RS: My God. Have you ever asked for your file?

PJ: No.

RS: You should.

PJ: It would be fun, I'd imagine.

RS: No, I don't know if it would be such fun, but maybe you ought to get it. Maybe it would put to rest some of the rumors, to see what they thought you were doing.

PJ: See what they thought I was up to. Of course, that was the end. They were always extremely nice—they never stopped my passport. Oh, once when I was in London, I noticed that I had misplaced my passport. My brother-in-law was in the C.I.A., which I didn't know, and he brought my passport back. The British were much cleverer at that kind of thing. They'd slipped my passport. While they were examining it, they called my attention to something else.

RS: He couldn't have been in the C.I.A.

PJ: Did I say that? I meant the M.I.1 or M.I.5 or whatever it was, British Intelligence. My brother-in-law wasn't American.[1]

RS: But there was no C.I.A.

PJ: It was the O.S.S. No, I'm sorry, I've got my dates all mixed up. It was after the war. It was the C.I.A.

But even then they wondered what I was doing. I visited Germany in 1949 for the first time since the war. Even then they were looking hard at my passport and where I was going. See, if you get your name started on one of those lists—

RS: Especially in those McCarthy years.

PJ: Yes, the McCarthy era. But McCarthy, of course—I wasn't a communist. But they just wanted to know where I had been. My God, what a lot of attention it takes on somebody's part to follow you around.

RS: But now with computers they do it much more easily. They can check all kinds of things when you're going through customs. You think they're looking in your socks; they're looking at more than that.

PJ: It was 1939, that winter I spent in Hidden House, in the little house behind the apartment buildings on Third Avenue, twiddling my thumbs and trying to figure out what to do with my life, which was unraveling, that I decided to go to Harvard.

RS: So, what was the impulse finally that shook you from your torpor?

PJ: Despair. Despair. Personal despair.

I'd wasted my life. I have a great sense of the Puritan, that rich people especially should do something. I didn't want to make money. But there had to be something of interest. I realized that I wasn't writing, I wasn't contributing anything to any cause, black, white, or indifferent. I realized that there was something terribly, terribly lacking. And I'd always liked designing, and I thought, if you like it, for Christsake, Johnson, what stops you from going to school? What had stopped me was my own infacility with my fingers in drawing. So finally, I just did it—although it scared me nearly to death at that age.

RS: Did you think to ask yourself whether you could ever get through Harvard in the normal amount of time? Earlier, you used to have those mental blocks.

PJ: That was all gone. You mean when I had to leave college for my mental troubles? No, I never had any more trouble like that again. They said it would come back. It never did. I never had any more great periods of despair, or writer's block, or anything like that. It was supposed to come back when I was in menopause, male menopause, but it didn't. So I was lucky there. And when I went to school, of course, it was the most wonderful thing in the world because I was better than they were.

RS: But how, at the age of thirty-four, did you just pick up the phone and call Harvard and say, "Can I enroll?"

PJ: Well, they were delighted because of the book [*The International Style*].

---

1. Johnson is referring to Theodate's second husband, Tony Kloman, 1904–1993, who studied architecture at the University of Virginia and was director of public relations for the Institute of Contemporary Arts in London.

Harvard

RS: Did you go to meet [Walter] Gropius? Did you speak to him directly?

PJ: Oh, no. I went up to see [Marcel] Breuer. I went up for an interview and told him my terror at trying to be an architect.

RS: You knew Breuer, of course.

PJ: Oh, yes, I had met him in Europe, and Gropius. But I didn't go to see Gropius for some reason. I guess Breuer was assigned to seeing new people. I said, "Do you think I could be an architect?" He was a nice guy. He said, "Let me look at your hands." I put out my hand. He said, "Well, I don't see anything wrong. The fingers all work." I said, "Yes." He said, "Well, then, why can't you be an architect?" You see, drawing, as we know it today, didn't exist and was of no interest. That "encouragement" enabled me to start.

So on a hot warm day in the fall, I left for Harvard.[2] That was the worst time, I guess, a low point in my life, because I didn't know how, as an old man—what was I then, thirty-four?—I could possibly go to a college with kids. And what would they say of my background?

Anyway, Gropius wasn't the dean. That was Joseph "Vi" Hudnut.[3] He was very, very broad-minded and a lovely man, indeed. When I said, "Can I come to Harvard as a student?" he was overwhelmed with delight.

I didn't go to Mies because I didn't want to go to Chicago. And I didn't think Mies was a very good teacher. I was right on all counts. I knew what Mies was all about. And I wanted to learn straight architecture.

Was that the year that the Shirer book[4] came out or was it the next?

RS: I think it came out the next year.

PJ: 1941. Of course, that is a wonderful thing to have happen when you are a student.

I took up lodgings away from the [Harvard] Square. This time I took a house down on the Charles River. I did it right this time. I had more money. The house is still there.

RS: In Cambridge?

PJ: In Cambridge. I had an Irish maid. Of course, in those days there were such things. It wasn't so long ago—forty-five years ago—but things have changed a lot in forty-five years.

2. Johnson as a student at the Graduate School of Design, Harvard University, 1941. Hugo V. Neuhaus Jr., 1915–1987, is seated in the back on the right.

3. Joseph "Vi" Hudnut, 1886–1968, dean of the Graduate School of Design, Harvard University, from 1936 to 1953. Hudnut (left) with Walter Gropius, 1942. According to historian Jill Pearlman, the nickname "Vi" was short for Violet, a fragrance produced by the Hudnut Company, although Joseph Hudnut was only distantly related to the family who ran the perfumery.

There was one boy who was much richer than I was, a Neuhaus from Houston.

RS: Would it be Neuhaus & Taylor?

PJ: No, Hugo Neuhaus.[5] No relation. Later he married the daughter of the head of Sears Roebuck, who said to him, "You build my daughter a house that has to cost at least $100,000."[6] Well, of course, a $100,000 house then is like a $2,000,000 house today. He said, "I don't know how to build it." So he copied my Oneto House,[7] a not very good idea.

But what I found at Harvard was that children don't learn very well; they are too stupid to take advantage of the chances offered to them. I got very angry at youth in those days because I felt that they didn't have the foggiest idea what they were missing. It is no trick at all to learn when you're older.

As an older scholar, say, using a library, you read about ten times the speed of an undergraduate or a high school kid. So as a thirty-four year old, I had no trouble with lessons. The only person I had trouble with was Christopher Tunnard.[8] Does that name mean anything to you?

RS: Yes, he was at Yale when I was there, a rather dull lecturer with a very good heart and probably a good head.

PJ: Tall and probably very intelligent. He was the local head of the Communist

-----

4. William Shirer recounts meeting Johnson in Berlin in his *Berlin Diary: The Journal of a Foreign Correspondent, 1934–1941* (New York: Alfred A. Knopf, 1941).

5. Neuhaus residence, Houston, Texas. Hugo V. Neuhaus, Jr., 1950.

6. Neuhaus's wife was Mary Stovall Wood, 1917–1979, daughter of General Robert E. Wood, chairman of Sears, Roebuck & Co. Mary was previously married to William Stamps Farish Jr., 1912–1943, son of a prominent Texas oilman.

7. Mr. and Mrs. George J. Oneto house, Irvington-on-Hudson, New York, Philip Johnson, 1949–51.

Party. They put out a magazine called *Task*. The few issues that came out are probably in the Avery Library.

And John Barrington Bayley[9] gave a course on housing, but that was wandering and useless.

Did Tunnard go to Yale after Harvard?

RS: Yes. And then he ended his career at Yale in a great academic scandal about the admission of blacks and other minorities who were underqualified. This was around 1969 or 1970.

PJ: He felt that they should be—

RS: Admitted, of course. He was always very liberal—a fuzzy-minded liberal.

PJ: A communist.

RS: I don't know if he was a communist at the end.

PJ: Well, maybe not. His wife was a distant cousin of Russell, so we always liked him. His course was simple-minded: "Housing in the War Period." We didn't get along, needless to say.

RS: Yet he was a very good friend of Barrington Bayley and Henry Hope Reed[10] and was responsible for a major exhibition on classical monumentality at Yale around 1950.[11]

PJ: You see, that's where the idea of monumentality—not housing—came from, from the example of the Soviet Union.

But at the time I didn't care where it came from. I was delighted to have an ally—we were as one. I mean, we all believed in architecture and monumentality as against just functionalism. Of course, in the early years, when the Russians were still functionalists along with Hannes Meyer, they were on the other side. But then they became monumentalists.

RS: After 1936.

PJ: 1936, wasn't that the time of the trials?

RS: Yes.

PJ: But that didn't convert all the American communists. When Tunnard was teaching social architecture at Harvard he was still very much a reactionary—I mean from our International Style point of view. It wasn't until later on that John Barrington Bayley became a monumentalist. Actually I don't know if that's true. When we went to war, 1941 or 1942, he was already a monumentalist by then, and we had a lot of fun.

RS: Was Bayley a person who had come to Harvard dedicated to the Gropius point of view and had a kind of conversion?

8. Christopher Tunnard, 1910–1979, landscape architect and professor in the Graduate Program in City Planning in the Department of Architecture, Yale University, 1945–75.

9. John Barrington Bayley, 1914–1981, architect.

10. Henry Hope Reed, b. 1915, advocate of classical architecture.

11. *Ars in Urbe*, Yale University Art Gallery, April 10–May 17, 1953.

12. Arthur M. Schlesinger, Jr., 1917–2007, historian and political writer.

PJ: I don't know. You see, he was a Party member and so he followed that line as it wandered. But later on, he became a good friend of mine simply on monumental grounds. We all laughed at the social pretensions of the Social Democrats, who became the enemy.

RS: So you were very politically—there were many political discussions?

PJ: No, absolutely none. I didn't know until the war was over and I saw Bayley afterward and he explained. Not at all! There wasn't a peep out of anybody as to politics. We all believed that the war was awful. There's no question about that.

I had a little trouble getting into war work because Schlesinger, Jr.,[17] who was the leading intellectual guide for the war group at Harvard, wouldn't address me. Plenty of the people did though; it just depended on whether they liked me or not. A lot of people did.

Then the war started and I stayed on as a student[13-18] and worked on my house. The day I was drafted I left my house and Bayley and I were in the same camp. He wasn't drafted till late either.

RS: Was he the same age as you?

PJ: Much younger.

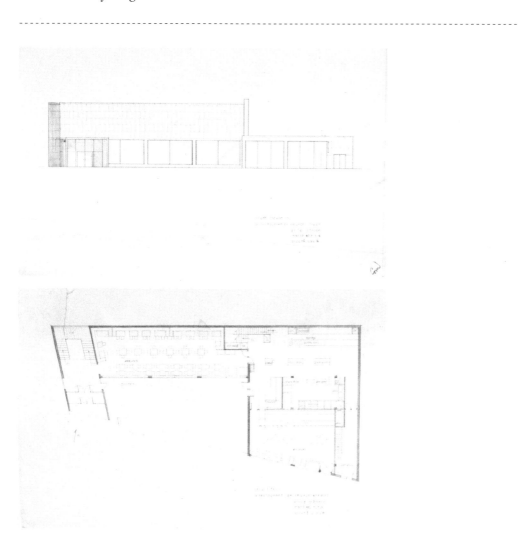

13. Church Street Restaurant, student project, 1940.
South elevation and ground floor plan.

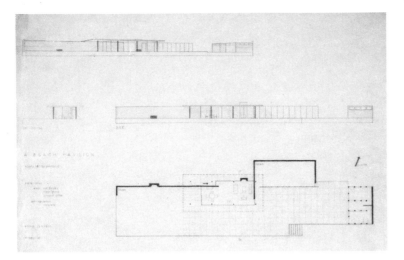

14. Beach Pavilion, student project, 1940. Elevations and plan.

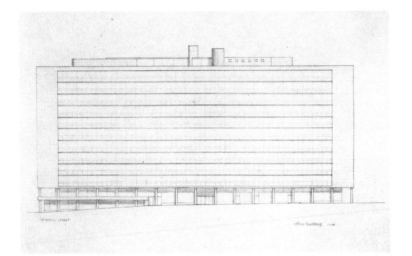

15. Office Building, student project, 1941. Congress
Street elevation.

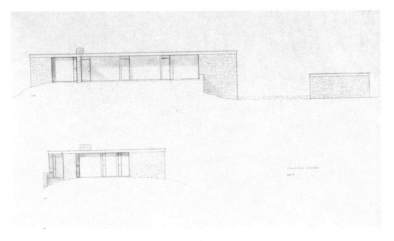

16. House in Lincoln, Massachusetts, student project, 1941.
South and west elevations.

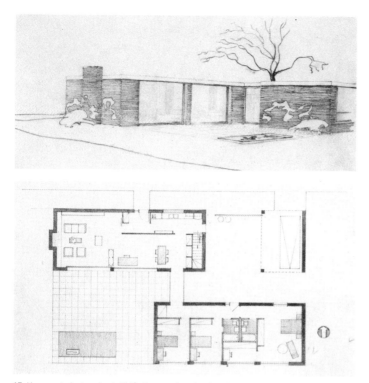

17. House, student project, 1942. Perspective sketch and plan.

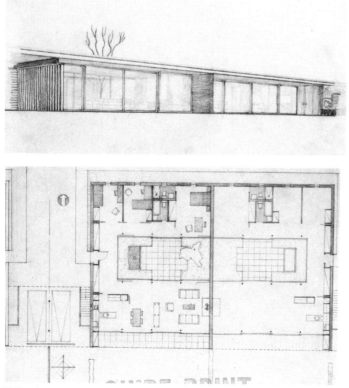

18. Row houses, student project, 1942. Perspective sketch and plan.

RS: Let's go back to Harvard. I'd like to hear about your experiences at school, who was there, your impressions of them, and so on.

PJ: Yes. The faculty had Perkins,[19] who taught history. He later became the person around whom things happened at Philadelphia. The [Louis] Kahn School was [dominant] while Perkins was the dean there. But I never saw him because our book, the International Style book, was used as part of the course. So they excused me from that course. It was very nice of them.

Then there was Bogner,[20] who tried desperately to keep up with the International Style. He had tenure, but he didn't want to be a joke.

Then there was an avuncular man named Frost,[21] who taught the beginning class. We put in a petition at the end of the class that we wanted to be taught another year by this very great teacher. He had that wonderful sympathy of a great teacher who can teach anything simply by saying, "Now, come on, what can you do yourself?" We all just blossomed. Almost exactly opposite of a disciplined teacher like a Mies who would say, "Come do it my way or get out." So we loved this guy.

I led a contingent who said, "Why don't we make all our models out of the same materials and the same color schemes so that the next time we show them they will all have a family resemblance." We did that to the horror of the school, but the kids and I, we all had fun.

Johansen[22] was my biggest supporter and good friend at school. My friends were all one year ahead, and I had only Carter Manny[23] in my class. But the classes sort of floated together, as they did at Yale.

RS: When you say "your friends," you mean the people you had a personal—

PJ: Personal interest in. We talked architecture together and could say, "Well, if you put the window there, don't you see—" We talked the same language. He's disappeared entirely. Yet I talked more architecture with him than with any other single architect.

RS: Carter Manny?

PJ: No. John Johansen, who was better than I was at drawing.

Naturally. That wasn't hard. I gave him something, I guess, that he was interested in. I always fought for him in the juries, because he was more like me in his work, and we always got beat up on by the teachers. But my class had only Carter Manny, who was pretty dim, architecturally speaking, although he was, and still is, a very honest and earnest man.

----

19. G. Holmes Perkins, 1904–2004, educator, urban planner, and architect.

20. Walter Bogner, 1899–1993, architect.

21. Henry Atherton Frost, 1883–1952, educator and architect, with student Dick Merrick, Graduate School of Design, Harvard University, c. 1938.

Then there was this strange dichotomy between the architecture school and the Fogg right across the street. Art was not to be mentioned by us. Gropius, I don't think, had ever stepped across the street himself, and that whole German, Bauhaus view of art filtered down to the kids. I thought it very strange, of course, because I came from the other side, the Museum of Modern Art.

The feelings I had were, in the first place, terror, and then I decided I would have fun. Because on the side I could do Miesian work, which I was rather familiar with. So my houses and buildings came out looking rather Miesian.

RS: When you say you were familiar with Mies, you hadn't ever worked with him at this point?

PJ: No. I knew just by osmosis and by looking at his architecture.

RS: And you lived in the room he designed for you.

PJ: That's right. So, of course, I knew his work. It wasn't strange at all, was it? It's hard to keep the sequence straight.

My first design was the usual little seaside house. It looked just like the Barcelona Pavilion. So it looked as if I was accomplished; I wasn't. They didn't know Mies at Harvard, you see. They—the other teachers—didn't know what a Mies building looked like, especially Stubbins.[24]

RS: Was Stubbins a teacher?

PJ: Stubbins was my teacher one year. That was the worst year. My best year was with Breuer, who as a teacher was very much like Frost. He was laissez-faire, very sympathetic to your own point of view, and not at all dictatorial. He was too much aw, shucks, old rocks and wood for me, but he was obviously a thinker. I respected him. His own house—have you ever visited it?

RS: No.

PJ: Well, it isn't an object to visit anymore. But it was so far superior to Gropius's and so much better than Bogner's. They were all together and we children were always allowed to visit all of them at the same time. It was impossible to think of Gropius living in that nasty little cottage.

RS: I have been to the Gropius house.[25]

---

22. John M. Johansen, b. 1916, experimental architect. Together with Johnson, Eliot Noyes, Marcel Breuer, and Landis Gores, a member of the "Harvard Five," a group of Graduate School of Design–trained architects who moved to New Canaan.

23. Carter H. Manny, Jr., b. 1918, Chicago architect, director of the Graham Foundation, 1974–93. Under the auspices of the Chicago Architects Oral History Project, Franz Schulze conducted an oral history of Manny in 1992 in which his memories of the Harvard years with Johnson are recounted.

24. Hugh Stubbins, 1912–2006, architect.

25. Gropius house, Lincoln, Massachusetts. Walter Gropius, 1938.

PJ: You have? Do you realize you had to go through his little study to get into the living room? You were young at the time you went there?

RS: No, I was quite old. I suffered such acute claustrophobia. Mrs. Gropius[26] was still alive and sitting queenlike in a corner. All I wanted to do was to plead migraine and leave.

PJ: I got claustrophobia too. I looked at Gropius, who was an enormous man like Mies, and he looked so silly in it.

RS: I never met Gropius.

PJ: He was handsome. He was the Warren Harding of architecture. I was nearly lynched at Eero Saarinen's[27] house in Washington for saying that one night. It was when Saarinen was working for the government. That really got me into trouble. But Gropius was very, very handsome.

To go back to being a student at Harvard. The rest of the kids tolerated me and, in fact, being older gave me a great advantage. Despite the fact that they could draw better, the emphasis at Harvard was so against drawing and making models—you can of course cover up a lot of sins with marbleized paper, which they had never heard of—that I found my way emotionally through those years better than I might have.

RS: Did you have any close friends at school?

PJ: Yes, Jeffries Wyman,[28] who was a biologist, a great scientist. I saw him practically every day. He and his wife used to live near the Harvard Yard. He was so brilliant and so incisive and so ruthless and so cynical that we got along fine.

I couldn't talk to anybody in architecture school. I don't think there was one person that I could talk to just the way we're talking. Vi Hudnut should have been, but he was soft as jelly and a wish-well, and he didn't have the intellectual equipment.

RS: And you couldn't talk to Gropius?

PJ: Oh, Lord, no!

RS: I would have thought that he was intelligent.

PJ: He may have been, but, you see, with my prejudices there was no way we could have gotten together.

RS: Also, your German background didn't—

PJ: Mies, you see. To him, the devil was Mies.

RS: Neither Gropius nor CIAM[29] liked Mies.

PJ: Kiesler[30] explained to me once how Mies was treated by his fellow members of the CIAM. He was discarded for two very good reasons. In the Barcelona Pavilion, he used matched marble. Well, you always lay marble—if your marble people are free to play, they turn the marble inside out and then sideways, book-matching. That's the normal way to do it. Mies, I don't think, even knew how it was being laid. I don't think that was one of his interests.

RS: His father had been a mason. I would think it would come second nature to him.

PJ: Yes, it was. I don't think he minded at all. Then he also answered, when I pointed the matching out to him, that it shows much more in the pictures.

See, in reality, the book-matching was just part of a general theme, but photography brings out those contrasts enormously.

The other reason Mies was not admitted to the inner circles of CIAM was that he used raw silk curtains, and, of course, that was bad. You had to use artificial materials or you just used blinds. You didn't use curtains for whole wall planes.

His playing footsies, as it were, with the silk industry was very much frowned on by the Gropius-type people.

It's strange but I feel even now that that line between what was represented in my world by Mies and what was represented by Gropius still exists.

RS: Was it not just your allegiance to Mies, but also that you had had a certain association with Germany?

PJ: Gropius wrote a letter to the Nazi people, "Couldn't you please let me stay in Germany?" Come, come. They're all Germans, basically.

Pevsner[31] wanted to go back to Germany, even after Hitler came in.

See, people forget.

The fact that Mies stayed too long in Germany is a fact, but it didn't seem strange to anybody at the time. Of course he stayed in his home country. Where else could he go? He never felt happy over here. He said, "Ich bin immer noch ein stiller Deutscher."[32] I'm still a hidden—what do you call it—underneath, underground—

RS: Oh, I can understand that, but I was thinking of something else. Once Gropius was at Harvard, he had to prove his own Americanism, given the politics. Therefore, an association with you—

PJ: —would connect him again with a pro-German. Well, that may be very possible. Sure. And he would have read that book by Shirer.

RS: I'm sure he must have. And the gossip would certainly—

PJ: That would certainly be part of his enmity. But the enmity with Mies was much stronger. [To Gropius] Mies couldn't design. He wasn't interested in social responsibility or teamwork.

No, I'm afraid I'm not sane on that subject, which he well knew. I never hid my feelings about Gropius. That's where Hudnut and I got together a great deal when I was at Harvard.

He was the dean and I was a friend of his and his protégé, as it were. He was very pleased I went to Harvard instead of to Mies's school. So we used to get together in hate Gropius-fests.

RS: He didn't get on with Gropius at all?[33]

- -

26. Ise Frank Gropius, 1897–1983.

27. Eero Saarinen, 1910–1961, Finnish-born architect.

28. Jeffries Wyman, 1901–1995.

29. Congrès International d'Architecture Moderne, the institutional standard bearer of modern architecture founded in Switzerland in 1928.

30. Frederick Kiesler, 1890–1965, Austrian-born experimental architect.

31. Nikolaus Pevsner, 1902–1983, German architectural historian who emigrated to Great Britain.

32. "I am still a quiet German."

33. Walter Gropius, master's class, Graduate School of Design, Harvard University, 1946.

PJ: Oh, couldn't stand him! Nobody that worked for him, except the little acolytes that later became TAC [The Architects Collaborative], who still are. Apparently the reason that I'm not invited back to speak to the students at Harvard, someone told me, is that when I was up there talking away, running on at the mouth, I said, "Of course, if you want to go out to Lincoln, to see Gropius's house, that's fine, but don't think you're going to see any architecture."

And the TAC-trained mass just rose as one man.

But it's true. Who ever heard of the Gropius house? It isn't considered a—

RS: It's not as bad as you say!

PJ: It certainly is. Go and look at it.

RS: I've been there. It is horrible, but it has a moment. If you look at it with a historical—

PJ: If you look at it with a historical eye, but it is nothing compared to the Breuer house.

RS: Nothing you would copy.

PJ: Now Breuer has an idea in his house out there.[34] It wasn't any more expensive than Gropius's. But how about that processional, walking in through that study to get to the living room?

RS: Well, I still like the canopy in the front. It's like a bar mitzvah palace. The angle and everything. It's where Morris Lapidus began.

PJ: That's where he got it from! I'll be damned! You wicked man. [Laughter.]

You're making it much worse. That's the only piece of design there is in the house.

RS: The screen porch with the gate and the frame beyond it.

PJ: The screen porch. Now, that's something. You've picked on what is really almost an original and architectural idea.

RS: The frame beyond—it's not bad.

PJ: Nobody else would do that.

That is a statement. I should be a historian.

34. Breuer house, Lincoln, Massachusetts. Marcel Breuer, 1939.

But we were talking about me as a participant in those battles at the school. Oh, Carter Manny, he was a friend. But he was about as good a one as I could get.

RS: He's not much to talk about.

PJ: I could make monologues at him, but there wasn't that much there to bat back and forth, not the way George Howe and I could. And it was nice to have Vi like me.

RS: What about people like Ed Barnes?[35] Was he there at that time?

PJ: Ed Barnes was so beautiful that I never could get a grasp on him. You see, he was so sexually attractive to homosexuals like Bayley and myself that we couldn't talk to him. When you're young those things can be very, very powerful. Then he married Mary Barnes,[36] whom we all knew, of course. She worked at the Museum of Modern Art.

RS: What was her maiden name?

PJ: Mary—a great liberal from the Chicago Coss family. She knew all the great liberals, the gurus of the time. She and Ed married very soon after I met him.

RS: He married when he was at Harvard?

PJ: Yes. She was always much stronger than he. It made a better team that way.

RS: She wasn't a student there, was she?

PJ: She's his partner now, so she must have been—

RS: I think she does color and things like that.

PJ: Just interiors, yes. She was so damn smart. And I loved her. Then, of course, she was somewhat like Catherine Bauer, the lady who later married Wurster.[37]

RS: Were there any women students then?

PJ: Sue Harkness[38] certainly was, so there must have been. She was Sue something-else then.

RS: Pillsbury.

PJ: Was she a Pillsbury?

RS: Sarah Pillsbury Harkness, yes. Sally, she calls herself now. And Chip Harkness[39] was there then?

PJ: Chip was there. They weren't married, of course. Chip was just a nice old bumbling guy. They were all—

The class that was good was the class just before mine: of Barnes, of Johansen, of Hale.[40] I now hear from him [Hale] all the time. He just thinks I'm God's gift.

RS: There were juries then? Because of course the Beaux-Arts system didn't have juries.

PJ: Oh, they didn't?

35. Edward Larrabee Barnes, 1915–2004.

36. Mary Elizabeth Coss Barnes, b. 1911.

37. William Wurster, 1895–1973, architect and dean, School of Architecture, M.I.T., 1944–50.

38. Sarah Pillsbury Harkness, b. 1914, later a member of The Architects Collaborative.

39. John "Chip" Harkness, b. 1916, later a member of The Architects Collaborative.

40. Peter P. Hale, 1916–1995.

RS: Not to my knowledge, no. They had juries which the faculty only would attend, no students. But you had open juries?

PJ: No, we had faculty juries, but we were allowed to speak.

RS: To present your own projects?

PJ: We presented our own projects. The faculty judged them but the other students also spoke up. At least I did. I remember defending a piece of Johansen's that they were throwing out. But then I was older than most of the teachers, you see. This annoyed them, it was very difficult for them. I was always much too outspoken.

Of course, the nicest period for me was the very end, when I could entertain them all in my house.

RS: What possessed you to build that house at 9 Ash Street?[41]

PJ: Well, the same thing that possesses you to build anything.

RS: Were you thinking that you would stay in Cambridge, and settle down to a quiet donnish life?

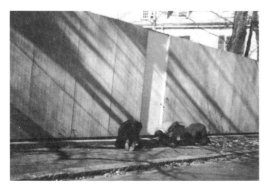

41. 9 Ash Street, Cambridge, Massachusetts. Philip Johnson, 1942. View from courtyard (top); Betty Bates DeMars, Vernon DeMars, and William Wilson Wurster in mock worship in front of entrance (left); Johnson with workman at construction site (right).

PJ: I didn't have the slightest idea. I knew I could get rid of it, I suppose. Well, Cambridge was as good a place as any, I felt. I'm always that way. Do you get that way? That wherever you are, you want to build a house and settle down?

RS: No, I don't have that problem.

PJ: See, I did that in Washington. I wanted to live on a wonderful street at the end of the Key Bridge that rises straight up. Those houses I could have gotten for $10,000.

RS: But you didn't.

PJ: I didn't buy one. I could have.

RS: So you would have a house in every city. You'd never stay in a hotel theoretically?

PJ: Theoretically. I always look around [to buy something].

Let's see, Harvard. That was really my only triumph—getting that house built and then getting that accepted as my thesis. Don't forget, I had a great friend in the dean, Vi Hudnut.

He was first hired at Columbia. He was desperately anxious to get in on modern architecture through George Howe. He was tight with George Howe. He admired him enormously, as I did. So he and George were the two older people who said, "Keep going, kid."

Vi felt lonely because he never got along very well with Gropius. Gropius dictated the policy of the school while he just kept the peace. He didn't have much influence on the kids because he couldn't talk the language of modern architecture. It's hard to understand that, because you'd think that he could have learned it by rote if no other way. That's what Bogner tried to do, you see.[42] He tried to catch on and learn as much as he could.

We always laughed, we kids, about the ineptness of his trying to learn to do a modern flat-roofed house. He designed a garage that came out, but it came out in a quarter-circle. Well, there are lots of things that you can do with an automobile, but curling up like a worm isn't one of them. So we said, "Ha, ha, ha." There was actually nothing wrong with it. The car could go in.

RS: He was trying to make space—

PJ: No, shape. But to our functionalist eyes, it was for the wrong reason. Therefore, it had to be bad, you see. If it was done for ornamental or for non-functional reasons, then it was forbidden. Isn't that funny?

RS: So Hudnut had no role in the studio?

42. Bogner house, Lincoln, Massachusetts. Walter Bogner, 1939.

PJ: He had no role with the studios. He didn't ever come to the studios and was never seen except by me as a personal friend.

RS: Did you have visiting critics at that time?

PJ: No, we did not.

RS: Was there any discussion of Mies?

PJ: There was a hatred of Mies that was palpable on the part of the faculty. There was the famous time when Mr. Stubbins[43] was going to flunk me.[44] So I said, "Well, I see what you are talking about. Just give me another week or so."

I did something I knew he'd like, pure Corbusier. It wasn't hard. Just look in the book and do a pure Corbusier building. I showed it to him. He said, "Fine."

I could see I was going to get my pass—there were no A's and B's. Then I pulled out my drawing—the one I had been working on the whole time, which was Miesian. I said, "You see, I had to do two solutions. One to get my mark and one because this is what I'm learning." He has never spoken to me since—to this day!

RS: How does Stubbins fit into the story? He wasn't a—

PJ: He was much younger than I. He was a young teacher from the South who wore plastic galluses—

RS: Suspenders?

PJ: These were galluses. They were suspenders, of course, but I mean they looked so funny because they were clear plastic. He wore octagonal non-rimmed glasses. He was a rube. Later he learned, of course. He's fine now. But we all snickered a lot. Isn't it funny? Young people are so vicious.

RS: What explains his ever being hired?

PJ: Very bright. Still is. But not in design.

I don't know where Harvard got its teachers. Perkins may have found them.

RS: I. M. Pei,[45] was he around at that point?

PJ: I. M. Pei came in very late because he was at M.I.T. He came over to Harvard graduate school to be with Gropius, just as a finishing-up thing.

[Paul] Rudolph[46] went somewhere else.

RS: Alabama.

PJ: Yes, and finished up at Harvard.

RS: What was Paul like in those days?

PJ: Not the way he is now. He's apparently gone completely to seed now and become grossly fat with terribly blotchy skin.

43. Hugh Stubbins, c.1942.

RS: That's funny. I saw him just a couple of nights ago. He was at a huge dinner at Columbia. I didn't notice him below the waist, but his face looked fine.

PJ: Wonderful. I must see him. I love him, always have. He and I didn't meet until after I had graduated. It's funny, Paul and Pei and I are the three most famous and we hardly knew each other at Harvard.

RS: Did you know Rick Franzen[47] at that time?

HARVARD UNIVERSITY
CAMBRIDGE, MASSACHUSETTS

GRADUATE SCHOOL
OF DESIGN

OFFICIAL TRANSCRIPT OF RECORD

Name PHILIP CORTELYOU JOHNSON Admitted with degree A.B. cum Laude (Harvard College) 1927 (1930).

Course	Grade	Course	Grade
1940-41			
A. S. 1a (History of Architecture & Site Planning before the Renaissance)............................	Cre.		
A. S. 1b (History of Architecture & Site Planning since the Renaissance)............................	Cre.		
A. S. 3^1 (Descriptive Geometry)......	A		
E. S. $7a^1$ (Statics)...................	B		
Arch. $1a^1$ (Site and Shelter).........	COM*		
Arch. 2a (Elementary Arch'l Design)..	P		
Arch. 4a (Building Construction).....	B-		
1941-42			
Arch. 2b (Design & Construction).....	Inc.		
Arch. 4b (Arch'l Engineering)........	B		
Arch. 5b (Mechanical Plant of Buildings)...........................	E		
Arch. $1c^1$ (Site Planning)............	A		

MARKING SYSTEM: A, B, C (lowest passing grade), E (failure), Abs. (absent from final examination), Cre. (credited), Exc. (excused), Inc. (incomplete), P (passed; no grades given in this course).
* MARKING SYSTEM: Com. (commended), Pass, Fail.

Awarded degree of: ----------------------- Date

Date issued ...... June 16, 1942

[signature] Dean

44. Johnson's official transcript, Graduate School of Design, Harvard University, June 16, 1942.

45. Ieoh Ming Pei, b. 1917, Chinese-born architect.

46. Paul M. Rudolph, 1918–1997, architect, chair of the Department of Architecture, Yale University, 1958–65, and editor of special issue of influential French journal devoted to Gropius's influence as an educator, "Walter Gropius: The Spread of an Idea," *L'architecture d'aujourd'hui* 20 (February 1950).

47. Ulrich J. Franzen, b. 1921, German-born, American-educated architect.

PJ: Rick came the last few months before I was there. He was the bright hope of the younger generation, from my point of view.

RS: He is much younger.

PJ: Oh, he is! Yes, he's much younger than Johansen and that crowd.

RS: Did you go to Chicago to visit Mies when he came to the States?

PJ: I went to Chicago quite often and we used to talk over that terrible enemy, Mr. Gropius.

RS: Did you show him your work?

PJ: No! No, the first thing I tried to show him was my house. I did show him my [Ash Street] house. He said it was terrible.

RS: This was photographs of the house?

PJ: No, this was the drawings. He was terribly kind. He said, "When ve do this kind of a court house, ve don't put quite so many columns in."

I had columns twelve feet on center or something like that. I didn't know much about spatial arrangements.

So I quickly fixed all that and invited him and Mary,[48] whom he was living with, to come and see the house when they were in Boston. They refused.

I always felt it was unkind. Of course, it wasn't. Now, I never go and see kids that think they do work "Oh, just like you, Mr. Johnson." That's the last thing I want to see.

But at that time I was quite hurt that he wouldn't come and look. Mary tried to bring him over. Of course, Mary Callery was a mother-of-us-all kind of person. You never knew her?

RS: No. She was not around at Harvard though?

PJ: No, except with Mies.

RS: She was with him almost from the beginning when he came to this country?

PJ: No, Farnsworth[49] was first. Then Mary wasn't around a very long time. She was too temperamental and he wasn't really able to screw much. He was too big and heavy. So it wasn't a satisfactory love affair.

I guess he got along better with Dr. Farnsworth. God, who could sleep with that woman? None of us could figure it out. Life is strange.

So that was my spiritual home. There were those evenings that Mies got very drunk with one or two martinis. He never became drunk but he became more interesting and he could talk about architecture, which he couldn't when he was sober.

I never knew Gropius well enough to know whether liquor would have helped or not.

RS: Breuer?

PJ: Breuer was married. He built the house after he was married.

RS: Oh, really. I always thought that was a bachelor's house.

PJ: I could be a liar.[50]

RS: Well, he wasn't hanging around with the students?

PJ: No, he wasn't. We went out there and he was always wonderful.

RS: How did the architecture school fit into Harvard as a scene? Or did it at all?

PJ: No. You see, we were so completely away from it. Ever since, there has always

----

48. Mary Callery, 1903–1977, sculptor.

49. Dr. Edith Farnsworth, 1903–1978, Chicago physician. Mies was sued over the house he designed for her after their romantic relationship ended.

50. Breuer married Constance Crocker Leighton in 1940.

been this interest: How are we going to integrate the design school into the business school? Or the planning into the economics? How can there be some interplay?

But Gropius was having none of that. He was running his own game.

RS: And his English was good enough so that he could—

PJ: His English was always better than Mies's. "Teamverk."

RS: So you stayed at Harvard and did three years or four years?

PJ: I only did three because I went into the Army in 1943.

RS: But you received your degree?

PJ: I got my degree a few months ahead of time. I would have gotten it in the spring but I got it instead in March or February when I left for the Army. They said, "What the hell, get him out of here."

The Army

RS: You were drafted out of school?[51]

PJ: Drafted from school. They were taking school kids by then.

RS: But you were thirty—

PJ: Thirty-five or thirty-six.

RS: You were sort of old to be drafted.

PJ: Oh, ridiculous. All my corporals and captains laughed. "Granddad." "Pop." I was a terribly bad soldier, of course.

RS: You were sent to do nasty fieldwork?

PJ: I was with the engineers. Mostly I was in basic training. Then the war stopped.

RS: Aside from being older, were you chastised because of the Shirer thing at this point?

51. Pvt. Johnson, 1942.

PJ: Not at all, except that they were watching me, no doubt. That's why I remained a Pvt. I was the only one that never made P.F.C.[52]

It's awfully funny how the intelligence service never caught up, though, because I was picked by a computer — or whatever they had in those days — because of my knowledge of German to go to prisoner interrogation school, which is a very important branch of intelligence.

So I went to intelligence school at Camp Ritchie. I had started the course and was doing fine and I was promoted to prisoner interrogation when somebody read down the list and saw a funny little mark. A day later I was sent back to engineering. So I spent the rest of the time digging ditches. One has to laugh.

And right in the middle of this, while I was working in the ditches, there was that famous trial of the fascists where the presiding judge died finally.[53] It went on for a couple of years.

RS: During the war?

PJ: Yes. Right in the middle of the war they were studying local fascism. I wasn't involved in any way, except as a witness. I never had to testify.[54] But Lawrence Dennis,

----

FEDERAL WORKS AGENCY
PUBLIC BUILDINGS ADMINISTRATION
WASHINGTON

OFFICE OF THE SUPERVISING ARCHITECT
IN REPLYING, QUOTE THE ABOVE SUB-
JECT, BUILDING, AND THESE LETTERS SA- ADM

June 19, 1942

TO WHOM IT MAY CONCERN:

I have known Mr. Philip C. Johnson, the bearer of this letter for eleven or twelve years. During that time he has to my knowledge been constantly employed in the study of the technics of contemporary building.

Mr. Johnson is a man of unusual intelligence and is also thorough and persevering. His character and reputation in the community are excellent. In my opinion his personality and qualifications make him excellent officer material.

GEORGE HOWE
Supervising Architect

FOR DEFENSE
BUY
UNITED
STATES
SAVINGS
BONDS
AND STAMPS

"REMEMBER
PEARL HARBOR"

52. Letter of recommendation from George Howe for Johnson's unrealized Army promotion, June 19, 1942.

53. See Gerald Horne, *The Color of Fascism: Lawrence Dennis, Racial Passing and the Rise of the Right* (New York: New York University Press, 2006), 112–39.

who was my friend from earlier days, was very much one of the leading defendants and he fired his lawyer and handled his own defense, very clever of him. He'd never done anything wrong either. This whole apparatus of the prosecuting attorney of the United States government was fascinating to watch because they were very bright people but they were dealing with something that was beyond their grasp. They just didn't understand where we were betraying our country, since the whole point—if there is a fascist point—would be pro-country, you see. So "subversive" could hardly be the word.

RS: It was a Catch-22.

PJ: Yes, they didn't know what they were prosecuting or persecuting. There was a long list of defendants, of which I was not one. There were a lot of kooks, of course, and then there was the one intellectual, Lawrence Dennis. The judge died so the government never bothered any more. But that kept me running to Washington to talk with the prosecution, because I was on their side, of course.

One of my best friends then was Lincoln Kirstein,[55] who was also at engineering camp, at Ft. Belvoir.

RS: Was he digging ditches also?

Dear Theo,

The axe has descended. Last Wednesday I was restricted to the Post, which means I was not allowed to leave to go to Washington or anything else pleasant. A horrible punishement for which they would give me no explanation. I thought it was probably to keep me under observation so they could get ahold of me when they wanted me. So Monday, I am to report to the Captain of the Company all dressed up; and I think it is for me to get a call to Washington to testify. But, and this is the worst: I don't know anything. What is to come? What will it be? Naturally all sorts of horrid things come to mind. Up till now my knowledge of innocence on my part is my best armor and I have not lost my courage except in spots, I mean now and then.

But gone forever is the old life here which was so swell, going to Washington every night and seeing the Wiley's and the architects. The last plan I had done pleased John Wiley immensely. He tore up his own plan and subsituted mine, so I felt that I was getting some where. Now I cannot even think architecture. I hope I can begin again soon unless things get too terrific

What would you think of sending for father if the legal part gets tangled? I hate to drag him into the thing. Would he rather be left out or in there fighting with me and for me? I really don't know. I think I shall call him tomorrow night and put it to him. I think he would be magnificent if he would help. And I am resolved to keep nothing back in my testimony. It is only the full truth as always that can do me any good. So really I have nothing at all to fear.

Will keep you in touch with things.

Love,

Philip

54. Undated letter from Johnson to Theodate, c. 1943, about potentially testifying at Lawrence Dennis sedition trial.

55. See Martin B. Duberman, *The Worlds of Lincoln Kirstein* (New York: Alfred A. Knopf, 2007).

PJ: No, he got into art interpretation and went over to Europe to authenticate the art in the salt mines—the stolen art business. No, he was a P.F.C.

I remember being told by a corporal who was digging ditches to get out of the ditch. I said, "Why? I'm supposed to be digging ditches. That's what you told me to do." He said, "You're confusing everybody. You can't dig a ditch. You're making everybody else look like they can't dig ditches. So you get out and sit over there until we get through digging this ditch." That's how poorly coordinated I was. That was the most humiliating moment in my life, I think. Those dumb asses. I was working five times as hard as they were, but probably just digging the earth and putting it back in the same place. I still don't know what I was doing wrong. It was just unbelievable. One remembers things like that. One remembers being offered KP [Kitchen Police] as a permanent job. See, I was the only one that worked at anything.

RS: But I've seen you open a letter, Philip, and I would think you'd be dangerous to yourself with a potato.

PJ: Oh, I can't do potatoes! We had a potato-peeling machine. That was nice for me. I still cannot peel a potato, nor open a letter. I open it just the way my father opened a letter. It's identical. We both had very short, stubby, unusable fingers.

Father wasn't prehensile. I mean he couldn't pick anything off the table like that. [Gestures.] I can't either. No, life was really hard.

The captain actually asked me once—he was a man who was very, very high up to me—to put a sign up on the board about where to do this and where to do that. Of course, I couldn't letter; we never learned lettering at Harvard. He couldn't believe that. He never said a word. Of course, you couldn't read a child's lettering.

RS: We never learned lettering at Yale, either. That was part of the whole reaction against the Beaux-Arts and against the establishment.

At the time you also built a building in New London, Ohio.

PJ: They now want to make that into a Philip Johnson memorial and erect it in the park that my father gave to the town.

RS: Isn't it on your family farm?

PJ: It was a farm machine storeroom[56] located on my family farm. I just wanted to build it. Didn't use it for anything. This man has offered to rebuild it on my father's place and they can put some memorabilia in there and all that. It's the silliest thing I ever heard of. That was my first building. It was rather nice.

RS: What were you thinking about when you designed that building?

56. Townsend Farm barn, New London, Ohio.
Philip Johnson, 1944.

57. Saarinen had opened a satellite office in Washington, DC, in 1943 to carry out work for the National Capital Housing Authority.

PJ: I did it while I was in the camp. Your intellectual life gets very strong when your daily life is digging ditches. That was the only time I could read French easily. I read Flaubert and I read *Le Rouge et Le Noir — The Red and the Black —* by Stendhal, all in French. I can't read it now.

But when I was on duty all night, let's say, watching machines, it was glorious. That's when I did the barn in New London.

RS: But the New London barn, I mean, it's rather unfarm-like.

PJ: It was purely formal, a palatial statement. I guess I was not a man who believed much in contextuality. I think a palace looks nice in the fields —

RS: Even if it has tractors parked in it.

PJ: Tractors fit through those big doors perfectly. Functionalism can work its way into a monumental building. It's not true the other way around: you can't make a monumental building out of a farmer's cottage. But you can always live like a farmer or any way you like in a palace. So obviously the place to start is with the palace.

RS: So you made those drawings and you sent them out to Ohio?

PJ: And they built it. There was nothing very difficult.

RS: You've been out to see it, I assume, many times.

PJ: Yes, I would go out there. Once our chauffeur was electrocuted and so I got a telegram to come home: "James killed." Of course, it didn't say who James was in the cable. They were very smart. So I got compassionate leave.

That was very easy to get because they didn't want you around in these goddamned camps. So I went home for a while and worked on it then.

I used to go into Washington every evening. One remembers very well the evenings in Washington and the sexual escapades and how I got to see Eero [Saarinen]. I don't think I saw him more than that once but it was memorable because there were other architects there and they were talking about architecture.[57]

It was just one of those unforgettable nights. The nights I've forgotten are when I had to go out with my *copains* from the Army.

RS: But I don't quite understand how if you were in the Army you had all this free time?

PJ: I had an automobile and I had "E" coupons from my tractors. You see, you couldn't drive in this country during the war even if you did have a car, but I could always get gas by using tractor coupons since tractors were for making food. Of course, people in the gas stations didn't give a damn what coupon it was so I could always drive. I drove a lot of the kids in every evening to Washington and stayed at George Howe's pad. That must have been when I visited Eero.

He had a good government job and a good staff and a good house in Georgetown and there were lots of architects around him.

Eero and I were very, very peculiar friends. We both respected each other enormously throughout our lives, but neither of us thought very much of the other's work. I guess we were both right. We were both able critics. We both knew what it was all about. Eero, of course, coming from a Finnish background and me more from the Miesian, German.

But we understood those differences of background and he was the one person I could talk to — besides Rudolph, and Rudolph and I never could keep up the same quality of conversation because Rudolph is an artist. That really, I suppose, has been his problem throughout life. He is a real artist. He knew what he wanted, knew what shapes he wanted. And he was more interested in those than he was in the—although there's nothing wrong with his intellect. He's a great teacher, as you know. Oh, my God, you were his student, weren't you? But somehow you wouldn't put him in that class of intellectual.

Yet Eero, who was a businessman basically, was just as intellectual as I was. We could talk, although he couldn't make a speech, he would mumble. But he was bright as all hell.

Although we disagreed a lot, it was the kind of disagreement that could make for excitement. I never could get on with his friends—Eames,[58] or his brother-in-law Swanson,[59] or Weese.[60] They were his closest companions and I wasn't. But he and I respected each other well enough so that we always wanted to see each other more and we always wanted to go on talking. Of course, I knew him when he was still married to his first wife,[61] whom I didn't like at all. But his second wife, Aline Bernstein,[62] was a wonderful, brilliant woman. We knew each other very well when she was married to Louchheim.[63] They lived right near me up in the country. Of course, when she married Eero it knitted us even closer. Usually marriage can break up a sort of *ménage à trois*, but we became better friends.

We would talk about other people's architecture, but very seldom about our own. But we knew we didn't like each other's work.

RS: You said Eero was a businessman. But wouldn't you say he was also an intuitive artist? Where did he come up with those shapes?

PJ: Mendelsohn.[64]

I guess art is the word.

It was also smarts. For instance, "the style for the job."[65] He developed this out of his knowledge of clients, out of his incredible feeling for the situation. He wasn't a great speaker but he was a great, great man at a business conference. I mean, General Motors hated his project. You could hear his clients rant at him all the time. But he could so fix it that he could get his way with the G.M. bureaucrats. It must have been much like working for the G.S.A. [General Services Administration of the Federal Government] He got that great airport [Dulles Airport, outside Washington, DC] built.

I remember feeling very inferior. He was so much older than I was architecturally. I mean, he had drawn all his life and became an architect when he was ten. So it came much more naturally to him. He could very well have been my teacher and I would

---

58. Charles Eames, 1907–1978, architect and designer.

59. J. Robert Swanson, 1900–1981.

60. Harry Weese, 1915–1998, American architect.

61. Lillian Louisa Swann Saarinen, 1912–1995, sculptor.

62. Aline Bernstein Louchheim Saarinen, 1914–1972, architecture critic.

63. Joseph H. Louchheim, 1908–1970, public health administrator.

64. Eric Mendelsohn, 1887–1953, German architect, emigrated to Palestine and then to the United States.

65. Eero Saarinen was known for inventing a different style for every job.

66. Eliel Saarinen, 1873–1950, Finnish architect residing in America.

67. The school complex designed by Eliel Saarinen in Bloomfield Hills, Michigan, 1926–40.

68. John Wiley, 1893–1967, career diplomat, ambassador to Colombia, 1944–47.

69. Isaiah Berlin, 1909–1997, Russian-born British philosopher.

70. Vladimir Nabokov, 1889–1997, Russian-born novelist.

71. Victory in Europe Day, May 8, 1945.

have loved it. I felt that—not inferior, but respectful. I looked up to him as my senior, which of course he was in experience as an architect.

RS: Did you know his father?

PJ: I knew his father[66] but didn't like him. I didn't like Cranbrook,[67] you see. I always thought Eliel's best work was in Finland. So I lost interest. And then, of course, don't forget I was so much for modern, as was Eero, by then. The school had won its prizes and everything, but it seemed too handicrafty to me.

RS: I'm sure Eero was trying to break away from his father.

PJ: Of course, he was.

RS: Did you hang around with the political crowd at that point?

PJ: No.

RS: Joe Alsop or people like that?

PJ: Joe I never saw. We didn't really become friends until later on. No, I never saw Joe.

But John Wiley,[68] our Joint Chiefs of Staff man, we got along just fine. I designed his house. You've seen it. It's the one with the pavilions with the pitched roofs and the water that goes in between the pavilions.

He had these evening dinners at his house and the most memorable guest was Isaiah Berlin.[69] We've been friends ever since. And Nabokov[70] was with him. We had marvelous evenings in their house.

But those things stood out a lot more to me than my routine work at the camp, which was KP mostly.

RS: So you were in the military for three years.

PJ: I was out before V-E day.[71]

The end was in sight and they let up on the gasoline rationing. It was clearly the end of the war. What could they do with somebody who was by then thirty-eight or thirty-nine and a PX Pvt? So I got out.

5. Philip Johnson, Architect

RS: So what did you do then? Maybe you thought you might settle in Washington, DC.[1]

PJ: That was the point.

I wanted to settle in Washington because I loved it so and I had a chance to buy a house opposite the Key Bridge for about $10,000. It seemed like I couldn't go wrong. Of course, had I done it, it certainly could have gone wrong.

But then I ran into Vi Hudnut, my great friend and advisor with whom I was always talking about Gropius and Mies and all that. He said to me, "You can be an architect in Washington if you want to, but if you want to be a world architect, you can only do it from New York."

And so I said, "Yes, sir," and came back to New York.

1. Johnson reviewing plans, c. 1950.

RS: What happened to your Cambridge house during your war service?

PJ: I lent it to a girl, a friend of mine who had a little daughter. They had no place to live at the time. They were poor, and I thought she would be a wonderful house-sitter. So she sat for the house during the war. Then I sold it.

RS: You hardly lived in it really.

PJ: No, I only lived there for about two years, from the time I built it to the time I went into the army.

RS: So you came to New York. What was it like after the Second World War? Certainly things weren't booming along?

PJ: I came to New York, and I got a room over on Lexington Avenue on the fourth floor and hired one chap to work for me. Through a girl friend—she was the wife of Ros Gilpatric[2] at that time—I met a man who wanted a house.

She was a friend of my sister and she said to this man, "Well, I know this Philip Johnson very well. He's awfully good."

Anyhow, that became my first house.[3] It was nice, in a way, that I didn't know the clients well because it gave me more freedom.

RS: They weren't perturbed by the fact that you didn't know anything about how to build?

PJ: They didn't know that I didn't know! You see, they never knew me and didn't even visit their house during construction. They just told me how many bedrooms.

RS: And they wanted a modern house?

PJ: Oh, yes.

RS: Or they tolerated a modern house?

PJ: They tolerated it, but modern or not modern, it didn't make any difference to them. They wanted somebody who could build them a house. They paid their bills. Isn't it extraordinary?

RS: Extraordinary.

PJ: Yes.

RS: I mean that's not the usual story for a first house.

PJ: Not the pattern, no.

---

2. Roswell Gilpatric, 1906–1996, lawyer and government official.

3. Mr. and Mrs. Eugene Farney house, Sagaponack, New York. Philip Johnson, 1946. Exterior and interior views.

RS: Who was the man you hired? Who was your first employee?

PJ: I have absolutely no idea. He hated it. He hated me. And the little room he worked in was something like a bathroom or a maid's room, stuck up near the attic. And he couldn't draw anyhow. Well, now, my first real office was in the Architect's Building, 101 Park Avenue, and that was a room with another architect. He lent me a room. I remember that attic, a tiny space.

Of course, I had money but I wouldn't think of spending it on setting up a place. I was terribly, terribly Puritan, still am, and I thought any money spent on fixing up an office was indulgence. I didn't indulge at that point. Business was business, and of course, nothing was coming in, as you well know.

RS: Tell me about the house.

PJ: Well, I did it in that one room with that one assistant. You don't need more than one assistant to do a house.

But standing on the unfinished platform of that house I thought, "Jesus Christ, I did this just from thinking about it!?"

RS: I still almost have a slight throw-up thinking about my first major project.

PJ: I don't. I must say I do keep away from the site now. But that's old age.

RS: I don't go to visit either, but I still am amazed that something out there is —

PJ: Is yours. Didn't you go to your first one?

RS: Oh, yes. Every minute practically. Yes.

PJ: Oh, the smell of that lumber! That was before the awful part started. I even put the closet in the wrong place.

There was wooden decking, of course, on top of the piles. And I remember I brought a bottle of champagne—because it's a hell of a distance, as it is now—and my sister and I had a great party there, to celebrate the groundbreaking, as it were.

Now, the Farneys I never knew well. It's funny. They were not communicative and they didn't tell me whether they liked the house or not when it was done. They lived in it and then they sold it without telling me.

Some clients become friends and some remain on formal terms. I've no idea what happened to them.

The new owners were very nice and they never changed a thing. They had to move the house two or three times. That's why I was glad that I had sense enough to put it on piles. I mean, to put it way up above the dunes.

RS: That was a very typical Harvard design.

PJ: A typical Harvard house.

I did one that wasn't. I designed one with an enormous berm. I thought you could do this on the dunes before I found out that you had to build on piles. See, I thought you just bulldozed the earth up around and made a great berm. The berm came up to the window sills. A Frank Lloyd Wright influence.

Or like in Alden Dow's[4] house, where the only thing you could see was the window band and the enormous roof that overhung four feet maybe.

Isn't that funny, to try something like this right in the middle of my International Style period.

But I found that you can't very well build a battered natural stone house in the

---

4. Alden Dow, 1904–1983. His studio and house were built
in Midland, Michigan, in 1934 and 1941, respectively.

sands. I would have had to hold it up with too many piles. The Harvard approach fit perfectly. If you put it on piles at regular intervals, you had your house.

But I was fascinated by this hugging the earth business, especially on the dunes, because I thought how horrible to plop-plop down an International Style box in that country.

RS: As soon as you came back to New York, did you go back to the museum?

PJ: In 1947 I did the Mies show, so I must have gone right back to the museum, which is awfully amazing, considering. But that was due to Alfred Barr, of course.

RS: But you didn't have illusions of working for another architect or apprenticing?

PJ: No, that never crossed my mind. I was much too old anyhow. I was forty.

See, when I started to work on my own house I used to take every weekend off and go look in the countryside for a site to build a house.

Oh come, come, you do it too when you see a hillside, you build a house there.

RS: Yes, of course.

PJ: I built something in Pennsylvania, in Long Island, and finally in Connecticut.

RS: You drew them yourself, or you didn't even draw them?

PJ: No, I didn't even draw them, just placed them in my mind's eye and said, "What a nice feeling here," and so forth.

Then I did the one that you know, I built the real one. The Glass House.

But by the time I built the Glass House in 1949 the drawings were already two or three years old, you see, so I must have been working on them since just after the war.

RS: There were other commissions in that period.

PJ: The Henry Ford II house?[5]

RS: I think that's right. But isn't there also a little house somewhere up near Pound Ridge?

PJ: Oh, yes, that was the first house, Booth, a crazy crippled guy.

That was another first for me. I know where it ended up: in the house for Jasper Johns [on St. Martin], that is, a cube and an 'L' making a court.[6]

The de Mandrot[7] is where it came from. And the "drop-off." We used the drop-off as the basis of the house, making one side, then the cube, then the 'L' completing it. You can look through but it still gives you a sense of *place*. The idea ended up still later in Miami,[8] where the cube is the Museum and the library and —

5. Mr. and Mrs. Henry Ford II house, Southampton, New York. Philip Johnson, 1950–51. Two views of model of unrealized project.

RS: That's right, but they split the two.

PJ: Yes. You had a choice. Then I had a long walk connecting both sides. It's funny, you get an idea early on in your work and it persists. I didn't really hug that theme, but it carried right through from the Booth house.

The Booths never had money enough for the cube and the ending of the path, so it was just a silly little block sitting there.[9]

RS: It's still there.

PJ: Still there, yes, built of cinder block, the world's most unsympathetic material.

RS: And you had no inclination to work for someone, to become a nice, well-trained, conventional architect at this point?

PJ: No. No, no, no.

I was conventional and still am, personally. Although I had radical ideas, I was a very conservative person. The current neo-conservative movement, you see, just fits me like a glove. That's politics, though. But I was always a genteel person, accepting of the world as it is.

RS: No, no, I meant something else. You didn't feel when you came out of architecture school that you should get a job in somebody's office—

PJ: Oh, no.

RS: —and learn about working drawings and things like that?

PJ: I was much too rich to bother about that. That only came up back to haunt me later when I wanted a license. But in those days, there was no license needed for houses.

RS: Did you have ambitions at that point to really be a serious architect and eventually build big buildings?

PJ: Oh, yes. That was all very conscious. I didn't know I'd build as big as I have, but I thought I was going to be a serious architect from the beginning, just like you. There was no question of that.

6. Mr. and Mrs. Richard E. Booth house, Bedford Village, New York. Philip Johnson, 1945–46. Model.

RS: So you felt that you could maintain your aesthetic commitment to this modernism and that it really would pan out, so to speak?

PJ: Oh, I was still a total believer in the modern movement, and I knew it would develop into God knows what it did. And so I never had any doubts about that. But I just also had a tinge of this other Wrightian, hovering-house feeling.

RS: Tell me about how you came back to MoMA.

PJ: I went back to the museum not really officially the first year out of the war or shortly afterward, I think.

RS: But you went back before the Mies show, presumably, which was 1947.

PJ: I must have been back already in 1945 or 1946, preparing that show. Yes, of course, I got out of the war early. That's right, I went back as a sort of unofficial job. I never was paid there.

RS: Never, not until the very last day?

PJ: I never was paid. I gave them money. What the hell is the sense of taking it back?

It gave me independence. It's a good thing to have in an institution because otherwise you can get ordered around. If you get paid, if you take money, you do what you're told, I always thought. And so I didn't.

RS: You've talked a lot about money, but you haven't actually said where the money comes from.

PJ: Oh, all right. Let's talk about that.

Well, my father was an extraordinary man who felt that you need the money when you're starting. When you're successful, what the hell do you need the money for? When you need it is that terrible first period. "Besides," he said, "how would you ever get used to spending money if you didn't have any? And how would you know the value of money if you didn't have any?" Because if he died all of a sudden and I got a lot of money, then I'd spend it. I'd do what younger generations always do.

- -

7. De Mandrot house, Le Corbusier, 1930–31.

8. Dade County Cultural Center, Miami, Florida, 1983.

9. Mr. and Mrs. Richard E. Booth house, Bedford Village, New York. Philip Johnson, 1945-46. Entrance facade.

He was of the opinion that if I wanted to lose the money that was perfectly all right. That's all the money there was. He died a pauper, with thirty thousand dollars in the bank.

RS: Having given it away and spent it?

PJ: He gave it to his kids, you see, because he thought we should make our own mistakes. I turned out to be more parsimonious than he ever imagined. My sister Theo was the opposite. She sees five thousand, she spends it. So we had to stop giving her money because it was getting expensive to the family purse.

But he was absolutely right. What is the sense of an inheritance when you're forty or however old I was when Father died?

So I started out with an independent income. I remember my income in those days was huge. One year I spent twenty-five thousand.

Father did speak to me about that. That would be like what now? Spending a couple hundred thousand in one year. I sure have wanted to spend it that way. He said, "It's your money, but if you spend it all . . ." I guess the income wasn't quite that much.

Because he was so generous I felt doubly guilt-ridden, and of course I stopped spending it.

RS: There is a story that your father gave you aluminum stock.

PJ: That's right.

What he did was say, "Look, I will divide the money in three. And I won't keep any, but somebody will have to take care of me. But the good stocks I'll give to the girls because they need the protection. The risky things I'll give you."

So he gave me his aluminum stock, which promptly went to five hundred times its value. That's quite a jump. So then Mother and Father came to me together and asked if I would mind giving half of the enormous wealth I had to my sisters.

I said, "Heavens no! It never was my money in the first place." So, of course, I signed over $250,000 to each of the girls, which they have been living on.

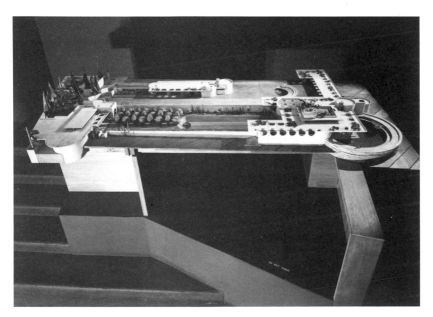

10. Gerald Loeb house, Redding, Connecticut. Frank Lloyd Wright, 1944. View of model from the exhibition *A New Country House by Frank Lloyd Wright,* The Museum of Modern Art, June 18–September 3, 1946.

RS: They got the Cleveland property.

PJ: They got the Cleveland property, which is fine. It goes on paying four percent or something. They just sold it and got a very nice profit.

But for forty years that's all they had. He thought I should never, ever get that much because he knew I'd want to work, because the work ethic was so overwhelming.

His partner was much wiser than he. His partner, another man named Johnson, said, "Look, I think it's the duty of people with money not to work." I took that very seriously.

I came to New York and worked with the museum on my own and I got much further—an Ohio phrase—working for nothing at the Modern than I ever would have if I'd looked for a job in my youthful Puritan way.

So that other man Johnson was absolutely right. If you are fortunate enough to inherit money, you better find yourself a job or a position, especially in culture, that doesn't pay, to get things further along in the world of art, which is my interest.

So that gave me a good start with Alfred Barr.

People do think I'm rich, you know. It's awfully funny.

RS: Well, you have just enough to be dangerous.

PJ: Yes. Anyway, when I came back I did the Mies show and I did a lot for Frank Lloyd Wright. I think I gave him individual shows, didn't I? One for that enormous house that wasn't built, that strange Loeb house.[10]

RS: Did you get a show for the Loeb House?

PJ: Yes. I was passionate about those double-vision things, stereopticons. So I put those all over the room.

RS: Didn't your mother have stereopticons?

PJ: We always had stereopticon slides in Mother's day. We had all of the Sistine ceiling in stereo. And it was great, see. I loved them. And the color in the little ones was so marvelous. So I put them around the room at eye height, and then an enormous model of the Loeb house, and that's all there was in the room. And Frankie was very pleased, naturally. So I got to know him better.[11]

RS: Were you still in touch with Russell?

PJ: No we never became unfriends, but we never worked together on anything after the catalog of the 1932 show.

---

11. Telegram from Frank Lloyd Wright to Johnson, September 25, 1946.

You see, when I was in my political period during the late 1930s I didn't see him, intentionally. I hardly saw Barr much, but I did keep up with Barr through the war.

RS: So Russell was not a close confidante, not in the way that, say, Kirstein is?

PJ: No. Kirstein and I had many other things in common, like gossip and age. Well, Russell isn't that much older, but he wasn't in the same world, sort of, as Lincoln and I were and still are. No, we never became close friends. That's funny.

I knew all about his sex life. But that wasn't interesting.

RS: Who were your friends at the time?

Oh, the main acquaintance through the museum, besides Nelson [Rockefeller], was Wally [Harrison], whom I liked very much.

His agony with the U.N. was very pitiable and he was sad. It was a sad occasion for him and for Corbusier, of course. But I only followed it from afar. It wasn't till the U.N. was pretty well finished in 1952 that he took me around, just before the opening, to show off his pride and joy, the Assembly Hall.

Of course, I couldn't say anything. I was so violently pro-Corbusier, and Harrison's and the committee bureaucracy's chopping it up was a great tragedy to me. Of course, I was such an idealist that I thought we should have the greatest masterpiece of the International Style by Le Corbusier here in New York.

But what I didn't understand at the time was that you just couldn't work with Corbusier. Corbusier was adamant that he was the leader of the world and people shouldn't question him. He was unlike Mies, who adapted well to the way we do business in this crazy country. He was impossible. But I didn't know that, so I took a very strong stand for Corbusier. I don't remember the critical talk of the time.

What I remember more is that Harrison tipped a dollar for a dollar-and-a-half taxi ride there. He was a very generous, easy, lovely man. But the building was too awful. My tongue was stuck in my throat. It just was a terrible building. It was very sad for the U.N.

RS: Who else was important to you then?

PJ: My big guru at that time was a man who later committed suicide, Bob Wiley.[12]

RS: Bob, the client who built the Wiley House?

PJ: That's right.

RS: He was not an architect.

PJ: No, no, he was a client and a great admirer of mine, I mean almost sexual. He was almost worshipful of me. And my father thought he was very able — he used to come out to the house — and I thought he was until I found his hands in the till. Then he committed suicide.

He took my money, and said he was working for White, Weld & Company.[13] Finally, a friend of Theo's called White, Weld and they had never heard of him.

RS: Oh, my. He was really that kind?

PJ: So I called him and said, "The people at White, Weld said you aren't a member of White, Weld."

In the meantime, he'd absorbed somehow — because he was my financial advisor too — about two hundred and fifty thousand. So I was worried and sick about it and

---

12. Robert C. Wiley, 1915–1956.

13. White, Weld & Company, a patrician investment banking firm founded in Boston in the nineteenth century, sold to Merrill Lynch in 1968.

called him and told him. This was when Mies was here in New York so it must have been in 1955. I never heard from him again. He killed himself in his room.

RS: Really? Incredible. You went into business with Wiley, didn't you?

PJ: Yes. We had a development company, which he merely used as a means of funneling money from my account into his.

RS: So there was also that little house built.

PJ: That one house, that was the only thing. Of course, we lost money on that.[14]

RS: Let's go back to the museum. It's 1947. You're doing Mies's show. What is the story of the show?

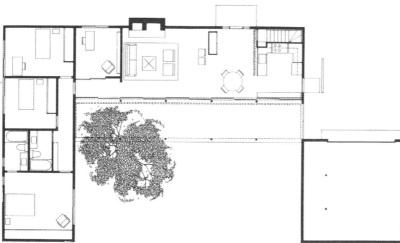

14. Wiley Development Company house, New Canaan, Connecticut. Philip Johnson, 1954–55. Exterior view and plan.

PJ: I made Mies do the designs for it. He was very pleased to, and he did.[15]

I remember he called me once from Chicago—a very unlikely event in those days.

He said, "Will you tell me if those columns in the Museum have chamfers at the corners?" I said, "No."

Mies said, "Well, that's fine because we don't want to have anything but the columns. Leave them."

Then he came here and, of course, he held it against me all the rest of his life.

RS: That there were—

PJ: That I hadn't checked on the chamfered corners. That's the way columns were built in those days, because it's much easier with a concrete column to have chamfered corners.

RS: It's very impure to have the chamfered corner if you're going to have—

PJ: Oh, shocking! So we had to sheetrock all the columns. Or plaster, in those days.

And only then did he install that show. But I had nothing to do with it. All I worked on was the catalog. That was agony for me since I can't write.

Then I had no office. I was working in my bedroom. My secretary came in every day and we would work on the book. I'd been to Europe and we got the pictures together. It was a major operation for me because it wasn't my natural activity in life. But there was nothing to build in 1946.

What was I working on? What was the next building? My own house, I guess. I remember the model sat around in my office for a year, and it was Lincoln [Kirstein] or somebody like that who came and said, "Why don't you build that?"

I said, "Build it?" I said, "I'm not that rich." "What do you mean, not that rich?" And I finally indulged.

RS: Tell me about how you got padlocked in New York.

PJ: A man came and said, "You aren't licensed to do your buildings." All perfectly true. Then finally he broke down and said, "Look, you got an awful lot of enemies, mister." He realized what an absurd situation it was.

15. Johnson and Ludwig Mies van der Rohe in the galleries of the exhibition *Mies van der Rohe*, The Museum of Modern Art, September 16, 1947 through January 25, 1948.

RS: Who was this man, someone from the American Institute of Architects?

PJ: Oh, no, this was the official police, the state officials, licensing officials.

RS: So you think there were political—architectural politics?

PJ: Someone didn't like me. You see, the A.I.A. existed, but I just laughed and was very mean, as I am still, to anybody from the A.I.A. I didn't think I needed the A.I.A. I still want to resign because it costs too much every year.

RS: So what did you do?

PJ: I opened an office in New Canaan.

RS: Well, you had to have built the house in New Canaan to have an office in New Canaan, and you didn't build New Canaan—

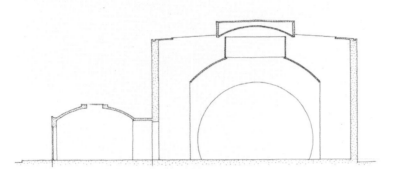

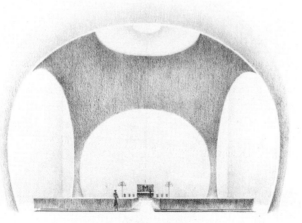

16. The unrealized Greenwich project is for a church, not a synagogue. Philip Johnson, c. 1949. Section and rendering.

PJ: Until 1948, 1949. But I rented a house out there.

RS: And where did you have your office?

PJ: Oh, I had my office over the grocery store on Main Street. It is still there, it's now the office of Eliot Noyes's successor firm.

RS: Did you think about building an office too?

PJ: I did have a design to build an office there.

Well, that was a beautiful building. All I've got are the sketches left for a synagogue based on the same design, which I didn't get to build in Greenwich.[16]

----

17. Lake Pavilion, Glass House estate, New Canaan, Connecticut, 1962.

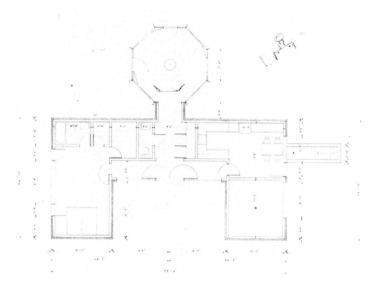

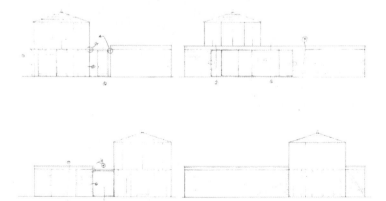

18. Proposed office for Johnson's architectural practice, New Canaan, Connecticut. Philip Johnson, c. 1949. Plan and elevation.

But it's a square box with a skylight. And inside the skylight was a bubble, a sphere, but cut off on four sides, with the feet round like this and toed out.

My favorite toe-out, the toed-out arch I used later on in my pavilion,[17] I got from Delaunay's St. Germain paintings.

So the white walls of the office[18] were to be lighted indirectly from the ceiling above. There was no other light in the room. You would never get to see the direct skylight, you see. And I made a twelve-foot-high mock-up of it and put it on the site. Hitchcock was ecstatic. He thought it was the best thing I had ever done. Of course, it was possible to stick your head up into the model. The ambient light that came from nowhere was wonderful.

I was going to make that into my office and headquarters. It was forty by forty or fifty by fifty.

RS: Up in New Canaan?

PJ: New Canaan. It was 1948, about the time I built my house, before I got my licenses and came back to New York.

You see, those were the days when I had leisure. It takes a long time to think of an idea like that and develop it that far. And it takes money to build such an enormous mock-up, with a sphere, cut sphere, that size. But, of course, that was my pleasure.

6. MoMA and the Practice in the 1950s

RS: Now it's 1949 and you're back at MoMA as the director of architecture and design.[1] How did you staff the Museum and how did you see the postwar mission?

PJ: I'm never good at staffing. I had no help at all. I had one secretary and that was all. I always ran everything myself and it was easier to do it that way than to train people to do it. I couldn't train anybody. I'm totally inept that way. So it was very simple. It was a one-man show just as it was before. I really don't remember that time at the Modern. Do you remember? Is there a list of shows that I did?

RS: First of all, there was Peter Blake[2] who was around and then Arthur Drexler and that was the period of the *Built in U.S.A.: Post-War Architecture* show [1952].

What was your relationship with Peter Blake?

PJ: When I built my house in 1949, he wrote an article saying that I had built the European house and Mies had built the American house.[3] I'm not quite sure what the point was, now that I think back.

It's the only criticism that my house got, the only criticism from my peers, as it

---

1. Johnson in the Abby Aldrich Rockefeller Sculpture Garden at The Museum of Modern Art in 1957. Philip Johnson, 1953.

2. Peter Blake, born Peter Blach, 1920–2006, German-born architect, journalist, and critic living in America. Curator of MoMA, 1948–50; editor in chief of *Architectural Forum*, 1965–72; author of several titles, including *The Master Builders* (1960), *God's Own Junkyard: The Planned Deterioration of America's Landscape* (1964), and *Form Follows Fiasco: Why Modern Architecture Hasn't Worked* (1977).

3. We have been unable to locate this article. Blake refers to the Glass House as epitomizing the European house and the Farnsworth House as epitomizing the American house in *No Place Like Utopia, Modern Architecture and the Company We Kept* (New York: Alfred A. Knopf, 1993).

4. Grace Rainey Rogers Memorial, 21 West Fifty-third Street, 1949–51. Razed in 1979 when the west wing was constructed.

were. I thought it was worth looking at for people who didn't like glass houses.

Peter Blake, being German, understood the whole story and its background better than any other critic.

There were people who thought the house was a progressive statement, but it was no critical work.

Those were the years that I built the Museum Annex,[4] and taught. I taught at Cornell and then at Yale in the early 1950s.

I had Arthur Drexler, who could write — still can — and we did that automobile show.[5]

RS: Yes, I remember that show.

PJ: Alfred [Barr] backed it and the British ambassador walked out of the dinner.

RS: Why?

PJ: Automobiles are not a fit subject for museums.

Of course, Alfred was just delighted, especially with the Jeep.

Henry Ford wrote me a stern letter that Jeeps were not art.

And that was kind of fun. I mean it was still possible in those days to take a firm moral stand for the importance of pure form in objects.

RS: On what was art and what wasn't art.

PJ: Yes, we knew. I mean, it was a thorough conviction, which has disintegrated since. It's all sort of diffuse by this time.

The principles of design were so clear then that we had no trouble doing design shows. We can't do them now because there is no clear-cut "take." But in those days, it was absolutely grand. That went for architecture, too.

RS: How did Arthur come to your attention?[6]

PJ: My attention? He worked for George Nelson[7] and he wrote in art magazines on design. And he wrote so well that I wanted to meet him. I found him brilliant and so I put him on as my assistant. When I designed the new wing at the museum, we

5.MoMA Exhibition #488: *Eight Automobiles: An Exhibition Concerned with the Esthetics of Motorcar Design*, August 28–November 11, 1951.

had desks in the same room.[8] No one could understand it but it was much easier than separate, tiny offices. So we had the only nice office in the museum, which I paid for. It was like the old days, but, of course, with the addition of Arthur, I had fewer problems.

Then I went on teaching and turned to my practice. I had that one house down in Bridgehampton[9] and I was working on my own house.

RS: Right. And the Glass House preceded the brick guest house?

PJ: No, they were done at exactly the same time. And I moved into the brick house on New Year's Night 1949. The Glass House[10] took a little longer to build.

RS: New Year's of 1949 or New Year's of 1950?

PJ: 1950. The night before I moved in I spent with Mary Callery. She took one room and I took the other. We celebrated until far into the night and then we had one other celebration in March for the opening, just Mary Callery and I.

RS: Just you.

PJ: Drunk again, yes. Then I commissioned her to do a work of sculpture for the lawn where the Lipschitz later was and nothing came of it. Her effort wasn't any good, and it was very embarrassing.

I met the de Menils[11] through Mary Callery. They were very young and very poor.

RS: They were poor, you say?

PJ: Well, they lived in a tract house. There was no money.

RS: In Houston?

PJ: Yes. So the house was cheap, $150,000. Even then, it wasn't very much. It's very small. You know the house.

RS: Only from the street and from some photographs.[12]

PJ: Very poor house, but the project was taken over by that strong woman. It was just the opposite of the people out in Bridgehampton. And of course, nothing could have been more fateful. Dominique said, "Would you come and design my house in Houston?" What a beginning!

6. Johnson and Arthur Drexler, c. 1950s.

7. George Nelson, 1908–1986, architect, designer, journalist.

8. Philip Johnson office with furniture designed by Johnson, Grace Rainey Rogers Memorial, The Museum of Modern Art. Philip Johnson, 1951.

9. Eugene Farney House, Sagaponack, New York, 1945–46.

RS: To be banal about it, in those days did you say, "Oh, Mrs. de Menil, we need to write a contract," and things like that?

PJ: Oh, Lord no. I never did. I still don't.

RS: You don't?

PJ: No, other people take care of that.

RS: And your people were doing that even in those humble—

PJ: No, I just plowed in. See, I wasn't quite rich, but reasonably well-to-do, so I wasn't worried about the money. If they didn't pay, I didn't even know it.

My accountant said, "You lost fifty thousand this year. You've got to change." I said, "Aw, shucks." You know, that kind of attitude.

Fifty thousand in those days is about a hundred thousand today. But fortunately, I didn't have to make a contract, because imagine doing that with the grand Mrs. de Menil. You don't do those things.

RS: She did pay?

PJ: I don't know. I think so, yes. Whether I ever sent a bill is the question!

RS: We'll leave those questions for the historians.

Was Mrs. de Menil a person of artistic taste?

PJ: She had violent artistic taste. She did not want a house with any architecture to it, and that's just what she got. In other words, she got exactly what she ordered.

The plan was rather good in many ways. I mean, it worked extremely well for her. It wouldn't work for anybody else.

She knew how to handle a house once she had it, but she wasn't particularly interested in the way it looked, and she still isn't.

She absolutely refused to see a real architect about her museum, and so she got what she wanted.[13] It isn't a building at all. It's just a warehouse with a fantastic ceiling. But she was interested in the lighting and the ceiling. But she had ineffable, great, perfect taste, in a sense, in painting.

That house I did was a struggle of satisfying the iron will of Mrs. de Menil and her

10. Johnson at the Glass House, July 1, 1949.

11. Dominique Schlumberger de Menil, 1908–1998, and John de Menil, 1904–1973.

daughter, who couldn't be out of her sight. So we had to make a secret passage from her bedroom to the de Menils' bedroom.

RS: Which daughter is that? Marie-Christophe?

PJ: Yes, she calls herself Christophe.[14] They were all very, very young, of course.

But it absolutely ruined the plan, and that, of course, to a Mies student was a very hard pill to take.

Mies would have refused the job at that point. He had houses lying around in his files that show him trying to please a rich client; nothing was ever built because he couldn't compromise. And the same thing with the Resors.[15] He could never fit their wishes into his straitjacket purity. That was the difficulty, of course, with that period and that approach. The plan was everything. And breaking the plan, which you had to do to live in it, couldn't be done. Whereas in the Wrightian approach, you could tack things on at the end of those hopelessly long corridors, two feet wide or whatever they were.

RS: So then the de Menil house was built, published.

PJ: No, never published; never will be.[16] She didn't want it published, and I was delighted because I don't think it's a very good house. You see, they were going to buy the land next door.

That's why it's got such a blank front, which I always regretted. But other people think it's an example of clarity and smoothness broken only by the kitchen window, which allows you to see who's coming.

I thought that was a very repulsive way to receive people into a house. So I was delighted not to publish it. As I said, the reason we did the blank wall was that they were going to sell off the front land. They were not rich, but the lot was not exactly cheap even then. Of course, they never did. They made money and went on.

Another reason that it is difficult to build in Houston is the climate. I didn't realize that it was so antihuman. I made porches and terraces on which there has never been a chair.

RS: Because it's too hot.

PJ: You can't step out. In winter, they're still so set on the summer that they don't go out. Fall and spring are marvelous in Houston. I would say, "Well, let's go out." They just look at you.

It's very much like here. You're in an apartment in New York. Why don't you

12. Dominique and John de Menil house, Houston, Texas.
Philip Johnson, 1949–50. Entrance facade and elevations.

open the windows? They're all operable. But that wouldn't cross our minds. They're perfectly good.

RS: It has crossed mine.

PJ: Well, because we didn't try to turn on the air-conditioning soon enough.

But you wouldn't like it if I opened that window because of the wind and everything. It's really habit. You're on a train and you decide you can't open the windows because soot's bad. But after the end of soot, you still don't open the windows. But the Houstonians are amazing—their lack of going outdoors.

Anyway, around the same time as the de Menils, I built a house up in Newburgh that no one has ever seen, the Wolf House.[17] It's on my list of works, I think. Somebody went to see it once and said, "Why should I come way over to Newburgh to see this?" They were right.

But I was concerned with the view up and down the river, you see, which is staggering from Newburgh. But the house was too far away and it was too difficult to get to and I was a very poor supervisor on the job. That's not my dish at all.

RS: In these early houses, did you do the drawings, everything?

PJ: Yes. I did everything.

RS: The working drawings, Philip? I can't believe this.

PJ: Well, working drawings, that's a pretty hard word for what I did. But when you do houses, as you well know, you can go as far as you like.

If you're interested in detailing, then it's really a good job but a hard job. But you see, I didn't know anything about detailing. Nor did I think it was important or necessary. It leads to much, much harder work, as you know.

But in the early days, if you got the plan right it was enough—remember the plan as the generator, the great Corbusier principle and Mies's, too, of course.

RS: Mies would do, or have people do for him, those meticulous drawings of brick coursing and reentrant corners and what have you.

PJ: Yes, entry corners and brick ceilings and all that, but it was still bare-bones architecture. Once he figured out the plan of the Fifty-by-Fifty House,[18] then it was done. Then it was just a plan and four columns and enormous sheets of glass.

RS: Were you teaching at this time?

PJ: Yes, and, the teaching part was interesting to me, especially teaching at Cornell.

- -

13. The de Menil Museum, Houston, Texas. Renzo Piano, architect, 1982–86.

14. Christophe de Menil, b. 1933.

15. Stanley Resor, client for unbuilt house in Jackson Hole, Wyoming, 1937–38.

16. Shortly after this interview, the house was published. See Rosamond Bernier, "A Gift of Vision: On the Opening of Her New Museum, Dominique de Menil Reflects on the Houston House Where It All Began," *House & Garden* 159 (July 1987): 120–29, 180.

17. Mr. and Mrs. Benjamin V. Wolf house, Newburgh, New York. Philip Johnson, 1948-49.

18. Fifty-by-Fifty House, 1950.

RS: Why especially at Cornell?

PJ: I didn't teach at Yale so thoroughly as I did at Cornell. I took a whole semester up there, I think [1950].

You could concentrate more because it was so far. It was a hell of a flight.

RS: You would fly out for two or three days and come back?

PJ: That's right. So you could concentrate more.

RS: Any good students?

PJ: Yes, Gatje[19] was my best student and later became head man for Breuer.

Let's see, that is now thirty-five years ago. You'd think some of them would have been heard from but only Gatje made it. But it was clear at the beginning that he was capable as well as a good designer.

RS: Paul Rudolph taught at Cornell then. Did you overlap?

PJ: No.

RS: Or Giurgola?[20] He was also up there.

PJ: It must have been after.

RS: So it was just you. What was your technique of teaching in those days?

PJ: I was not a good teacher because I don't think I had enough empathy for the student as such. I was also a very permissive teacher. I didn't force any directions. I was more like Stirling,[21] but I don't know how he actually does it. He helps each one in the direction he's already going in. I mean, there's no school of Stirling the way there is of Mies.

RS: No, but then he just gave a prize for the scheme that is closest to the way he has actually designed the building already.

PJ: No!

RS: Yes!

PJ: That's very interesting. Then why is it that it isn't a recognizable class of work that emphasizes Stirling? He does it that way?

RS: That's the way he does it. Well, I mean, when you were at Yale, my recollection is that you would give a problem and say: design a house in the manner of Mies, Le Corbusier, or Wright.

PJ: That was what I started at Pratt.

That was a course that I gave: work in Mies, work in Le Corbusier, work in Wright. I thought students should get exposed to that.

That was a very Miesian technique, but it didn't last too long. Then, you see, I assigned them a regular house. Your mother's house, you know, the usual tripe. But I was never a strong aesthetic direction leader, in any way.

But I was at the same time strangely arrogant. Once I flunked one of my students, Richard Foster. He later became head of the office. And he reminded me about it ten years after. He said, "You flunked me on that design on the theory of architecture." That was the course; it was called "Theory of Architecture." I felt historical courses were all right. It wasn't a class where you were trying to learn how to design.

RS: I see. It wasn't a studio but a seminar kind of situation.

- -

19. Robert Gatje, b. 1927, architect.

20. Romaldo Giurgola, b. 1920, Italian-born American and, later, Australian architect.

21. James Stirling, 1926–1992, architect.

22. Landis Gores, 1919–1991, architect.

PJ: Yes, a seminar, and this was their thesis, as it were. They could choose what they wanted to hand in.

But I was too unsure of myself to be a good Miesian, you see, and I resented the Miesian straitjacket teaching. And I didn't have a strong enough direction of my own. I would now, but I didn't then. I regret that, but I just didn't.

At the same time, I was starting to build my first [public] building, which was the addition to the Modern. Gores[22] was then a partner of mine. He was a fellow Harvard man. He hadn't gotten polio yet. He was a very bad administrator and supervisor, as I was, and the Modern got very upset with me and with him.

One remembers these little troubles, doesn't one?

RS: So here it is 1950, modernism is on the upsurge. You're here. You're not taken so seriously as an architect.

PJ: No.

RS: How are you struggling to overcome your 1930s bad-boy reputation?

PJ: That's interesting. The bad-boy reputation has become much stronger in the last ten years than it was at that time. It's very strange.

Everything was so close that we couldn't see the forest for the trees. There was no reexamination of the Holocaust. The word hadn't been invented, for instance. I didn't know about it, of course, during the war. None of us did. That has gradually grown on us. The horror, you see.

So there are really more books per year on it now, I guess. Then Shirer was reprinted. At the time the book came out it was 1943 or 1942, and I went right on in school. Nobody bothered. It has sort of snowballed since.

I don't wonder! But had we known at the time what we know now, I suppose we'd have been more horrified. So it is worse now than it was then, being brought up by everybody. At the time it wasn't a bothersome thing.

But you are right on the other thing. I was a critic and was taken to be such. It was Frank Lloyd Wright[23]—I guess you've heard this story a hundred times—who blasted me out. That was 1953, I guess, when I left the museum again. He said, "Look, you should shit or get off the pot. You are either going to be a critic, which is fine, or you're going to be a practicing architect. But you simply can't do both." Drexler found that out for himself when he built a house. He quickly went back to criticism. Hitchcock found

23. Johnson and Frank Lloyd Wright, c. 1953.

24. Addition to James Thrall Soby house, Farmington, Connecticut. Henry-Russell Hitchcock, 1935.

that out when he built a wing on Soby's house.[24] You've never seen it, I hope.

RS: Only in photographs.

PJ: Sad. But it never hurt his eye as a critic. So I had to struggle with that dual role, which I'm still struggling with, I suppose. I mean, I'm still an extracurricular architect. I'm better known as an advisor and picker of architects rather than for my work, which naturally annoys me because I enjoy doing the work.

Okay, let's see, we're back to the monuments, as Russell calls every little outhouse. The de Menil house, and then that almost begins the collaboration with Mies, doesn't it? 1954.

RS: Yes, but there's the guest house for Mrs. Rockefeller. Where does that fit in?[25] At this point you're being taken up by Mrs. Rockefeller, the Rockefellers.

PJ: I was always an old friend of Nelson's but not his architect.

RS: That was Wally Harrison.

PJ: Wally was his architect.

Although I knew I was a better architect. But the friendship was too strong and Wally was too closely, umbilically attached.

But Blanchette always liked younger people. At that time, I wasn't much younger than she, was I? But she was so grand.

RS: Younger? Aren't you older than she?

PJ: Older than she, but she seemed always older in the sense of class difference. I won't call it class—positional difference.

RS: Well, she was a woman Rockefeller and had some money on her own, besides.

PJ: She was a woman of position and power at birth. So I was in awe.

She said, "Well, aren't you an architect?" I mean, that shows you how much I wasn't considered an architect. I said, "Oh, yes."

She was my first patron, if you will.

The job of her house was my first regular commission by anybody. And it came through the Museum because she liked my *beaux yeux*.

25. Johnson in January 1974, during his tenancy in the Rockefeller Guest House, 242 East Fifty-second Street, New York. Philip Johnson, 1950.

It was as simple as that.

She said, "Well, what about your doing my house?" She almost had to persuade me into it, but we got along fine and it went well.

I don't think that she knows anything about architecture, ever will, or ever did. She has had a series of favorites. Her next one was Eddie Barnes, for a long time. She never took to Pelli.[26] Pelli was chosen by a group of us.

But she was a patron and you cannot, as an architect, do without patrons. The cultivation of patrons becomes an important part of the grand game, as no doubt Mr. Lutyens[27] knew.

RS: So she doesn't care about architecture. Does she know anything about architecture when you come to present her with an idea?

PJ: No, she knows even less—which was a great blessing because it's not a very practical house, in case you've ever been there.

RS: Indeed I have, when you lived in it.[28]

PJ: Yes, that's right. Anyhow, she always said afterward, "Well, Philip, we built it for art, didn't we?" whenever something perfectly horrible happened.

RS: She never meant to live in it, did she?

PJ: No, that's why she didn't care. But it was hard to go to the johnnie, you see, without being seen from the street. That was a difficulty, and other things like that, minor things.

But she felt that that was quite all right, that it was done for the sake of showing art. In other words, her head was in the right place.

She had no feel for art or taste. She didn't say, "But I don't like that." Because she wouldn't know whether she liked it or not. And she still doesn't.

I remember taking Mies to the house. He must have been visiting here—it was at the time when we were starting to think about Seagram's.

RS: Now, who are the Boissonnases? You did some houses for them at this time, or a little later, in the mid and late '50s.

PJ: The Boissonnases are very much influenced by the de Menils in taste. Mrs. Boissonnas[29] and Mrs. de Menil are sisters, and both came into this fantastic wealth.

RS: But you did better architecture for Mrs. Boissonnas.

PJ: Yes, because she and her husband were hands-on clients. They were interested in the art of it. They were interested in the development.

RS: The synagogue comes in somewhere about this time too.

PJ: The synagogue[30] I was doing out of guilt, partially.

RS: How do you mean?

PJ: Well, I built it for nothing. I didn't take a fee. They knew about my background, of course.

RS: So there was some sensitivity.

PJ: Must have been. That was also true of my advisor, the one who later committed suicide and for whom I built a house—Wiley.[31] He was my sort of business advisor and was very helpful.

----

26. Cesar Pelli, b. 1926, architect of MoMA expansion, including Museum Tower Apartments, 1984.

27. Sir Edwin Landseer Lutyens, 1869–1944, British architect.

28. Johnson shared the Rockefeller Guest House with David Whitney in the 1970s.

RS: And he said, do it?

PJ: He said, "You have never built a big building. What does it cost you? Thirty or forty thousand dollars. What's that to start a career? You do it and do it for nothing. It will help with the past—it will help you do other things."

So I made the offer and . . . maybe they understood. How much they understood, we never discussed it. So that was a very good job.

RS: Had they come to you or did you just get wind of it?

PJ: I must have gotten wind of the job and somehow got an interview. They came up to the house in New Canaan, the committee, and they finally couldn't resist. It was a lot of money, of course, for them, and synagogues always need money. I enjoyed that very much.

RS: They executed it pretty much the way you designed it?

PJ: They did. Oh, I was right there. The faults there are mine. I can't say that the clients influenced me too much.

For the stained glass, I went to [John] Johansen, because I thought he was an *artiste* and I wasn't artistic enough to pick the colors.

29. Silvie Schlumberger, 1912–1999, married to Eric Boissonnas, 1913–2005. Pictured above are two views of the Mr. and Mrs. Eric Boissonnas house, New Canaan, Connecticut. Philip Johnson, 1954–56.

30. Kneses Tifereth Israel, Port Chester, New York, 1956.

I don't think I'd make that judgment today, but that shows you how tentative everything was in my own mind.

RS: Well, you still fall back on Mr. Kaufman.[32]

PJ: I used Mr. Kaufman.

RS: You could have picked the colors yourself.

PJ: Not as well. Besides this is too delicate a thing. Color is too important to leave to the architect, just as some of the architecture is.

I'm particularly aware of color, but not of how to use it in the right amounts. For instance, the bright green in this room, the picking out of the molding strips—I never would have done that. I'm not sure it's necessary either. But that's the kind of thing—it's the amount and the balance between one color and its contrasting colors that's so hard.

I feel inadequate, and properly so, in the practical side. See, you and Rudolph and all those people—Gwathmey,[33] don't seem to feel that way.

RS: No, no, that's not true. We just don't tell you.

PJ: Oh! Why would you?

RS: I have other people do those things. I'm totally inadequate.

31. Mr. and Mrs. Robert C. Wiley house, New Canaan, Connecticut. Philip Johnson, 1952–53.

32. Donald Kaufman, b. 1935, and wife, Taffy Dahl, b. 1940, color consultants.

33. Charles Gwathmey, b. 1938, architect.

PJ: I don't believe it for a minute.

RS: Well.

PJ: Anyhow, I've always felt so inadequate.

RS: It's hard to design buildings.

PJ: We're private in here, aren't we?

Yes, it's impossible. And to find that fine balance, without hurting *amour propre* all around, is one of those delicate things. Because people do want to work for you, they know what they're contributing.

[Richard] Foster, my enormous friend, always knew that he was doing all the work. What was I doing? Just making some sketches? And what was he getting out of it?

RS: He wasn't even getting the glamour.

PJ: No, so he finally left.

RS: And nobody's ever heard of him since.

PJ: No one has ever heard of him since. Actually, he has work now. It's all right. Because he's very eager, a carry-outer. I've always searched for a person to carry me along. First I got Charles Abbe.[34] Of course, he wanted some fantastic sum of two hundred dollars a week. In those days, thirty years ago, there wasn't any such thing as two hundred dollars—that'd be what, twelve hundred now? And he said, "You just can't afford me." So I had him find me other people, and we got along a little bit that way.

Then I had Foster. He was working for me at Pratt when I was teaching there. He came to work in the course of just the normal turnover.

RS: So you had this small office in New York with a variety of people trooping through.

PJ: Trooping in and out. I remember the day I fired Foster and then Wiley walked in. Foster had been managing the office as well as me, as well as my affairs. Wiley said, "You absolute blithering idiot. This is the one good man. He should be head of your office as soon as he's a year or two older. You're going to regret this all the rest of your life. Now, you get him back here."

RS: In those days, were you seeing George Howe?[35]

PJ: Yes. George is the man I think of more than any single person of that era because he was always so very open to new ideas.

----

34. Charles Abbe, 1907–1993, architect.

35. George Howe in the 1950s.

And rather like a pixie, I amused him. You know how he was. He wasn't a bit stuffy. And he found Philadelphia stuffy and Mrs. Stotesbury[36] stuffy. I mean, his great claim to fame is that he refused to build a house for Mrs. Stotesbury.

RS: Oh, I didn't know that.

PJ: Yes. You didn't do that if you were a Philadelphian. She had houses all over, like confetti, from Maine to Florida. She was the big patroness of architecture and for Mellor, Meigs and Howe[37] to refuse to build her a house in 1932, or whenever it was—in 1932, you didn't turn down any jobs. But he was quite proud of that and rightly so.

I used to go to Philadelphia and we'd have lunch at his club. Did you ever do that?

RS: I didn't know him at all. He was dead before I got to Yale.

PJ: George got Kahn[38] to build the Yale Art Gallery. He was a great patron when he knew that he couldn't be a designer. His patronage showed in his favoring of me, the same way I try to help kids in my way.

RS: Getting Philip Goodwin[39] basically fired on the Art Gallery job must have–

PJ: Oh, it was Goodwin's job at Yale?

RS: Goodwin before Kahn,[40] yes, probably on the strength of—

----

36. Mrs. Edward T. Stotesbury, 1865–1946, grande dame of Philadelphia society.

37. George Howe's firm from 1918 to 1927, specializing in French Norman-inspired country houses.

38. Louis I. Kahn, 1901–1974, architect.

39. Proposed addition to Yale University Art Gallery, New Haven, Connecticut. Philip L. Goodwin, c. 1950.

40. Addition to Yale University Art Gallery, New Haven, Connecticut. Louis I. Kahn, 1951–53.

PJ: The fact that his name was on MoMA.

RS: Yes.

PJ: Imagine Goodwin! Of course, he's from Connecticut too, and Yale.[41] Goodwin was from Hartford and very well connected. I never knew that. What do you know!

No, Howe was determined to get a good building at Yale and he thought that Kahn could give it to him. He talked quite openly with me. Of course, I wanted the job myself, but that wasn't possible. I mean, I was just a beginner, hadn't done anything. I had no track record. He was quite right to pick Kahn. It was quite perceptive of him to see that there was somebody like him who wasn't a kid anymore but who represented something new.

RS: Did you have a friendship with Kahn at that point?

PJ: I never was friendly with Kahn.[42] I always helped him whenever I could. He used to call me and say, "They're trying to take away my"—whatever he wanted at the time—and I'd call everybody I knew at Yale. Never successful, but I used to try to be.

Then, of course, we later gave him a show at the museum, but that was under Arthur [Drexler]. I liked his work better than I liked him. Did you know him?

RS: Yes, I did know him, reasonably well.

PJ: He didn't die till—

RS: 1974.

PJ: He was seventy-four, the same age as the century. But I never found him the great lovely guru-type. I couldn't stand all those long monologues about belief in truth.

I can't stand truth. It gets so boring, you know, like social responsibility. Did you see that thing? They're all having a protest, the Architects for Social Responsibility?[43]

RS: But you can't be against social responsibility, can you?

PJ: Oh, I can. You don't have to be for it.

RS: Well, *you* can. You've had your day at being against social responsibility.

PJ: Yes, I have a long, long reputation.

RS: In fact, you'd be more suspect if you came out for social responsibility now.

PJ: I know. People would say, "Has Johnson changed his spots or what?" Social responsibility!

See, in the 1930s, that was the euphemism for membership in the Communist Party. I have nothing against the Communist Party. If it had only won! But it was a hopeless cause always.

----

41. Class of 1907.

43. Activist organization, now called Architects/Designers/ Planners for Social Responsibility, founded 1981.

42. Johnson and Louis I. Kahn, 1966.

And I didn't like the fronts that they used all the time: social responsibility, progress, and freedom. You know, the word freedom was adopted by the communists before it was adopted by Hitler. Hitler called the mission of his Zeppelin going around the world "Freiheit und Friede," freedom and peace. Shit. But all these fronts and euphemisms drove me up the wall. Why didn't they say, "Look, I like Russia." I could certainly have understood that. But, no, they had to cover it all. So, of course, this isn't that. This is do-goodism.

Anyhow, where are we?

RS: We're with George in New Haven.

PJ: George in New Haven. He was the one person that I could talk to, the way I can to you now, and cut through things. We could always get right to the essence because we knew what we were on earth for. Just as you and I do. We don't have to deal with any bullshit, we don't have to have arguments. See, the problem with the rest of the people, like Eisenman for example, is that people talk as if the writing of books, the producing of books, is the end.

The end, as you and I know, and as George always knew, is what the building really looks like. Of course, he was much better than he knew. But it wasn't till later that I discovered Mellor, Meigs and Howe.[44]

RS: They were great.

PJ: I had no sense of how well he, or somebody down there, understood stone. You see, we could never do this today. Or the way that he simplified things in his own house.[45] It was beautiful. But he came to think that all hand craft, all reference to history, was somehow suspect. He too was much converted to the modern, as was I.

44. Arthur E. Newbold Estate, Laverock, Pennsylvania. Mellor, Meigs and Howe, 1921–24.

45. High Hollow, George Howe house, Chestnut Hill, Pennsylvania. George Howe, 1914–17.

It's a shame because he would have bridged the whole period if he had lived. He wouldn't be dead yet.

RS: He was born in 1886, the same age as Mies.

PJ: Excuse me, he would be dead. A hundred years. Yes, exactly. Same age as Mies?

RS: Same age as Mies.

PJ: But he was much more fun to talk to back then. I was much encouraged by the fact that he existed. I myself must have been somewhat like that for the kids at Yale. It's good to know that someone can make it, can deal with the world.

RS: For the bright kids, you were a breath of fresh air.

PJ: That's right. For the rest, I was the most despised. Still am. I didn't care about the rest. Neither did George. He was not a common man with a common touch. He was an elitist from way back. See that was another thing we had in common, like Lincoln Kirstein and I have always had. Elitism is the only proper philosophy, but you cannot, simply cannot, I repeat, talk about it.

RS: Except to other elitists! But then you don't have to.

PJ: Then you don't have to, you see. So the word elite never crosses Lincoln's and my lips. Just once in a while when Lincoln gets really angry. He says, "Goddamn, I'm an elitist and I'm only going to dance for people who can stand it or can tolerate it."

46. Kirstein Tower, dedicated to Lincoln Kirstein, on the estate in New Canaan, Connecticut. Philip Johnson, 1985.

Oh, my new tower is called the Kirstein Tower.[46] Yes. It's fascinating. It's a study in staircases—I thought I'd never get up it because of the way I designed it. It is too precarious.

But it's a fascinating physical experience to walk right up it. I never had a piece of architecture—I suppose it's architecture, or is it sculpture?—where the participation in it is the point of it. I don't know, it's not beautiful, maybe. I don't even know that. But the participation is delicious. And the ins and outs are fine.

RS: Lincoln was your longtime friend and close confidant. Did you have any other relationship before David Whitney of an enduring kind?

PJ: Oh, yes, John Hohnsbeen[47] was the first, second, and third Mrs. Johnson. Yes, John Hohnsbeen. And if you don't know, he's a playboy. He lives. He inherited money from an unloved uncle.

We thought he was going down the tubes. We didn't know who was going to feed him because he was not much at getting jobs. But then he got a telegram that his uncle died and left him a very rich farm. So he's going through that money now, and when that goes he won't have anything. He's from Oklahoma. You never ran into him?

RS: I've never heard his name.

PJ: Because he doesn't come into the art world much. He was an art dealer, but unsuccessful and not very interesting. He worked with one of the early dealers. And we were together for a long time at Fifty-fifth Street.[48]

But where were we? George Howe was the first of my real architectural friends whom I could talk shorthand with, whom I always depended on.

RS: So you would see George down in Philadelphia. Also presumably in New York?

PJ: No, only in Philadelphia, and in Washington during the war. I stayed at his apartment when I came up from camp, whenever I could stay all night. He wasn't there much. He was the "Architect for the United States" at that time, a wonderful title which used to put him into stitches.[49] Of course, he had nothing to do. No bureaucrat does. He felt deserted and I would buck him up and he would buck me up because I was in camp. I was building out in the country, my little tool house out there. I built a tool shed on the farm while I was in camp.

RS: What about Stonorov,[50] Howe's partner, who was important?

PJ: I never became friendly with Stonorov. The whole Philadelphia milieu was something that I just never understood. I didn't get it even in the time of Giurgola and Kahn. I never was woven into that group. It's funny, isn't it, because you'd think that was a natural. And considering what a center Philadelphia became.

RS: George Howe invited you to Yale to teach?

PJ: He may have. I don't see how else I would have gotten there.

RS: And then there were all these bright young students there then.[51]

PJ: There were, indeed. I don't know whether they were bright or not. That was before you came. I had more impact, I think, when I first wrote on the wall, "You cannot not know history."

RS: Right.

----

47. John Hohnsbeen, 1926–2007.

48. Johnson's New York pied-à-terre on East Fifty-fifth Street, between Park and Lexington Avenues, where he lived before moving to the Rockefeller Guest House in 1972.

49. Howe's official title was Supervising Architect of the Public Buildings Administration.

50. Oskar Stonorov, 1905–1970, German-born American architect who worked with George Howe and Louis I. Kahn.

PJ: The kids wrote all over the walls, of course. The graffiti was very good. We were in the old hall, Weir Hall. So all over the rooms where I took my [Connecticut State architectural licensing] exams, as I remember, you could look up and see the "Yale box." The Yale glass box was a picture of my house. A photo taken and put into various contexts: it was a bank, it was in the desert, it was a church. The students made very good fun of it, and for very good reasons, so anti-symbolic was it and Miesian.

51. Top: Johnson, Paul Rudolph (seated center), and Vincent Scully (standing, center right), at Yale student review, c. 1960. Standing directly behind Rudolph is Charles Gwathmey; behind Gwathmey is Michael Hollander, b. 1934. Standing behind Johnson is George Buchanan, b. 1937. Partially visible on the far left is Jean-Paul Carlhian, b. 1919.

Bottom: Paul Rudolph, Johnson, and Robert Venturi, b. 1925, in profile at right during Yale student review, c. 1960.

52. Illinois Institute of Technology chapel, 1952.

Like Mies's church,[52] it looked like an outhouse. And Mies's outhouses looked like churches. I always made the joke that the powerhouse at I.I.T. is a much more religious building than the chapel.

RS: Absolutely.

PJ: So they made that kind of fun of my house, perfectly justifiably, a good point. And they did it by these humorous graffiti sketches all over the wall. So there I was, feeling so humiliated and drag-ass, since I didn't have a license yet, and I look up on the walls and my house is all over the place. I took the exam for my Connecticut license in that room.

RS: Yes. A number of times, didn't you?

PJ: Yes, two or three times, because I kept flunking design. I think we went through this before.

RS: No, we talked about it before, but not on tape.

PJ: I couldn't get my license. Design was the only part I flunked. I had no trouble with structures. Oh, I did have a little trouble at first with city planning. What do you call that?

RS: Site planning.

PJ: Yes, with arranging: "Arrange these houses on these lots." Well, I didn't know that you just copied the latest suburban subdivision. So I tried to do something classical and monumental and flunked. I learned better when I went to school; I finally went to cram school. "How do you pass?" I asked the man. He was terribly nice.

7. Seagram

RS: What about Mies, Phyllis Lambert, and Seagram?[1]

PJ: Yes, we'd better get it straight; that's a good idea.

Phyllis's[2] father[3] was going to build a skyscraper and he had a very bad architect. Luckman.[4] Good old Charlie.

Charlie did a quick scheme and Bronfman sent it to Phyllis because she was the one interested. But he had one passion in life and that was to get his daughter back—she lived in Paris. There had been the usual family arguments between generations. He said, "Well, if you're so smart, you come back and build the building."[5]

1. Johnson, Ludwig Mies van der Rohe, and Phyllis Lambert, c. 1955.

She did. A woman of enormous energy, of fantastic single-mindedness almost to the point of absurdity. She decided that the way her father was proceeding was no way to find an architect and certainly no way to build a building.

She didn't know why but she felt something was wrong. So she went around asking different people. I never knew really how many people she asked before she came to Alfred Barr.

Alfred Barr, quite wisely, said, "Well, we have a Department of Architecture. Why don't you go across the hall and talk to Philip Johnson?" So I said, "Well, here's a list of architects." Then she asked me to go with her to interview these people, except for Mies, whom she wanted to see alone. That was fine with me because I knew Mies too well and didn't want to get involved. But we went to Saarinen; we went to Pei. We had Pei to lunch out at the house. He was young.

RS: Well, what were these interviews like?

PJ: They were funny—mostly about how she felt personally. She was very impressed with Saarinen, but Saarinen oversold. Pei undersold. Saarinen thought he had the job and he could be an extraordinarily pushy man. Well, that's why he got ahead! But he kept calling and that frightened her.

I forget what in particular set her off against Wright. I think it was some insistence on his part that she give him half a million[6] up front as earnest to start right in. It was just the wrong approach to use when you're trying to impress somebody who has a mind of her own.

I, fortunately, kept completely still. Finally, she went to see Mies. And I remember riding the train. My God, there were no airplanes in those days. We were going from Detroit [where Saarinen's office was located] to Chicago [where Mies van der Rohe's office was located]. She said, "You know, I've made up my mind." I said, "Well, what?" I didn't have a clue. "I've picked Mies van der Rohe." It was as simple as that.

---

2. Phyllis Bronfman Lambert, b. 1927, Canadian architect and founding director of the Canadian Centre for Architecture.

3. Samuel Bronfman, 1889–1971, president of the Joseph E. Seagram Company.

4. Charles Luckman, 1909–1999. Initially trained as an architect, Luckman eventually became the head of the U.S. branch of the British soap company Lever Brothers. He was involved in the planning for the company's American headquarters, Lever House (Skidmore, Owings & Merrill, 1952), but was fired over the building's high construction cost. He returned to architecture, practicing with William L. Pereira (1909–1985) from 1951 to 1959. After 1959 the pair split, forming separate firms, William L. Pereira & Associates and The Luckman Partnership.

5. Seagram Building, 375 Park Avenue, New York. Ludwig Mies van der Rohe, Philip Johnson, and Kahn & Jacobs, 1958.

6. This story, which may be apocryphal—Phyllis Lambert believes it is—is also muddied by Johnson's recollection that the figure demanded was $500,000. Robert Stern remembers hearing the figure $50,000 when the story was told.

RS: Did you go to see Wright?

PJ: I don't think so. I think we decided—or I decided—that he hadn't a track record or interest in business architecture. His work was ideal, not real—he hadn't done the Mile-High yet.[7] Had it been a museum or a small enough building, one would have talked to him, but I didn't advise it under the circumstance. Did she go and see Breuer? Yes, that didn't last. Oh, she went and saw, of all people, Walker.[8]

RS: Ralph Walker, really?

PJ: Ralph Walker was the A.I.A.'s "Architect of the Century." Special medal [1957], never granted to anybody else. He oversold. Took her out to, of all things, General Foods.[9] Do you remember the old General Foods?

RS: Yes.

PJ: He showed her how he could handle a great big job. He could indeed, but she was so appalled by the looks of that building. I didn't go with her. So she did see the head of the profession.

The people who were most seriously considered were Saarinen and Mies. Of course, I didn't come into question because I had never built. So that was easy. Besides, I always had my other hat on. That's that ambivalence that you mentioned: I was between stools. I could be of help to her and I was, I think.

The Bronfmans were under the influence of the best builder in those days, Crandall,[10] the president of the Fuller Company. An absolute genius and very sympathetic to architecture, and a leader. None of us had ever built a building, let's face it.

Mies never built a building. He was like me that way. We're not hands-on builders. Crandall was essentially an extraordinary courtly man who got the confidence of the old boy [Samuel Bronfman] and of Phyllis, of Mies, of me, and he handled us all the way one only wishes to be handled.

The money I didn't know about; he took care of that. He took care of the programming. He took care of the subcontractors. I wanted to use a two-inch granite because it was cheaper. He said, "We in this office use four-inch granite." Well, now, that's a good builder. All right, it cost Mr. Seagram a little more, but he knew that wasn't the point. The point was to make a monument. He didn't mind when the old boy said, "Well, why don't you make it out of *that* material," looking at the doors of the Daily News Building—bronze.

Mies said, "That's wonderful," and I was left to deal with the bronze companies and they nearly died.

RS: They'd never built anything with that much bronze.

PJ: No! They said they couldn't. They couldn't extrude a thing that big. And I said, "Well, I bet you if you work hard enough and put enough engineers on it, you could." And they could and they did.

You see, another reason we don't have craftsmanship in this country is that there's no mass demand.

RS: I've been saying that.

PJ: I know. Well, we both have.

We've preached this all our lives, haven't we?

RS: You only get what you ask for.

PJ: You only get what you ask for.

The same with the client. That's why you and I are so successful with Gerry.[11]

We know what buttons to push. We know what he wants, really, is the fame and the reputation of being a fine builder.

So this man Crandall was a Hines, but as a builder, not a developer. He set the thing up and said, "Look, if you're going to have this mad genius, that's quite all right. But for heaven's sake a) tie him to another architect who knows how to design and has been through the factory, and b) get him to come and live here [in New York]."

Of course, that was unheard of. Mies balked. He said, "Look, I can design as well in my armchair," where he always worked, "in Chicago as well as I can in New York." Adamant! Crandall wouldn't hear of it. So we found a place in town for Mies to live.

RS: Did Mies actually spend chunks of time in New York?

PJ: He spent time here, sure. We got him a suite at the Barclay. He was happy as a clam and sat all by himself in a room about this size.

I said, "What do you do all the time?" He replied, "Ve think." I see now what he was talking about because I cannot work with all these meetings and telephones.

I get my time Friday, Saturday, and Sunday. I come back with a lot of yellow paper, but most is in my head.

But he was right. It's the thinking time that's the important time in architecture. You see, the reason I got into the Seagram project was that they thought he ought to have an interpreter who was on his side, but a person who was a little more able to talk English and had experience as an architect, at least slightly. I had built the Rockefeller house and enough little things so it was all right. So he said, "You can be co-architect," which is a name I have never used. But I did do some of the work. The interiors of the dining room, of course. He and I didn't get along very well for obvious reasons. I wanted to be an architect and all he wanted to do was to have a draftsman or executor who would carry out things the way he wanted.

RS: Well, there was Kahn & Jacobs, also.

PJ: Kahn & Jacobs[12] did the working drawings. They worked extremely well because they had a very good spec writer. In some offices the spec writer really calls the shots. This man had built piles and piles of buildings. We never had to see Jacobs or Kahn. I had a terrible fight with Kahn the very first meeting so he never came back.

RS: Oh, really?

PJ: It was marvelous, a glorious meeting in our offices. Kahn said, "I tell you how we do it, Mies. We start in with a ground plan and then we work the elevator core out. And in this building it would be about this many elevators to do the job quickly. And then we start decorating the door like this, you see."

Mies was a very, very quiet man, but right in the middle of this long speech—he must have been talking for ten or fifteen minutes—Mies stood up and hit the table, an enormous thing, with his hand and said one word, "No."

-----

7. Frank Lloyd Wright presented a 26-foot-tall, 6-foot-wide drawing for the Illinois Building, dubbed "Mile-High," in Chicago in 1956.

8. Ralph T. Walker, 1889–1973, architect. The Barclay-Vesey Building, 1923–27, which he designed while working at McKenzie, Voorhees, and Gmelin, is frequently cited as New York's first Art Deco skyscraper.

9. A pioneering suburban corporate headquarters building designed by Voorhees, Walker, Foley & Smith in White Plains, New York, 1953.

10. Lou R. Crandall, 1893–1978.

11. Gerald D. Hines, b. 1925, developer.

12. Ely Jacques Kahn, 1884–1972, and Robert Allan Jacobs, 1905–1993, founded Kahn & Jacobs in 1940. The firm was preceded by Buchman & Kahn, founded in 1915.

It was the end of the meeting. We never saw Kahn again. Mies said it very loudly and very emphatically. He never—he was good that way. He would let things sort of flow until they ran into a stone wall.

But, you see, I didn't do my duty because I didn't stay and supervise all the work. I kept running out and finishing the synagogue or whatever I could find to do.

RS: Did you have an office at that time?

PJ: We had an office for the building on Forty-second Street which looked out on Forty-third Street, near Third Avenue.

RS: By this time, you had become a registered architect at last. You must have.

PJ: Yes. In between was the business of failing exams all the time.

RS: And Mies was at the Barclay a lot?

PJ: He came and lived at the Barclay. Then, naturally, he'd go for a week or two back to Chicago. When he was gone, we used to get little things accomplished. For example, we had to change the bronze trim from seven-eighths to three-quarters because of the method of fabrication.

Mies came back and saw the change and said, "Vi don't you build it the way I drew it?" I tried to explain to him that there were certain processes in making the thing and his detail just didn't work. But I couldn't explain it to him. He drew it and said, "You build!"[13]

Of course, there were lots of things in the Mies project that couldn't be done. He didn't mind once he realized it was impossible. My other contribution was in the lobby. He wanted verde antique,[14] dark green. Kelly,[15] the lighting man, pointed out that it would be so gloomy. There'd be no way to light it and it would be very unpleasantly dark.

Well, there are dark lobbies, like the one in the RCA building.

RS: Sure. The Daily News Building was black originally.

PJ: That's right, and Mies liked that dark, noble feeling. Kelly said, and I think rightly, that the way to use the walls and the floor was as reflecting surfaces. I've just done a black bathroom floor;[16] I know the problems. It's all right if the floor's wet.

So that was a big battle because Mies loved travertine. But it was all right; he accepted the change very well.

---

14. A type of dark serpentine stone from Vermont.

15. Richard Kelly, 1911–1977.

16. Johnson is referring to the bathroom floor of his guest house on the New Canaan estate.

13. Ludwig Mies van der Rohe and Johnson in front of the Seagram Building, c. 1958.

RS: You did many of the interior details. I'd like to hear about the restaurant. Also, didn't you design the plumbing and the hardware?

PJ: Well, I filled in the little holes where Mies either didn't want to or didn't complete things. And then I did design fountains, which Mies hated. I changed them to suit Mies. That was kind of expensive because we'd gone through to the working drawings, and Kahn & Jacobs sent in a bill for extras—I remember the amount, $22,000—and they wouldn't pay it.

RS: The fountains were figural?

PJ: No, they were elaborate waterworks. I had them mocked up in a place in Massachusetts. The water would go bub-bub-bub-bup-bup-bup. You know, playing waters. And much, much more. They weren't small the way the fountains are now. They went all around the building.

Mies just said, "No." And Phyllis said, "Look, Mies is the designer." I said, "He certainly is, Phyllis, if he wants it that way we'll do it that way." And he did much better, of course, adding the trees. Mine was all water. I think the trees are very important. So he was right.

Then I designed the two entrances to the building from the side. They added those when they realized nobody was going to go around to the front door when it was raining. There was no way to approach the building and get out of the rain. They said, "We just can't rent the building that way." I'm not sure they were right, but that was the owner's decision. So I filled in those entrances.[17]

Then the interiors. Mies was working on the restaurants. Finally, he put down his pen and said, "For heaven's sake, will you please do this?"

17. Fifty-second Street entrance to the Seagram Building.

In other words, he was impatient with anything that had too elaborate a program. No one could decide how to get into the restaurant. The more expert you are, the less convinced you are that you have the only way of getting from a kitchen to a dining room. How do you get people in? There was no precedent for bringing people in from down below and walking them up.[18] Americans don't do that.

But actually I suppose they do. You see, you do the beautiful shell, which shows in a way that Mies was right. Somehow or other. Look at the palaces, they followed no set programs. The architect just said, "Well, I'll make a wonderful stair hall," or whatever he was interested in. People just fit in.

Look how I fit into the Glass House. It's probably the most inconvenient house in the world, but I don't know it. Of course, this is the source of my original statement that I'd rather live in the nave of Chartres Cathedral and go out of doors to the john.[19]

Funny, that still shocks people, that approach.

RS: Well, function is something we can hang onto; it's tangible.

PJ: We can talk about it, you see. And clients love to talk about it, and experts love to talk about it. The new topic is the hot one, though—the wind, the pedestrian and the wind.

They say people will fall down if you build a building this way. Well, do you fall down every time you stand in front of the Seagram on the plaza? You damn near do. I know the feeling. It doesn't happen often enough.

Yesterday the owner knew I'd be in the building. He told our engineer—his favorite pastime is to upset architects by saying, "Yah, we caught you functionally, you're going to have terrible trouble with wind." I'm not going to have trouble with wind.

Fortunately the owner said, "Oh, phooey, that's something that happens one percent of the time. I don't care about that." An old-fashioned owner would have said, "Oh, that's a functional mistake." But where were we?

18. Four Seasons, Seagram Building. Philip Johnson, 1958.

19. The well-known quote by Johnson is: "I would rather sleep in the nave of Chartres Cathedral with the nearest john two blocks down the street than I would in a Harvard house with back-to-back bathrooms!" See Vincent J. Scully Jr., "Doldrums in the Suburbs," *Journal of the Society of Architectural Historians* 24 (March 1965): 36–47, also published in *Perspecta* 9/10 (1965): 281–90.

RS: The restaurant. Whose idea was it to enter through the lobby?

PJ: Oh, that was always the way to do it. Mies designed those steps. I had designed steps to slow people down.

RS: More baroque. You have to make a—

PJ: Yes. Make a turn. In Mies's version you don't turn. You sweep up right to the Picasso, which we didn't have yet. But he was right not to slow people down with a little minor eight-foot stair.

We took the stairs full width. The only thing that was wrong was what the city made us do, which was to put those railings in. I always thought we'd take them out afterward, but, you know, owners don't want to do that kind of thing. They got used to them and even I don't notice them anymore.

RS: They go away.

PJ: Isn't it funny? Yes.

RS: You did the elevator cabs.[20]

PJ: The elevator cabs of woven wire. That material was new in those days. You can't get it anymore.

Elevator cabs, the restaurant. It was fascinating working on the restaurant because we had no budget. We just bought things. I didn't know about budgets in those days.

RS: Was Sam Bronfman an active client?

PJ: No, he just sat there with Crandall. The building was, shall we say, a little over anybody's conception of what buildings should cost.

Once Crandall went to Sam directly with some drawings. He called me into his office—the only time he ever did—and he said, "I want you to tell Phyllis about this. I want your opinion as one of the architects." You see, he really accepted me.

RS: You mean, Sam, Sam Bronfman.

PJ: Sam, himself. He didn't usually interfere in the building, but he said, "This I've

20. Elevator cabs, Seagram Building. Philip Johnson, 1958.

got to do. Mr. Crandall has brought me these drawings."

Of course, I was so angry about it, but I did keep still, I think. It was no business of the builder's to make drawings and take them to the owners. That's not the chain of command. I got that point across later.

But in the meantime, Sam said, "I want your frank opinion. What would this do to the building? I want to know the relative importance of the harm we'd do the building."

I said, "It's very simple. This would totally ruin the building and nobody would build it." He said, "That's what I wanted to know," and threw the drawings away. In other words, he was a pretty straight guy in spite of his foul temper.

RS: Oh, did he have a foul temper?

PJ: Turn that off.

RS: No, it's on.

PJ: I don't want to go on record. Well, why not?

The Museum was asking him for money, and Mrs. Rockefeller isn't the most tactful woman in the world but she's very insistent and a very good fundraiser. She said, "Mr. Bronfman, you've had a building built by a man whose work we've also honored. Will you give ten million"—or whatever the amount was—"to the Museum of Modern Art?"

He called me in his office and said, "You tell that Mrs. Rockefeller to go fuck herself."

RS: [Laughs.] The message was not conveyed?

PJ: The thought of it is just absolutely fabulous. He used to say, "We've got no money." But he was a very, very wonderful client in that he just kept out of the way.

RS: And Phyllis, what was her role?

PJ: Her role was that she went to all the meetings and, of course, just her presence meant that there was no hanky-panky, nobody cut corners. It wasn't that she knew anything about buildings but it was like having the crown prince present.

RS: She didn't interfere; she didn't offer her opinions?

PJ: Not one bit. She was so devoted to Mies, and still is, that he could do absolutely no wrong! That was the amazing part about getting the bronze. That was Bronfman's idea. But Mies then worked it out to look so much better than those metal things that have to be painted. Sam saw the advantage right away. But that was his only big interference, if you will. That was his leadership. He never interfered in the restaurants.

RS: In the restaurants, I think you were the first to collaborate with a graphic designer and an industrial designer. It was certainly a modern way of going about it, a contemporary way.

PJ: Yes, I enjoyed the collaboration with Kelly, of course.

RS: Who designed the Four Seasons? Who conceived of the idea of Four Seasons?

PJ: That was Joe Baum,[21] who later did Windows on the World in the World Trade Center. He said his favorite hotel in the world was in Hamburg and that he wanted to call it the Four Seasons after that.

RS: Munich.

PJ: No, Hamburg. Well, there was one in Munich, too, but his favorite was the one

---

21. Joe Baum, 1920–1998, food consultant.

22. Alvin Lustig, 1915–1955, graphic designer.

23. Emil Antonucci, 1930–2006, artist.

24. Elaine Lustig Cohen, b. 1927.

in Hamburg. So Four Seasons was a good name. I didn't mind. Then I got the graphic designer.

RS: Was it Alvin?[22]

PJ: Oh, no. Antonovitz — that isn't right.[23] We still use him. He's a very modest, very varied painter. A single, one-man office. He's not a Vignelli machine. The graphics of the building were done by what's-her-name, the wife now of Cohen.

RS: Elaine Lustig?

PJ: Elaine Lustig.[24] She picked the Egyptian tack that we used and it worked all right.

RS: How did you find Garth Huxtable[25] to do the tableware?

PJ: Garth was not very helpful. It was done for obvious reasons: to get good notices in the *Times*. I can pick them, you see.

Joe Baum said, "Wouldn't it be nice to have Garth Huxtable?" And they credited both Garth and Ada Louise. I don't know what her particular role was, but he did the bowls that fell over so much that we never used them. He picked the china and the knives and forks. I think I picked the tablecloths, but I don't know. I left it as much as I could to Garth, because it built him up, you see. But anyway, I didn't know much about that, that was Joe Baum's business. But it didn't work. Joe should have known something wouldn't work. Oh! Then we had great support from the decorator, who was my partner at one point. He was one of the most famous decorators at that time.

RS: William Pahlmann.[26]

PJ: Pahlmann. He did not help so much as his great assistant, who later did the Zum-Zums, who died.

That central fountain was their idea. Pahlmann was a wonderful fellow. And he was, again, picked by Joe Baum. Phyllis thought that it was only right to get a firm that had done the decoration of restaurants.

Then came the big battle of where to put the Picasso. Again, he was very helpful figuring it out.

----

25. L. Garth Huxtable, product designer, 1911–1989. His wife, Ada Louise Huxtable, b. 1921, was an architectural reporter for the *New York Times* and became its first architecture critic in 1963. View of bowls designed by L. Garth Huxtable.

26. William Pahlmann, 1906–1987. He also designed the Forum of the Twelve Caesars restaurant in Rockefeller Center, which was run by Baum.

RS: But you commissioned the Lippold?[27]

PJ: I commissioned the Lippold. It helped to lower the ceiling there. That was one of my more successful commissions. Some of them aren't so successful. Then I bogged down completely in the big room above the fountain room. It was just a corridor, so long and nothing. It's not bad now; what we've done is to put a Rosenquist[28] there — we commissioned a big Rosenquist painting there. I like it.

Gesamtkunswerk was the idea. Very rarely is it a success.

RS: Was it you who decided to terrace the room?

PJ: Yes. Well, no, it had to be terraced because we had trucks coming in there that needed truck docks and things, so we had to elevate it. It was Joe Baum's idea to make it flexible. I hate flexibility. Those doors that open and join the Rosenquist room to the big one—that was my idea. The railing details were mine, of course. The lighting was me and Kelly.

RS: The curtains?

PJ: The curtains were mine. I wanted Austrian jalousies and I then worked at it with Marie Nichols[29] and she fabricated it. It was even much copied. But the fact that they waved was pure accident. That was an interesting battle. But the owner came to me the day after they started waving and said, "Now I really believe in architects." I didn't say anything. We knew it was going to be good.

RS: And you did work on the faucets in the bathrooms?[30]

PJ: Oh, I was just coming to that. The harder job was the rest of the building. That was where I was least accomplished and where I had the most trouble. The V.A.T. [vinyl asbestos tile] is horrible stuff but carpeting hadn't come in. There were two decisions that I wish could have been changed later on. One is the tall door. In those days, they were horrified when I said, "Well, obviously, doors go to the ceiling." They said, "There's no such thing as a nine-foot door. They can't make them." You know, the old argument.

---

27. Richard Lippold, 1915–2002, sculptor. His installation hangs over the restaurant's bar.

28. James Rosenquist, b. 1933. The painting discussed is *Flowers, Fish and Females*, 1984.

29. Marie Nichols, textile designer.

30. Bathroom. Seagram Building. Philip Johnson, 1958.

Kahn & Jacobs, who were doing the work for us, said, "We can't—we don't know what you're talking about." It was a hopeless mess. So we picked standard doors, fire doors. We had so many different heights that I said, "Let's make them seven feet throughout." Because some of the ceilings aren't nine. I would rather have had special doors made for each ceiling height drop because of the air conditioning. But I said then I thought that uniformity was more important. Well, I don't think it was.

Later it changed. All doors of Gerry Hines buildings go to the ceilings and everything is carpeted. The elevators are all nine feet now. But when you're on the firing line for the first time and you have Kahn & Jacobs—I can see why I didn't insist.

What I could do was the faucets. And I made the bowls, too. I made them as part of the architecture: square, with the oval in it, rather than a lot of oval bowls. That was my design and the fixtures are still used in a bastardized way by Speakman and American Standard. And we decided to use the brushed stainless. They'd never heard of brushed stainless for the fittings.

But I had time to battle these things out because I was pretty much left out of other decisions. Richard Foster was the one who executed the building.

RS: And you didn't have very much work besides, did you?

PJ: Not that much, no. I was finishing up the synagogue, I guess. Anyhow, Mies said I was never there. Mies finally said, "I don't like Foster," and fired him. Well, he took him back the next week. Foster was the only man who knew how to build buildings.

RS: Was Manley[31] working for you?

PJ: Manley worked there the whole time, but he is not an execution man, he's an ice cream man. I mean, he likes to be on the design side, but what he's actually good at is drafting. He's a one-man office. He did the theater [New York State Theater] later. He's been with us now for thirty-five years, I guess. He's working now on the buildings down in Washington.[32]

RS: So the Seagram Building opened—

PJ: In 1958. We were the first tenants.[33] And we're just now leaving. It was a great success.

RS: Was there a great opening ceremony? Was there an occasion? Did architects appear?

PJ: I showed architects through the building before it was done. They didn't understand a single thing I was talking about.

Oh, when I talked to them alone, of course, they were so jealous. I mean, this was the job of the century.

Paul Rudolph said I was a damn fool to be under a big man, that that was a hell of a lousy way to start to be an architect. But I got my foot in the door by working with Mies. Paul said I'd just be swallowed up.

You know his passion for independence. He's never even had a business manager. That's one of his troubles. And so he's sort of disappeared now. It's a shame because he's certainly the most intelligent, intellectually, of all the architects. Remember him as a critic? Wouldn't you rather talk to him about a design problem than almost anybody?

RS: Once I would have liked to, but now I feel—

PJ: Oh, you'd rather do your own.

----

31. John Manley, b. 1925, architect.　　　32. Tycon Towers, Vienna, Virginia.

RS: No, no, no! I love to talk to people, but I think he goes his own way and he can no longer see beyond his own self.

PJ: No, he can't.

RS: He's lost perspective, which was his greatest asset.

PJ: Which he used to have. He could follow what you wanted and explain better what was wrong with what you wanted—I mean, where you hadn't fulfilled what you wanted—better than you could yourself.

RS: Did Saarinen come to see it? I'm sure people were talking about it.

PJ: They must have been. My father always hated the building. Of course, the great moment was when Mumford's article came out in the *New Yorker*. [34]

RS: Mumford liked the building.

PJ: Mumford liked the building.

RS: It was a very intelligent piece—I read it the other day.

PJ: Did you, really?

RS: Yes. I just filmed Phyllis telling her side of the story for the television program.[35] That's why I'm very interested in getting you to talk about it.

PJ: Oh, I'd love to hear her side.

RS: Well, her side is pretty much the same. The only thing she talked about was Saarinen. She felt that Saarinen had a very intelligent take on what the building could have been, but he kept referring to Mies as the standard of what could happen. Therefore, she thought, "Why not go to Mies if everybody's talking about Mies?"

PJ: Oh, that's wonderful. I didn't know that at the time, but, of course, that's the way it happened.

RS: But she didn't mention at all going to Pei. Of course, on television you edit

33. Johnson in his Seagram Building office, c. 1958.

anyhow. We didn't have the luxury of sitting and talking as we are here.

PJ: I didn't think she'd remember Pei.

RS: She didn't say anything about him.

PJ: We met him for a lunch at my house.

RS: But these were the days you were having architects, too, who came in little groups to discuss, to chart out the future.

PJ: Oh, yes. That continued until just a few years ago. That was the kind of thing that was really good in those days, I think, to have that kind of a conversation. The next time we had it was at the Century. But it ran down.[36] Everything runs down.

RS: Yes, you get bored.

PJ: Then we go on.

RS: But Le Corbusier didn't visit it with you?

PJ: Corbusier never came. I mean, if he saw the building, it was on his own. Saarinen never saw it, but, of course, he wasn't a Mies fan anyhow. Oh, when he was working on the Black Rock,[37] of course, he said that it wasn't simple enough and that he was going to do the ultimate simple building in New York.

RS: He did. Isn't it boring?

PJ: It's so boring.

RS: It doesn't even have a door.

PJ: Well, I think the worst mistake is going down into a building.

RS: What about the night that Mies visited the Glass House?

PJ: Oh, yes, the night, the famous night when Mies—well, when we first got the Seagram job, Mies came East a good deal.

We were working one Saturday night—Phyllis and he and I—in the country because Mies hadn't seen the Glass House at night.

And after dinner, Phyllis went off to stay where she was staying. Mies was going to stay in the guest house. At about 10:30, he got up and said, "I'm not staying here tonight. Find me another place to stay."

He talked quietly when he was really angry.

And I laughed. And about ten minutes later he said, "I don't think you understood. I'm not staying in this house another minute and you've got to find me a place to stay."

This was getting late. There are no hotels up there. So Wiley, my advisor who had built a house further up the road, took him in.

What had caused it was I said, "Mies, I see what you see in Behrens. But I don't understand what it was in Berlage[38] that interested you so much." And that just set him off. I never knew what layers of meaning there were. Phyllis never understood either.

RS: It had nothing to do, in other words, with the room he was in?

PJ: I think it did, but I don't know.

----

34. Lewis Mumford, "The Sky Line," *New Yorker* 34 (September 13, 1958): 141–48, 150, 152.

35. *Pride of Place*, an eight-part PBS series on American architecture hosted by Stern, 1986.

36. A series of architect-only dinners held at the Century Association. See Richard Plunz and Kenneth L. Kaplan, "On 'Style,'" *Precis* 5 (1984): 33–43.

37. CBS Building, 1961–65.

38. Hendrik P. Berlage, 1856–1934, Dutch architect.

RS: Do you think it could have been that the "Soane Room"[39] was too much for him?

PJ: Could have been.

RS: The decorative quality of it?

PJ: No, I just think he felt that my bad copy of his work was extremely unpleasant. He also deeply resented my inquisitive attitude, making him verbal when he wasn't. He was a groan-and-grunt man, as you may remember.

RS: I never met him.

PJ: He was always a very morose type. And something happened inside him and so he just stalked out.

RS: The next day it was all over? Or he took the train back to New York?

PJ: He went right back to New York. And we went right on as if nothing had happened.

----

39. The bedroom of Johnson's guest house contains a vaulted structure with a roof mounted below the actual ceiling and supporting columns on the interior of the room. He took some of the inspiration for this room from the breakfast room in the house of Sir John Soane (1753–1837, British architect), which contained a similar masonry canopy.

8. Lincoln Center

RS: Philip, we should talk now about the Lincoln Center period.[1] I'd like to find out how you propelled yourself—or got propelled—from a house architect who said things in the press and was a clever museum curator to being entrusted with these more significant kinds of public buildings.

PJ: Well, there are two threads that come together in Lincoln Center: one is my personal relationship with Nelson Rockefeller; the other is my shift to historicism at a ripe early age. The third element I want to bring out is the inside and outside problem. My theater[2] was one of my, shall I say, "inside buildings." The outside has never been satisfactory and wasn't when I did it. It isn't yet today.

Because both of us had interests in culture and sex, I had a personal friend in Mr.

1. Johnson in the 1960s.

Lincoln Kirstein. He is still my best friend. He always had the dream of building a grand theater of the dance in Central Park that he would dedicate to Balanchine[3] and that would be the epitome of American culture.

And he thought I was the only architect in the world. He still has that fallacious opinion (which one wishes all one's clients had): total faith. He doesn't care what I design, it's perfect.

So he's the perfect patron. The first thing we did for him was Dumbarton Oaks.[4]

RS: What did Lincoln Kirstein have to do with it?

PJ: He commanded it right straight through.

RS: Really?

PJ: Oh, yes. The curator was a rather weak little Harvard-Fogg creature who collected drawings in the proper Fogg fashion.

So Lincoln was the strong man there. And he knew Mrs. Bliss, the great lady.[5] I met Mrs. Bliss, and we made beautiful music. From there on, Lincoln got his way.

In other words, he's the kind who's a hands-off patron. He got Nelson Rockefeller to give him money for the theater. Nelson personally admired Lincoln, and me, a little bit because of my work at the Museum of Modern Art. And Lincoln also worked through Mrs. Rockefeller Jr., who had a great influence on Nelson. Nelson was in his forties and he was getting powerful. He was governor of New York state. But he also had his memory of a relationship with me and Lincoln when we were young, Nelson and I, at the time of the opening of Rockefeller Center.

RS: No.

PJ: This was before the RCA Building was finished. So it was in the [early] 1930s and I was still at the Museum of Modern Art. Nelson was very young and he couldn't get his foot into the Todd organization in spite of his name. John Todd,[6] as you know from history books, was a very, very strong man. Nelson felt so frustrated that he

2. New York State Theater, Lincoln Center. Philip Johnson, 1964.

3. George Balanchine, 1904–1983, Russian-born ballet choreographer.

couldn't get into design—he was a Phyllis Lambert of his day, you see. And to get his father to pull him in, Lincoln and I and somebody else made a corporation to design and market souvenirs of Rockefeller Center. And Nelson rented a shop on the street to sell souvenirs of the building.

We started with a few little gewgaws on the outside of the building, which was rather fantastic. We set out to make matchboxes and little objects. In the middle of this design period—we hadn't actually done anything—John Todd lowered the boom and said, "You're not going to do anything of the kind. We're not going to have such nonsense going on in Rockefeller Center." Nelson caved in and canceled the whole corporation. I remember my father saying, "It isn't so hard getting into a company with Nelson as a partner. The problem will be getting out." He said that long before it ended, very prescient. That was the end of that.

But Nelson kept, his whole life, a sentimental affection for that period, and two people that he always associated with it were Lincoln and me. For no reason, because we were never budsy-wudsies and we never had much in common. His ambitions then led him off into entirely other directions, but he always thought that he was the great cultural pope and that he would someday ride a white horse in a Louis XIV saddle. Whoops. We mixed a few metaphors on the way.

So he'd always had this dream. And Lincoln always had his dream.

It just happened that Johnny[7] had to fill up that site that he'd rashly started out to develop. Now, that was another whole story that I knew nothing of at the time, the Moses[8]-and-Johnny-Rockefeller-and-whoever-the-heads-of-the-Met-were deal.

But the Philharmonic was easier to understand. This third site wasn't at all certain until the state came through with the money. That was such an amazing thing. Lincoln

4. Dumbarton Oaks Research Library and Collection, pavilion for the Robert Woods Bliss Collection of Pre-Columbian Art. Philip Johnson, 1963.

5. Mildred Barnes Bliss, 1879–1969, donor of the Dumbarton Oaks house and grounds to Harvard University.

6. John Todd, 1867–1945, development supervisor for Rockefeller Center.

was so happy. Of course, I did not have the qualifications that Harrison & Abramovitz[9] had. Young people don't.

But I had some reputation—maybe wrongly—attached to the Seagram Building. That gave me some credibility, enough for those two to put me in august company. Of course, since I was so much brighter than the other architects, I had a lot of fun. Being young and much too brash—I mean, I blush now thinking of some of the meetings we went to—I just assumed that I might as well take over everyone's job. They seemed to be hacking it up. But the great question was when we would meet—four of us because there was Saarinen by then. Saarinen, Wally [Harrison], and me—three pushers-arounders.

Now, Wally by this time was sick in his head about the horrors of life and not being successful and still getting these enormous supervisory jobs like the U.N. So he wasn't going to stand up and fight and he kept rather quiet. I had just arrived as a team member and they were still discussing the overall plan with this foreign architect, Sven Markelius,[10] and Gordon Bunshaft.[11]

That's a history that could be looked up, but my memory is Markelius came and did not get his way. So he said, "There's no point in my being here." And he was quite right.

Then Bunshaft came in with drawings that showed all the buildings in one—it was his favorite theme. He had done a building [the Venezuela Pavilion] at the World's Fair, too. He thought, quite rightly, that a crystal palace somehow—a vast, grand experience in architecture—was a better way to do things than to parcel out projects to your friends and political appointees and make a mud hash of affairs.

The same thing he thought here, each of us, of course, was thinking too, playing the same game: Why don't you give the whole thing to me and it will be much better? But I don't know why I thought that. Wally was the only one who kept a steady hand and was reasonably quiet. Then I came in with my arrangement, which is more or less where the buildings are today, except of course, my proposal had the fatal flaw of wanting to unify the court.[12]

Wally said, "Philip, who do you think is going to let you build a facade right in front of his building?" That was perfectly true. He said, "I like the idea, but nobody is going

---

7. John D. Rockefeller 3rd, 1906–1978.

8. Robert Moses, 1888–1981, New York parks commissioner and development czar.

9. Max Abramovitz, 1908–2004, architect and partner of Wallace K. Harrison.

10. Sven Markelius, 1889–1972, Swedish architect.

11. Gordon Bunshaft, 1909–1990, design partner of Skidmore, Owings & Merrill.

12. Proposal for arcade to enclose the main plaza at Lincoln Center. Philip Johnson, 1958.

to let you." That was his quiet way of slapping me on the wrist. I moved the site. See, I wanted to be on the next site, away from all of this sort of fuss-and-feathers. That was the round-fronted[13] site, the next block north where the Juilliard School is.

RS: Oh, you wanted to be completely out of the main action. You wanted to be able to play your own game.

PJ: To play my own game. Why should I follow a lot of rules?

Brisbane was a proof that round-fronted opera houses were quite a good idea. Unfortunately, my design ideas were not equal to my concept ideas, and I just repeated that screen around. The building might certainly have been better than the one we built. But I was pushed back by the people above my level, I suppose.

RS: Well, the state wasn't going to build its building off on the side, I'm sure.

PJ: It would have been more prominent. It wasn't the state. No, it was the internal politics, the idea that I should flank Max. Then we got down to saying, "Okay, let's accept that tripartite plan." That way everybody got a front seat. And that was my idea, to have the grand avenue go up to the main building, which everyone agreed would be the Met, and that we would flank it.

Then we got to the question: should we set up any rules? Unfortunately, the rules we set up were mine: a twenty-foot bay dimension and travertine material. That's still there. The first design in was Max's. He was way ahead of us. So he had a twenty-foot bay. I changed it to twenty-forty, which is a little more amusing but not very good. But in that kind of atmosphere it's so easy as an architect to say, "Oh, well, I was forced into this design because of the pattern set up by a committee." Well, in a way it's true and in a way it isn't. I mean, baroque architects were always being forced into that and somehow they managed to create some of their best works around a court.

RS: I think the problem was that there was such a paucity of a vocabulary with

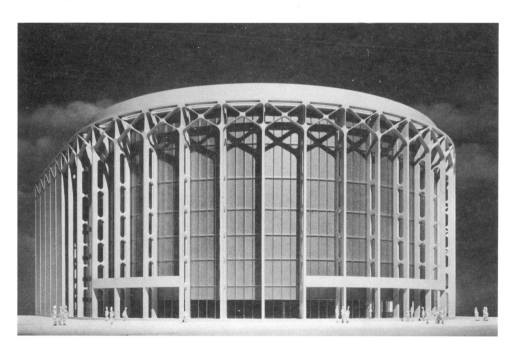

13. Proposed New York State Theater, Lincoln Center.
Philip Johnson, 1958.

which to explore. Once you got past the twenty- or forty-foot bay, there wasn't much else left in any of those designs.

PJ: Well, a more original architect than I or than any of us might have been able to work with it. But then Saarinen came along and broke the rules anyhow.

Then the big battles began of who should do the plaza, you see. Wally again kept still. Wally had terrible trouble with his arches. He wanted to make them like Dartmouth[14] and I said they'd just pull apart. But if he had done that he would have been able to create a unifying cornice line. So what we have now is no better, strange to say, than Dartmouth. Is it really?

RS: No.

PJ: So I did absolutely no good, probably damage.

RS: No, you just messed it up.

PJ: Wally was a frightened, frightened man, design-wise. I don't blame him. He had a terrible time.

So I more or less went along with that twenty-forty rule, but I designed quite an ugly column, as Hitchcock very pointedly pointed out. So the exterior of my building isn't any better than the others, or anything to write home about. The interior, on the other hand, is the right way to do a proper opera house: that is, to have a grand entrance room, promenade, and then the theater behind it in a horseshoe plan.

But the next big battles were among Belluschi,[15] Saarinen, and me over the exterior. Finally, out of exhaustion, they just said, "Well, all right, you do the front court." They got so tired of my screaming, I suppose.

RS: Saarinen got to do his own court anyhow.[16]

PJ: Well, that was a big part of it. I finally went out to his office in Michigan and

----

14. Wallace K. Harrison's Hopkins Center (1962), Dartmouth College, Hanover, New Hampshire.

15. Pietro Belluschi, 1899–1994, Italian-born architect practicing in Portland, Oregon, and then Cambridge, Massachusetts, where he was dean of M.I.T.'s School of Architecture from 1951 to 1965.

16. Vivian Beaumont Theater and Lincoln Center Performing Arts Library and Museum. Skidmore, Owings & Merrill, Eero Saarinen (1910–1961), and Jo Mielziner (1901–1976), 1965. Henry Moore's sculpture *Reclining Figure*, 1965, is in foreground.

sat down with him and said, "Look, you are trying to design the court in front of my building as well as your own court. Why don't we draw a line like the Church did in South America? This is the Portuguese on this side of the line and the Spanish on that side. Then you do your garden and I won't say a word. I don't like your garden and you may not like mine. But why don't we just back each other?"

Saarinen was the most powerful presence in architecture at that time. He was the first one—well, we talked about this before—to choose the style for the job. He didn't have a straight stylistic line, the way his father did. I never liked the plan for his theater and I still find it very difficult to get around that pool.

RS: That's all right. Nobody goes to the theater, anyhow.

PJ: To that theater! Well, it's empty, isn't it? Somebody's performing there this fall.

Then he had his own battles with Bunshaft. Bunshaft had more or less shrugged his shoulders. That's why he was such a good man at Skidmore. He could say, "Oh, well, fuck it all," and walk out, as he did on many buildings that he's sort of connected with. But when the client did something or other he didn't like, why he'd say, "You finish it," to his partners. He thinks that's the best way to do architecture when you get into a jam. I'm beginning to sympathize. There are some clients who are physically impossible to work with. The higher you get in the world of business, the worse it gets.

But he got into my battle with Saarinen and he ended up backing me. He thought I was a contentious worm—not worm, annoyance, which of course, I was. So we were friends up to that time because I had more or less got him around to my way of thinking, just by dinners and things. Boy, the time one had to spend in those days!

Well, of course, you cannot do a job as big as Lincoln Center, I suppose, without this kind of recrimination and backbiting. So everybody pretty well hated everybody. And you've seen that picture with Johnny Rockefeller in the middle of the model with all of us sitting around just blissful?[17] We weren't speaking by then. We just sat there glaring at the camera.

But it was a normal thing, which I didn't know at the time. You see, my problem was that I was an inexperienced architect, even though I was older. I was older than Saarinen by a good deal, and still am. That was one battle.

17. Group portrait of the Lincoln Center Architects Group posed around a model of the proposed Lincoln Center for the Performing Arts in the basement of Rockefeller Center, November 28, 1959. Back row, standing, left to right: Edward J. Matthews, 1903–1980, Johnson, Jo Mielziner, Wallace K. Harrison, and Pietro Belluschi. Front row, left to right: John D. Rockefeller 3rd, Eero Saarinen, Gordon Bunshaft, and Max Abramovitz.

RS: What about John Rockefeller 3rd? He was in charge.

PJ: He was the head man. Without him there wouldn't have been any center. He raised the $170 million or whatever it was in those days. It's much like raising a billion today. I was amazed that he could raise it.

But he was non-visual and cantankerous and exactly like one of my new clients, the head of New England Life. He'd be swayed by whoever talked to him last. The great fight with him over Asia House[18-20] was that it wasn't all glass. "Philip, I like glass buildings."

Mr. Rockfeller's favorite building was by Bunshaft. Happy's Bank, it was called, the one where you look into it at Forty-third and Fifth.[21] It was his favorite building in the world. His was a type of mind that would say, "Ah, now here's some logic. It's a bank, so why shouldn't you see the wheels go around? Glass is the only logical material." And he could hang onto that concept like a bulldog. I would never, never admit to this. See, I was getting very much more historically minded by this time. I think it was about the same time as my signs went up at Yale.

RS: That's why you did the alternative facades?

PJ: Yes, and one that I did was the Bunshaft facade, as I called it, much to

18. First proposal for Asia House, 112 East Sixty-fourth Street. Philip Johnson, 1958.

19. Asia House, 112 East Sixty-fourth Street. Philip Johnson, 1959.

Bunshaft's fury. It was built as just a curtain wall, something that was then just coming into its own. But it's an interesting curtain wall in that I used white. That's about the only difference. No, well, it has other interesting features.

RS: What about Nelson? He was an architect *manqué*?

PJ: Yes, but you see he was out of the picture because he was so busy spending money getting to be governor and trying to be president, even then. So he played no part.

And Lincoln played no part, although he's intensely visual, but in his own quirky way. For him, I'm the only architect in the world, and Noguchi[22] is the only sculptor in the world—he just has that settled. His real interest, though, as with all verbal people, is in the word and in his poetry.

So then I didn't have any help. I thought I might—from Belluschi, though, so I said, "I'm going to Johnny Rockefeller." Well, of course, I didn't do that, although since I knew him through Blanchette (I'd done Blanchette's house, you see, some time before) I mistakenly thought that I could talk to him.

Ed Young[23] said, "Sure. Go and talk to him." Of course, Ed Young, being very experienced in handling Johnny, knew what would happen, what was he going to say. So I went to him with the purpose of getting rid of that ridiculous stairway up to Belluschi's building.[24] It wasn't only a matter of the baroque—I didn't want it tucked off to one side so that you had to crawl up and around.

It isn't a space that's usable in any case, but if we had connected it by making the whole thing a stairway—At that time money hadn't reared its too-ugly head, but, of course, Saarinen didn't want to hurt his *hortus conclusus* theory by having the stair become part of a grand scheme that led to what? So Johnny said, "No, we're doing it that way. End of subject."

----

21. Manufacturers Trust Company (Skidmore, Owings & Merrill, 1954) at 510 Fifth Avenue. The provenance of the building's nickname is uncertain and may have not been bestowed on the structure until after Nelson Rockefeller married his second wife, Margaretta "Happy" Large Fitler Murphy (b. 1926) in 1963. However, the Rockefeller bank was the Chase, so the connection is not clear.

22. Isamu Noguchi, 1904–1988.

23. Edgar Young, 1908–2007, chairman of the building committee for Lincoln Center.

24. Juilliard School of Music, 1969; the stair was removed as part of an extensive renovation by Diller Scofidio + Renfro, 2007–9.

20. Alternate design for Asia House, Philip Johnson, 1958.

And he wouldn't even see the points I was making. You get used to that kind of disappointment, but when you get it early on, the first few times can be lacerating. Strange, we had no press against us yet. There were no critics. I don't know whether Ada Louise [Huxtable] was even operating at that time.

RS: Barely, she was barely going at the time you were planning Lincoln Center.

PJ: She wasn't running the country as she thinks she is now.

RS: No. And it was the time of Robert Moses.

PJ: Yes. And Moses—there wasn't even that much anti-Moses sentiment. Isn't that extraordinary!

RS: We were still riding the crest of his 1930s popularity.

PJ: That's right. Well, he was the one who put the land together.[25] It was he who kept that park [Damrosch Park] that ruins the court. That's what Markelius said. "What are you doing taking a three-block, 800-foot-long site"—it was a square, a 900-foot square, something like that—"and taking a bite out of it for a park that obviously should be part of this great scheme?" Of course, coming from abroad he had a sense of urban space and he was absolutely right. But he knew nothing of Moses, of his horrors. And the only price that we had to pay at Lincoln Center was that Moses kept that park.

RS: That stupid band shell, which you can't even hear a concert in.[26]

PJ: You can't hear, no. Spatially it makes no sense. It's off in one corner. Although Moses was not stupid. But then again he was not a visual man, he was a can-do man, parks, you see.

RS: It was the only solution that would work.

PJ: Well, it was possible, really. I mean, the two flanks were logical because otherwise how would Wally have an address on the main avenue if we couldn't put our two buildings there? We couldn't put three in a row.

RS: What about the idea of cutting through to Central Park? Were you involved in that idea?

PJ: Only peripherally. That was Nelson's great dream. So he picked me out of the whole bunch—well, naturally, because I knew him best—to draw up a bridge over the entire intersection.

RS: Well, you didn't know him best. Wally Harrison knew him best.

PJ: That's right! But he knew Wally was no good. He has always told me that. Toward the end he said, "Philip, come and help him. He needs help." I said, "Well, Nelson, of course, but why would he accept my help? Think of the human possibilities here." "Oh, Philip, there must be a way—you're so smart that way." The last time was on Battery Park. That first plan wasn't Wally's, that was Nelson's.

RS: Oh. Terrible.

PJ: I sent a note, "I don't know who did that plan, but it's just awful." Nelson said, "Is it really?" I said, "Yes." He said, "Fine." Then he was too busy to do anything about it.

But he was a very, very strange man, willful, but not a follow-through type of man. I think he would probably have been a very bad president. Then I didn't know till later that the secret was dyslexia. He couldn't write and couldn't read. He never could write

----

25. Robert Moses was serving as chairman of the Mayor's Slum Clearance Committee, which obtained permission from the New York City Board of Estimate to designate the Lincoln Square area for urban renewal.

26. Daniel and Florence Guggenheim Band Shell, Eggers & Higgins, 1969.

till the end of his days. He took a year off to write his book because he knew so much. I doubt that the first sentence ever appeared from his hand. He had a staff of writers. He surrounded himself with the best.

RS: It never occurred to him to talk into a tape recorder?

PJ: That wouldn't do any good—that type of mind.

RS: Just couldn't organize his thoughts.

PJ: David [Whitney] is dyslexic, can't write. I can't either but I don't have any hindrance. I'm just not a writer's writer. Nelson was always compensating by getting into fields where he didn't have to read and write, or getting somebody to write his papers, or whatever.

RS: That's why he liked art probably, especially abstract art.

PJ: Yes, he did. I'm not sure how genuine that was, actually, but he knew he should like it. Visual arts are easier and you don't have to write anything. The verbal arts are more dangerous. But as president, of course, he would have had to organize his thoughts better than he ever did. But he was also intensely personal.

It was a great thing for him to do, to celebrate Balanchine. Well, of course, without Lincoln nobody would know Balanchine. But without Nelson and also without me— I just mean I played a small part in making the greatest art that we've favored in my lifetime.

RS: And from that came all kinds of dance, which Balanchine—

PJ: Oh, dance is big now. But it was nothing then. Balanchine created it single-handedly, and he is still the greatest choreographer of our time. That was the result of this Lincoln Center potpourri. The Met didn't improve; the Orchestra didn't improve. The playwrights under Jo Mielziner's[27] kind ministrations didn't work because the whole premise was wrong. But Kirstein had the premise right: the court ballet was something you could translate into an American visual experience.

RS: What was your working relationship with Balanchine?

PJ: I never spoke to him; Balanchine couldn't talk. I would say, "How wide do you want the proscenium? How high? What depth of stage? What kind of a floor?" The things I'd have to learn from somebody. "And what kind of pit?"

He said, "I want the highest proscenium possible." I said, "I'll make it higher than any other theater. I'll do whatever you say, Mr. Balanchine." It was too high; it was never used.

But no one ever talked to George Balanchine, Lincoln finally told us. But Lincoln was not interested enough to follow the process of designing a building. Strange!

So the result is that there are millions of things wrong with the theater, which came about because I had to get my knowledge where I could, which was naturally in the field, at Broadway shows. In other words, the reason there was no orchestra pit was that Richard Rodgers[28] said, "What do you want an orchestra for? It just takes seats away." Which, of course, it does. But then along came theater people who said, "What am I going to do? I can't talk to my people over there and over there. I've got to have them here." So we chopped it up.

RS: So there was no orchestra pit to begin with?

PJ: Well, there was one. It was a Broadway orchestra pit, just big enough for

---

27. Jo Mielziner, theater designer.   28. Richard Rodgers, 1902–1979, popular composer.

a Broadway show. They don't bother about this on Broadway. In fact the fewer instruments, the cheaper the show. Then there were the floor lights.

The faults of that theater—besides architectural ones—are that I didn't have enough briefing. Balanchine was no help, and Lincoln less so. He was the kind who'd say, "It's absolutely marvelous," then storm from the room—on the first sketch!

Nobody was there to tell me that I needed a dark gray floor. I hate gray. But of course, if you put a very strong spotlight down on any other color, all your dancers are lit bright red. Any fool would know that! Or at least somebody connected with the ballet.

RS: You had no consultants?

PJ: I thought I was talking to Balanchine's people. Blithering idiots. They may know what they're doing in their own field, but if you can't communicate it, it's a problem. There was no interaction between that group and me. I also had a bad acoustician. But I didn't know enough to get your Columbia man, Cyril.[29] So there were lots of catastrophes along the way simply because of the lack of communication.

RS: But I can't imagine as sophisticated an operation as that without somebody saying, "Don't pay any attention to Mr. Balanchine. This is the way it's going to be."

PJ: Of course. Somebody should have said, "This man is an idiot even if he's a great choreographer." Of course, he wanted a big stage. So he got his big stage and he got his coming-out all right. And he never complained himself. But some of the staff finally complained that their big offices and dance halls had no windows. I said, "You don't need windows in the dance halls, it just a nuisance with noise and all that." Actually they have little slits so that people know if it's raining or not. We also had the lights in the wrong place. I said, "Well, where were you when we were designing this?" But you can't say that too much because they were—

RS: Paying the bills. What about the art inside the theater?

PJ: That was my fault or privilege. I had the idea, since I was rather meager in my detailing knowledge, shall we say, of a classical language, and the areas looked awfully plain to me, as indeed they are. So, except for Lincoln's insistence on the big statues in the foyer, in the upper foyer—

RS: That was his idea, to blow up those figures?

PJ: Oh, yes. He always thought it was a good idea. He didn't care about the actual finish. He wanted them to be enormous.[30] I didn't mind; it filled the place nicely. We did get little complaints on that. But even then, where were the little ladies in tennis shoes saying that they don't like pudenda up ten feet high?

RS: Well, nobody complained about that. I think people thought they were silly.

PJ: Well, they are. Sure, silly and balloonish. The main thrust of the objections that I heard was that they were disgusting.

RS: Well, I never heard that. But the idea of putting in a full program of contemporary art, on permanent installation—

PJ: You mean that stuff downstairs?

RS: Yes. Whose idea?

----

29. Cyril Harris, b. 1917, acoustician and professor of electrical engineering at Columbia University.

30. The statues are based on the papier-mâché maquette *Two Circus Women*, 1928–29, by Elie Nadelman (1882–1946), in the Glass House.

31. Jasper Johns, b. 1930, American painter.

PJ: It was all mine.

RS: Your idea. Were you and David Whitney friends at that point?

PJ: Yes, but I didn't consult David. He was an eighteen-year-old or something. He was a student up at RISD [Rhode Island School of Design]. No, no, I didn't consult him.

We met because of Johns's[31] flag painting. He said, "Why did you buy that flag?" It was his first question to me in the world. He just came up to me after a lecture and said, "Why did you buy the flag?" I said, "Because Alfred Barr told me to." I told the truth too soon, as usual. So then we got started. No, David had no influence at all at Lincoln Center.

But my instinct of looking at art and wanting to use it as decoration for the too-blankness of modern, was a holdover from Mies. Mies always made me think that if you have blankness, only art can help. But it worked less well here. I relied too much on making it like a museum, instead of letting architecture do the hard work.[32]

RS: You never quite finished about this whole notion of bridging over the street to Central Park.

PJ: Oh, yes, we were talking about that. Nelson dreamt of persuading the city to condemn the land from the center over to the park. Nobody else thought it was feasible. And Wally was so practical. That's what made him Wally. Obviously that was one reason Nelson came to me. He couldn't get Wally to take the idea seriously enough to design the bridge. Can you imagine the cost? The bridge would have spanned maybe 150 feet.

RS: And can you imagine condemning the YMCA and the Ethical Culture Society?

32. Johnson inspecting the fountain at Lincoln Center,
March 7, 1964.

PJ: Heavens. Anyhow, somebody stopped Nelson in time. I think it was the cost of the bridge that finally made him realize that the whole thing was not in scale. He said, "I don't see any sense in having Lincoln Center if it isn't on the park."

It's the same reason I told AT&T, "Why don't you buy the block in front of you?" Of course, in those days they had money.

So we ended up not being on the park. That's all that happened.

I still think the only good thing I did there was that one big room [in the New York State Theater].[33] I still enjoy going out to get a drink there.

RS: The idea of a big room was Nelson Rockefeller's or yours?

PJ: I just said, "I won't build a building that doesn't have a bar." Lincoln and I knew Garnier,[34] you see. We knew that the theater was the least important part.

Circulation and promenade. Lincoln understood the importance of the grand stairs and the big room, and that's what he and I talked about, and the cost. So that was all done. I don't think there's anything else amusing to say on this.

33. New York State Theater, Lincoln Center. Philip Johnson, 1964. Grand Promenade with untitled sculptures by Elie Nadelman at either end.

34. Palais Garnier, home of the Opéra National de Paris, 1860–75. Charles Garnier, 1825–1898.

9. The Institutional Commissions

RS: After Lincoln Center you started to build museums around the country and big institutional commissions.

Let's start with the Museum of Modern Art here in 1959 and then 1964, when you added onto it.[1] I'm thinking of the role of Mr. Paley,[2] of course, when he comes on the scene.

PJ: Mr. Paley had nothing to do with it. It was all decided on the staff level—by Alfred Barr—so I really wasn't conscious of the more powerful people. Paley liked my addition here, that is all I remember. Everybody liked the garden,[3] of course, except René.[4] René was a strange patron. He realized that because I was sitting there he had to pick me. I was just there. I was so there that they couldn't go around advertising for other architects very well. So my first garden was very bad.

But he never told me this. He said, "Nelson thinks that it might be a good idea if we did this and that." I never knew till years later that he was behind things.

RS: What do you mean by your "first garden"?

1. The Museum of Modern Art, Fifty-third Street between Fifth and Sixth Avenues, New York. View c. 1964 showing original building (Philip L. Goodwin and Edward Durell Stone, 1939) in the center, East Wing (Philip Johnson, 1964) on the right, and Grace Rainey Rogers Memorial (Philip Johnson, 1951) on the left.

2. William S. Paley, 1901–1990, chairman of the Columbia Broadcasting System and president of The Museum of Modern Art from 1968 to 1972.

3. Abby Aldrich Rockefeller Sculpture Garden, The Museum of Modern Art. Philip Johnson, 1953.

4. René d'Harnoncourt, 1901–1968, director of The Museum of Modern Art from 1949 to 1967.

PJ: The first one at MoMA, before we added the back part.

RS: Oh, why do you think it was bad? I thought it was wonderful.

PJ: Well, yes. It was, but only after he fixed it. My first first, I mean, nobody saw except René.

RS: Did he really fix it, in your opinion?

PJ: He pointed out a few key, little things. One of them was that there was a dead wall to the street, which is bad enough. But when it was completely dead, it was just a nasty elbow crack at the town.

One tends to remember the good things, like remembering the pretty nurse at the hospital, not the disease. I really can't remember why it was so poor, but I just ripped it apart and then came up with a new design. He said, "Now, you see?"

Same thing with the wing here. My first one was completely modern. It was layered but different—I just kept a bar across.

I put the windows—the walls, glass walls—on different planes. And it was so brutal, so horrible, that I then got into my television-window mode and it came out better. But that was due to René too. René was so smart that he never even let you know that he was changing your design. He was such a master at handling people.

RS: That was his strength.

PJ: He was the Museum of Modern Art. That's why I say I never went to Paley. There was no board of trustees. René was so strong, and he realized what was inevitable. I was inevitable to him, so he handled it.

RS: Then you did the New York World's Fair.[5] Tell me about that.

PJ: The World's Fair was a battle again. This was between the governor, Mr. Rockefeller, and Mr. Moses. Mr. Moses wanted to have Nelson's state building in the fair. He was selling space like mad.

5. New York State Pavilion, 1964–65 New York World's Fair, Flushing Meadows, Queens, New York. Philip Johnson and Richard Foster with Lev Zetlin, 1964.

RS: You were not involved in the preliminary planning for the fair?

PJ: I wasn't in the preliminary planning at all. That was a Moses/Wally [Harrison] business.

RS: I do remember that I was in your office, and we were looking out at the construction, which you could see all the way across the river in Queens. I said, "How come this building is taller than any other building at the fair?" You said, "Well, Nelson, wants it that way—"

PJ: That was Nelson's pact with them. I didn't want to do those towers. Actually, they didn't fit the design in any way. I had a big egg in a circle, and he said, "Where's the height?" I said, "There are the rules. The rules of the fair are this is the height."

He wouldn't sign off on it. "Well, I guess we have no building," he told Moses. He just plain held him up. Once Nelson got his way, he used to come and criticize in the office. He was more interested in this project than in Lincoln Center. It was more his. He didn't like Johnny [John D. Rockefeller]; nobody liked Johnny. Nothing is more disruptive than a family problem. So this was his baby, a state fair thing, and he followed it reasonably closely.

Then the next battle was that it cost ten times what the budget was, fourteen million. Of course, that was an unbelievable sum in those days. It was ready to build within a month, and George Dudley,[6] a close friend of Nelson's, went to Albany and buttonholed people—it was the time of year when you stop the clock in the Senate chambers so that you don't have to stop the session. By law you're required to stop it on a certain date, but if the clock doesn't move, you don't have to stop it. So this was one of those times when the bills were piled up high and he got somebody to stick in that fourteen million at the last minute, no backing of any kind.

Like the state educational system, it was never paid for. That was Nelson's problem.

But so on the last day, after everyone had given up, money came through. All due to George. He said, "Look, tell me what it's really going to cost. I'll just speak to Anderson." I guess it was Anderson.[7] They just bulldozed it through because Nelson was the governor and had some favors to cash in.

Same thing with Niagara Falls [Convention Center], which I did around 1970. At the same time that I was doing that I was working with Ruth Carter Johnson.[8]

RS: Tell us about her.

PJ: Ruth is an extraordinary woman. She's now using her extraordinary strength at the National Gallery since she married the chairman of the board.[9]

RS: How did you get to Texas?

PJ: That happened through the de Menils. John de Menil was a big promoter. But he was a very strange type. He resigned from the Museum of Modern Art board in a rage. Still he remained violently friendly with his people, those that he was really friends of. The de Menils became my patrons through Mary Callery. So he was the one that invited me to dinner with Ruth. He knew she was going to build a new museum. That's where that started. Well, my first building outside of New York was actually Utica.[10] But that's not in a center like Houston.

---

6. George Dudley, 1914–2005, architect.

7. Warren Anderson, 1915–2007, prominent New York state politician.

8. Ruth Carter Johnson, b. 1923, philanthropist.

9. John R. Stevenson. They married in 1983.

RS: Utica preceded Amon Carter?[11]

PJ: Oh, yes. That was my first big job outside New York.

RS: How did you get Utica?

PJ: I have no idea. I got it away from Saarinen. He was furious. You know, he was a very competitive guy. I thought you got jobs just by being nice.

But Carter was my introduction to Texas, except for Mrs. de Menil, of course. She's a patroness by gift and nature and temperament. And she and I get along simply splendidly as she has with every architect since.

RS: What is she like?

PJ: Very, very strong, very Texas, very brittle seemingly.

Brittle. But warm enough to patronize architecture. She is a patron by instinct. She likes to collect architects in that world's fair way. She got Paul Rudolph and she got Kevin for the School of Communication at Trinity.[12]

RS: Was she involved with the Roofless Church in New Harmony?[13]

PJ: No. I also met Jane Owen,[14] the New Harmony lady through the de Menils, through John at a club. And he was very pleased. And I was pleased to get the job, needless to say.

One day Jane swam up to me and said, "Will you build me a—?" She had an idea of sex, of course, as part of the background. Her interest in me was physical. And that made for a stormy relationship. She was into sex to such a degree that it inhibited one's architecture.

But after a little hanky-panky, well, we got down to business. And her whims and wishes were really too strong, you see, to make her a good patron. A patron has to realize that he's only one part of the equation.

10. Munson-Williams-Proctor Arts Institute, Utica, New York. Philip Johnson, 1960.

11. Amon Carter Museum, Fort Worth, Texas, 1961. The first addition was completed in 1964, and a subsequent addition by Johnson and Burgee was completed in 1977. The most recent renovation, 1999–2001, again led by Johnson, removed the previous two expansions and increased the museum's overall size by 50,000 square feet.

RS: Aside from her wanting to climb into bed with you, did she also want to hit the drawing board with you as well?

PJ: She was in love with you as long as you could keep that relationship on keel and work. She was quite good. But she's too crazy.

That never worked out as a good patronage job. It should have. It should have been the perfect job.

RS: I've never heard you talk about that commission for the so-called Roofless Church [1960].

PJ: That's her name for it. I didn't like it, of course. That was a fascinating thought. I was into stupas, and what I thought were stupas, although it wasn't in any way a stupa.

I was very fascinated by mathematics, as you remarked in your article.[15] The two things that start me off always are geometry and the processional.

RS: I've never heard you really talk about geometry. I've heard you talk about processionals.

PJ: I never thought of it until I read your article. My God, you mean I'm interested in geometry? I know nothing of geometry. I didn't do well in the darned subject. But there was a kid in the office who was a dynamo.[16] Of course, we didn't have any computers in those days.

RS: That must have been an amazing feat.

PJ: He took weeks and weeks just to make the calculations. It's a crutch, I suppose. I mean, I think architects like me need crutches like history now, or mathematics, or materials. Gropius always had to use new materials.

RS: Technology or whatever.

PJ: Yes, technology. Mies was, of course, Schinkel on the one side and building, *Bauen,* on the other. But I suppose everybody needs something.

Well, on mathematics, I suppose my interest came about through early work with the golden section, through Corbusier, and through Greek proportions of the

---

12. Kevin Roche, b. 1922, architect. Johnson is mistaken; Roche actually built at Texas Christian University in Fort Worth, Texas.

14. Jane Blaffer Owen, b. 1915, philanthropist.

15. Robert A. M. Stern, "Four Towers," *Architecture + Urbanism* (January 1985): 49–58.

16. Johnson is likely referring to James Jarrett, b. 1926, who had been a student of Johnson's at Yale and later worked for him.

13. Johnson seated in front of the Roofless Church (1960), New Harmony, Indiana.

Parthenon and the square root of two crap. And I thought the plan was the whole thing. Of course, in early Mies's time you didn't have to do elevations. From Corbusier's talk, you'd think the plan was the generator, you see. So I was totally gone on that. So the plans of the various parts of the church pleased me very much. And then the thought of a great dome over a sacred statue—well, I've always done that, right down through to AT&T.

RS: That's right.

PJ: From the idea of the chryselephantine statue, which was too small for its niche in the Parthenon, right through to this one,[17] which is too small for its niche, the idea of a sacred thing appealed to me.

Then the temenos, the idea of a sacred place, a walled place, was absolutely fascinating. I mean you step through into another world. And of course that's what Saarinen was trying to do in his unfortunate thing in St. Louis.[18] The sacred place was one thing. The Hindu molded thing, which I interpreted as a stupa . . .

RS: Well, most people interpret the Roofless Church as a kind of pumpkin dome out of Hadrian and see it as related to your classical interests.

PJ: Probably more than I knew. You see I thought it was pure abstract, and just picked a little bit into history. But you're right, it was more of a melon shape. And the melon changed as it went down to meet the ground. I had trouble with the elevation, in every other way except geometrically.

The eggs at—the bases were, I think, nice. Those eggs are very good. Sometimes you hit, sometimes you don't, I guess.

So I was, in general, pleased by the idea of this sitting in a sacred courtyard.

RS: Whose idea was it to collaborate with Lipchitz?

PJ: [Laughs.] Mrs. Owen's. She said, "The great artists should all collect together." And I said, "Oh, sure. Oh, sure." And then he, of course, had only one intention, which was to kill the architecture. He did it before in Blanchette's house, where he put in a piece so big that the house just shrank under the load. That thing that's now in the State Theater, at the end on the left as you go down to your seats, is another Lipchitz, very fitting from a hundred-foot view. I forget the name[19] but it's sort of abstract. It isn't but it looks it. But he was very aggressive, did you know?

RS: Yes.

PJ: A very, very aggressive man, and a very good sculptor. His early work, his cubist work, was the best. So I always like to collaborate with architects and artists—too much probably. So Lipchitz tried to demolish any view of the temenos by putting those gates in and making them bright gold. In the end it just became meaningless. So I always entered the other way, as everyone does. And that worked out very well. But it was just the opposite of my original thought there.

RS: What else did Ruth Carter Johnson patronize you for?

PJ: She built the Water Gardens.[20] That was a marvelous commission. It was in the wrong part of town, and still is, by the way, for a city. It doesn't link up with the action of the city, which all went north to the Basses and the Tandys.[21] So she picked wrong there. But the land was available, and she bought it and said, "Well, what do you want to do?" Our idea was a garden, but no water. There again, mathematics and the processional were the only two guiding principles, the way we began. But it has been, in a way, the most popular thing I've ever done.

RS: Now, when you were in this Alfred Barr phase of collecting, you didn't really hobnob with artists at all.

PJ: Never did. Alfred didn't either. He always felt that he'd be influenced. And I never talked much to artists. They don't talk much. The better the artist, the less they are able to verbalize. So I prefer critics.

RS: But with David Whitney, you have had more friendships with artists.

PJ: Through him, I know Jasper Johns quite well, but in a silent way. One communes with artists, quite properly, by means of grunts. And I did his house down there on the island of St. Martin.

I reused the first principle I used in the very first house I built in Mt. Kisco.[22] I got it from Corbusier's de Mandrot house, I realize now. My God, when you're old you remember things. I didn't think at the time that I did get it from de Mandrot, but I did. I took the idea of a single square plan and then a long element and then one more open square with a pool, so it made it a sort of court.

That's right. Same idea, but different, of course. Nothing fancy. It was just a plan because Johns hates architecture, which I knew. So I did just a plan and he had other people finish it. And they didn't help it, shall we say. But the court is there. It's the right way to live in the Caribbean, and it worked out very well. But there was no communication from him. I would ask, "What'll I do in that corner?" Grunts. I'd say, "Well, perhaps we'll do this, and that, and that. Here's a pencil." He built it. Wonderfully carried through. He's very well organized mentally, but it's very hard to make a type of friendship with him like you and I have. You see, we can talk objective things. But I don't think you can with any artist, really. David doesn't care because he's not an intellectual himself. But you don't talk to artists the way you talk to architects.

RS: David makes wonderful small talk with artists.

PJ: Artists communicate very strangely to my mind. Like Andy,[23] how do you talk to Andy?

RS: No, you can't possibly. He always asks you how much something costs.

PJ: Wonderfully interested in money.

RS: But let's talk about some of the other projects of that period. What about the Bobst Library at NYU?

PJ: NYU is a strangely unsatisfactory commission. Hester,[24] the president, was very supportive. It amounted to twenty million, or something like that. In those days, that was a lot. But I was in one of my worst periods. Foster had left, you see. So I was wandering around alone, didn't have a partner, which I needed so much for my psyche. And so I was a one-note designer. I mean, all I had was a negative column, which I see now in Bofill's Marne-la-Vallée.[25]

RS: That's right.

---

17. The statue in the Roofless Church is entitled *The Descent of the Holy Spirit*, 1960, by Jacques Lipchitz, 1891–1973.

18. The Jefferson National Expansion Memorial Gateway Arch. Project conceived in 1948, groundbreaking took place in 1959, and actual construction lasted from 1963–65.

19. The sculpture is *Birth of the Muses*, 1944–50.

20. Fort Worth, Texas, 1974.

21. Two prominent local families who built extensively in the area of Sundance Square in the 1970s and 1980s.

22. The house being referred to is the Booth house, actually in Bedford Village, 1945–46.

23. Andy Warhol.

24. James Hester, b. 1924, president of New York University from 1962 to 1974.

25. Ricardo Bofill, b. 1939, Catalan architect. The complex in Marne-la-Vallée is called Spaces of Abraxas, 1978–82.

PJ: Of course, Bofill was crazy about that building of mine. It's the only building in New York he would visit.

RS: Oh, really. It was conscious?

PJ: Absolutely. I never mentioned it, of course, this is the truth. Oh, yes, he's the only one who really likes my work. To him, the most important thing in the world is the top of that building. He's completely stuck in postmodernism of your period. Fascinated. Where were we though?

RS: NYU.

PJ: NYU. So I never got to loosen that building up. Looking back it's much easier to see—the way Le Corbusier hated Weissenhof.[26] I used to talk to him about his early work. He certainly didn't like that.

RS: Oh, really.

PJ: Oh, yes. He felt very strong about it. He didn't publish it, any more than I'm going to talk about the NYU work outside this.

But it's that business of being modern in the sense that the plan was the generator, that the module was the key. The third dimension—I mean Frank Lloyd Wright's great passion—was lacking. All I did was to work on the elevation in that building and to see that it did fit the plan behind. But that leads to a very—shall we say flat—facade, although, God knows, it has a three-foot-deep reveal.

RS: No, but it is flat.

PJ: The bulk of the mass, the stodgy, froglike mass didn't interest me at all. How could I miss that?

So that was a period when I was sort of despairing. We didn't have any work, not much to keep going. So I got Foster back to associate with me on the building. Then Wrightsman[27] insisted on locking me in the library of his yacht to work on it. Well, I don't work that way.

RS: That's a terrible thing to do.

PJ: Well, he did it so that he could charge off the trip, of course. He also charged off flowers that he sent to Johnny Walker. It was in the newspapers.

RS: Who was Johnny Walker?

PJ: The director of the National Gallery.[28]

RS: Why did he send him flowers?

PJ: Oh, I don't know. He was sick or something. But he marked it down as a deduction. I mean, really, it was seven dollars and a half.

RS: A yacht's another thing. That's not seven dollars and a half.

PJ: No, it was fifty thousand a week, whatever. The whole constellation somehow wasn't the kind of thing I get stimulated by. As you do by Gerry [Hines].

RS: And what about the big room, on the inside of the library?

PJ: The big room started out all right. But somehow the marble floor and the stone walls don't go together. The roof was never glassed the way it was supposed to be, and again, no articulation.

I had an awful time with the railings because of the local people telling me,

---

26. Le Corbusier designed two villas for the Weissenhofsiedlung, Stuttgart, Germany, 1927.

27. Charles Wrightsman, 1895–1986, oil baron and donor to NYU.

28. John Walker, 1906–1995; director, National Gallery of Art, Washington, D.C., 1956–1969.

"Somebody's going to jump over."[29] Nobody ever has, of course, but that's why there are those horrible spikes.[30] But I mean it is very boring, indeed, just to pile up a lot of balconies. I didn't think it would be. The proportions are off. It's too tall for its width, and the materials arc funny. I don't know what else is wrong, probably a lot of things. I thought the stairway would save it.

RS: No, but anything repeated that much—it's just so dizzying.

PJ: That's the word, repetition. The same with the outside—the bays, the bays, the bays, the bays. It may have worked in Mies's case. I don't know if it did really.

29. Elmer Holmes Bobst Library and Study Center, southeast corner of Washington Square South and La Guardia Place, New York. Philip Johnson and Richard Foster, 1973. Interior court.

30. In 2003 there were two suicides in the library, and plastic barriers were installed.

But you see, I wasn't far enough along to get the textural thing straight. That finally happened in Republic.[31] That's the way to do it.

Oh, it was a very hard job. If it isn't hard, it's hardly worth working on. But I headed into the job from a wrong premise, I think. I loved the material. That worked out very well. But the building sits on the street without any sense of welcome. It doesn't have any of the French hôtel way of going in.

RS: One of the things that I think you did pioneer at NYU was the galleria over the street. I'm not sure if anyone else had proposed such a thing at that time.[32]

PJ: Of course, they wouldn't do it. Which one of the buildings would bear the expense? And also André Meyer[33] hated it. He wanted his building not to be under a goddamned galleria. It's the same problem in shopping centers. The true powers in a shopping center are the two Sakses or the two Neiman Marcuses at the ends, and screw the stuff in between. That leaves no money, no chance for doing shaped bases or anything. We gave up one scheme right in the middle, the LBJ one in Dallas.

----

31. Republic National Bank, Houston, Texas, 1984.

32. Proposal for redevelopment of New York University's Washington Square campus. Philip Johnson and Richard Foster, 1964.

33. André Meyer, 1898–1979, investment banker.

34. Sheldon Memorial Art Gallery, University of Nebraska, Lincoln, 1963.

35. Full-scale mock-up of Sheldon Memorial Art Gallery facade in Italy.

But that's not our subject. The period we're talking about is the low point. Including the museums. Of course, the worst one of that type is Nebraska,[34] which is a purely modern building.

RS: You really don't like that building?

PJ: No, I do. I went back to get an honorary degree there and I once more liked that period. Of course, it's beautifully maintained, and incredibly well detailed. Foster went to Italy and they mocked the whole thing up full scale.[35] We took pictures of it in the mountains in Italy. And it all got put together, and she paid for it.[36] It worked very well. There are some contradictions in the lobby. For instance, the modern stairs don't fit with the—

RS: Well, the detailing is not quite classical, it's concrete in travertine.

PJ: That's right, concrete done in travertine.[37] Absolutely right, the first job of that type was in concrete.

RS: But I have seen it. I thought it was beautifully put together. Improbable to come upon this palace there.

PJ: Isn't it strange? They love it, of course.

The modern sense of mixing modern and classical—we were trying to be restrained. I ended up being block modern with repeated units, you see, and the repeated units cover different kinds of functions. Like the entrance hall.

RS: Also like the Boston Public Library addition [1972]. It doesn't read as a library except by its size.

PJ: It doesn't say, "I'm a library." A bank should look like a bank. All that style-for-the-job business came afterward, I guess. But you never know what period you're in or why you're doing things.

The trouble was that the building doesn't have any emphasis. Repetition, and nothing to cross it.

RS: This is also the Museum of Modern Art addition period, of course.

PJ: That was about the same period. I was very tired.

----

36. The patron was Olga Nielsen Sheldon, 1897–1990.

37. Sheldon Memorial Art Gallery, Lincoln, Nebraska. Philip Johnson, 1963. Exterior and interior views.

RS: It was your most wayward—

PJ: Well, I was wanting to break out, and I didn't want to do any more of that damned thing at Lincoln Center, with the stupid classical column that doesn't fit the cornice. So instead of that, I said, "I'll be modern, but I'll soften it." This is what I called my television-windows period. I thought by these windows I could gain enough richness. Of course, I didn't. The only thing that saved that building, if anything, was the fact that it was so small. It only had five bays, and five you can hold onto. It's when it gets to be endless, like the library, that you can't afford to be boring. But I was still modern. I thought I could dress it up.

RS: What turned your practice around? Is Burgee the cause of a renaissance, or did he just help you implement that renaissance?

PJ: Well, you see, I don't know. But I was the one who pursued him because we were trying to get a job with his boss, Carter Manny. I said, "This is a great guy, just exactly the answer to an architect's dream." And I said, "Won't you come to New York?" And he said, "Oh, hell no, I'm going to be head of this company here. Why should I come to New York?" I said, "Well, think about it." And then a year later I called him from the airport because I was in Chicago. And he thought about it and brought Gwen [Burgee's wife] here.

Then he insisted on being full partner, and then later a little more than full partner, all of which was fine with me, because the age thing works out fine.[38] But he wasn't yet a partner, although we were working together closely, when the guy from IDS came in.[39]

That was the big shift. They had a local architect whom they brought in with these designs, and they said, "Would you please put a facade on this, that's all. Design a fifty-story blank facade."

The first eleven stories were a garage. And there we had sense enough—now John did a lot on this—to say, "We will not build an eleven-story garage." So if we don't get the building, we won't do the facade. We're not facade decorators. So they said, "No." That's a hard decision—you'll get to it too in your work—when to say "no."

Mies accepted to put a facade on a building, you remember, and it never came about. And what was wrong with that? Just to get a start, to get your foot in the door?

Anyway, they came back after lunch and said, "You can have the whole building."

So John Burgee was in his glory. He was at his most helpful and cooperative and collaborative. Because I would not—I was too timid to take an aggressive attitude with IDS and say, "You darned fools, why build up half a block in Minneapolis? Buy

38. Johnson and John Burgee, 1980.

the rest of the block." So help me, they did, otherwise we couldn't have done that plan. So the urbanistic part worked out fine. We had the obvious advantage of the bridges. I think it's our best building.

RS: I'm not sure it's your best building, but certainly it's one of the most important urbanistically.

PJ: Urbanistically it's the most important.

RS: And to use glass that way—it realizes Mies's conception of how glass should be used.

PJ: Yes, well, that was almost accidental, the return. The idea was later used, of course, in lots of buildings.

RS: But Burgee was not your partner yet.

PJ: No, he wasn't. Right in the middle of that job, he said to me in an airplane, "Look, Philip, I want to be your equal partner." I said, "You got it." Because he was doing the work. He was doing the traveling. He went out once a week, and that's a hell of a ride. He's going out to Phoenix tomorrow for a new job, and I said, "If you can't sell it, I can't." "If you can't start it, there's nothing I can do." I mean, after all, I'm nearly eighty. I'm not going to go traveling around to everybody who wants to see a sketch of a building.

You can see where my mind's at right now. He has a much more aggressive

39. IDS Center, Minneapolis, Minnesota. Johnson/Burgee Architects, 1973.

personality than I do, in funny ways. I'm a better salesman, I guess. And of course I'm the figurehead.

RS: You're the famous architect.

PJ: I'm the famous architect. No way out of that. As they told us at the new job in Hartford, "We got you because of your name—your face was on the cover of the *New York Times* Sunday section. We need your name to get the job." Fame is a silly thing, very silly, as you will find.

RS: That's right. Then you're the famous architect and you're too busy to do the job.

PJ: Too busy to do it thoroughly.

RS: That's right.

PJ: And you can't resist.

RS: "Will you concentrate, Mr. Johnson?"

PJ: "Are you gonna concentrate on this job?" "Oh, yes, certainly. I wouldn't want—" You start crossing your fingers, and you say every time, "Oh, I'll put my whole personal attention on it. Nothing is as important as this. For you . . ."

Shit.

It's embarrassing, isn't it?

RS: It's embarrassing to be caught with one's own truth.

PJ: Well, we're talking to posterity here so it's all right.

RS: It is! But John is not a good salesman in that sense?

PJ: He's a wonderful salesman, but he's a businessman too. The business people always feel much relieved when he appears on the scene. But they are also after the image, you see. Only in America is architecture dependent on private feelings.

RS: It's true, as it was in the days of Raymond Hood.

PJ: Of course, it was, as you put it in your article.[40] Exactly the same. You get the prestige that way. That's why Hood made his buildings all so different. I can't do what Bunshaft did, do the same building three or four times around New York. Ski jump buildings.[41]

RS: Ski jump, yes.

PJ: He copied them from Burgee's firm anyhow.[42] You can't do that anymore.

They say to me, "Oh, you do such original buildings. We want to be just like AT&T. Front page of the *Times*." Pretty silly.

RS: But what does John Burgee do in the design of these buildings?

PJ: What he does is to act as a severe critic, as a business leader. For example, he always stops me up short, "No, that material will not do what you think it will."

As short as that. Or, "What you've done there is to spoil the very point you started with, which is this half circle." In relation to our new office, I had been playing with making notches and things. He said, "The whole theory of a half circle is, there it is. We gotta emphasize that."[43]

---

40. See Robert A. M. Stern, "Four Towers," *Architecture + Urbanism* (January 1985): 49–58.

41. The Grace Building, 41 West Forty-second Street, 1972, and 9 West Fifty-seventh Street, 1974, are nearly identical.

42. The allusion is to the First National Bank, Chicago, Illinois. C. F. Murphy Associates, 1969. Burgee worked for the firm and its predecessors, Naess & Murphy (1958–61) and C. F. Murphy (1961–65).

43. After twenty-eight years in the Seagram Building, Johnson moved his office to the "Lipstick Building" at 885 Third Avenue, in 1986.

Perfect. He's marvelous. He's got a good eye, and he will never try to design himself. Never instigated a design that we used. But on the other hand, I never get very far without starting to work with him on all these things because his perception is so clear.

RS: Well, Foster didn't quite function that way.

PJ: No, Foster was nowhere near as good. He was a technical builder; he saw that it got done in the field.

RS: So who did you interact with at this time? Young designers in the office, or Manley?

PJ: Manley, and still do. Manley is the only man who can design with me. He does all the work as if I were there, but I can't be there all the time.

When I come back, the things I've been dreaming about have somehow slipped into place. He's the key man in our office—and they hate him, of course. Everybody including John hates Manley because he's prissy and because he can't work with people and he can't meet clients.

I had him working on the library in Boston before Burgee appeared. They hated John Manley so the job practically ran into the sand. And that was John's [Burgee] first job. He practically lived in Boston trying to get it back on track.

RS: But Manley has never demanded a silent partnership?

PJ: Oh, he doesn't want it. Even when I made him a partner, sort of, and gave him that office, he wouldn't go into it. He can't run the business.

You see, John Burgee does all his business—insurance, contacts with clients, picking contractors, all that, as well as the legal stuff—the piles of lawsuits that just appear like mushrooms.

It's something you have to look forward to with great pleasure. You don't really get the suits until you get big. The pockets aren't deep enough until you get five million, ten million dollars worth of insurance. Then, of course, the vultures appear. Americans are getting more litigious, not less.

RS: That's insane. So Manley has been content to be the senior draftsman.

PJ: My amanuensis, I believe the old word was. The man who writes, the man who gets the ideas into workable form. And he will also say, "Well, look that's too steep for what you're talking about."

But as for me, I have to see too many people. So now I have designers on each job, as you do, probably.

RS: Yes.

PJ: And that spreads one thin: "How thick is a pilaster?"

RS: "Mr. Johnson, just tell us what you want." "Well, I don't know what I want."

PJ: [Laughs.]

"If I knew what I wanted, I would have told you long ago."

[Laughs.]

Bob, I'm afraid you and I have too many similarities.

Well, wait till the critics turn on you. That'll be fun.

RS: Oh, don't worry. In a small way, it has been happening for years. Not so seriously. I'm doing harmless stuff.

PJ: Yes, you're not into the stuff where you really— Who do you want to hit next?

There are a lot of buildings that you've kindly left out of the discussion that aren't so important, that you do in the course of a practice like mine, where you have to be very cheap. Like Denver.[44] Or what's another one we don't talk about? Never mind.

RS: Denver's not so good. Well, the lobby's not bad.

PJ: That lobby was an afterthought. All that room, so I said, "Well, let's have fun in the lobby." But it has nothing to do with the rest of it. Well, of course, the entrance isn't finished yet. It's just going up now.

RS: Well, I'll wait.

PJ: Never mind. That's another one where I thought cutting through the window would be enough to make the building different or something. It didn't.

RS: It is different. It may be the best building in Denver, but that's not . . .

PJ: That's not saying anything.

RS: You used to have people like Jarrett and other young people work for you.

PJ: They never did this kind of design. And now I've got two or three. Raj Ahuja.[45] The Indians are very good. Raj and I are partners, you know.

RS: No.

PJ: Yes. Made him a minor, I mean, a minority partner. And he's very good but very rambunctious.

Of course, the bigger the organization, the more time you spend on organization. You must have found that already.

RS: Yes, I hate it. I find it a nightmare. With sixty people, you can imagine.

PJ: You've got sixty—?

RS: We're going down. Some people are leaving and we're not replacing them.

PJ: You have been up this high? We never went over sixty.

RS: Well, you know, houses take a lot of pencil mileage.

PJ: And they don't make money.

RS: Yes. I don't think they make money anymore for me, either.

What about Gerry Hines?

PJ: He was an incredible client.[46]

The day he called me and said that Fifty-third Street [885 Third Avenue] wasn't right, I was sunk. I went around for days, "My God, if that isn't right, what is?" And I changed the whole thing. The only reason it's good now is that Gerry called me.

----

44. United Center Bank Tower, Denver, Colorado, 1984.

45. Raj Ahuja, b. 1941, Indian-born architect.

46. Johnson with Gerald Hines, c. 1985.

47. Johnson's four office towers proposed for Times Square, designed for New York developer George Klein, b. 1938.

48. In Transco Tower, Houston, Texas, designed by Johnson/Burgee, 1979.

RS: Really?

PJ: I'm the type of architect that you've got to hit over the head before I will start again. I did not do it at Forty-second Street.[47] I'm now trying to do it and it's too late.

Gerry knows—as you know too now—that his judgment was accurate and prejudiced and clear. We either did good or we didn't. And if we couldn't persuade him, we did what he said. But there are very few patrons like that among developers.

That's the very best kind of a patron: the kind who will pull you up short, sometimes for the wrong reasons, but usually because—I trust Gerry's eye.

He has a quirkiness, as he should have, but he also has a fine fingertip feel, which he doesn't know he has. He loves architecture and is an architect *manqué,* of course.

To let us go ahead with Republic, for instance—no other developer or patron would have done it.

And he's suffered. To go to his office,[48] you have to go to the top and come down. So when you want to leave, you punch the up button on the elevator, contrary to nature. Things like that didn't bother him if he could have a beautiful tower. In other words, he was willing to warp the definite requirement of an office building in order to get that kind of glory, and to pay for the five-million-dollar fountain, which he didn't know was going to be as successful as it is.

RS: It's fantastic.

PJ: Isn't it? I had a lot of problems with that design, but we won't talk about them.

RS: Technically, you mean?

PJ: Technically it was agony. Nobody was right; everybody was wrong. They were wrong, we were wrong, our consultants were wrong, our engineers were wrong. There wasn't one single thing that went right. I guess it's inevitable in any new technique that we get into. That one was especially vicious.

But, I mean, there is real patronage. Again, Gerry wins out as the best.

RS: But you don't think he's such a patron anymore.

PJ: No, he was corporate before. Now he has just lost his interest in architecture. So all my work now—all our work for him—is for his kids. They now give out orders as if they were Gerry. He won't cross them up. He used to. He'd say, "Oh, I'll fix that in the morning, Philip. You're absolutely right." Then he'd go and slap them down. But he can't do that anymore. So we switched our lines of allegiance, as it were.

Well, that's marvelous, in a way, but you need a little more. That's why Gerry is the perfect mixture, because he can say, "Look, Philip, I've got to change this window. It's too far in, and the returns are costing me five to ten million. Could you move the window farther out near the outside? Now, I'm not forcing you, I'm asking you. On a scale of one to ten, how much does that rate?" "Gerry, that's an eight, only we won't have to move it as far . . ."

In the Republic, it's very important to have that amount of depth. But he understood the techniques, the pricing, and all other restrictions of developers.

See, with any other developer, I never could have done that tower. It's the most inefficient way to end a building you've ever heard of. Just a short little elevator. And those steps on the facade. They get so narrow. One of them at the top is about twenty feet across. How are you going to rent that?

10. Patronage, Competition, and the New Generation

RS: I thought that we should talk a bit about the social aspect of your whole career. How, in the 1950s and the early 1960s, the Glass House became a real social center for architecture and perhaps for other things as well, how you were entertaining important people coming through, and so forth.[1]

PJ: Well, let's go further back, to Seagram's. I was at the Museum of Modern Art and I was only taken aboard because I was already there. So I introduced Phyllis to all

1. Johnson in the Lake Pavilion (1962), Glass House estate, 1964.

the architects. I have always leaned over backward.

But the house was, of course, the center of activity.[2] Do you suppose that it was something of a feeling of inadequacy on my part, of not being part of the game, part of the creative side at that time? And of wanting my house to be a center so that it would be liked and would become famous?

Of course, I had a passion for publicity, I suppose, much more than I realized. But with my publicity I wanted to be among architects and especially the kids.

I did leave the Architectural League out of our discussion.

But I hear more about the Glass House now, even to the extent of its appearing in the article on early Stirling in the new Stirling book by that Cornell man, Colin Rowe.[3]

I can see the influence of New Canaan in the discussions of the period. It did become—you couldn't be a Yale student if you hadn't been down to see it. That was toward the end of this period when you first came down.

RS: Right.

PJ: But I was still welcoming people. I didn't shut the gates tight until later. I think the last man to come was Chuck Moore when he became dean.[4]

RS: Which would have been 1966–67.

PJ: Yes, you see, he was brought down by the then-dean, Gibson Danes.[5] Mr. Moore was not interested and Gib wasn't, of course, a great man. And I didn't think Mr. Moore was a very good architect. His little houses in New Haven were not very good, do you think?

RS: I think that he was better in California.

PJ: Yes, he's a California architect.

RS: I think the Eastern situation didn't agree with him. By and large—there are a few exceptions—but the East Coast projects are not among his best. But the West Coast—

PJ: —is where he blossomed.

2. Johnson in the Painting Gallery (1965), Glass House estate, 1966.

3. Colin Rowe, "Introduction," in *James Stirling: Buildings and Projects*, eds. Peter Arnell and Ted Bickford (London: Architectural Press, 1984).

4. Charles W. Moore, 1925–1993, chairman, Department of Architecture at Yale from 1965 to 1969, and then dean of the Yale School of Architecture from 1969 to 1970.

5. Gibson Danes, 1910–1992, dean of the Yale School of Art and Achitecture from 1958–1968.

RS: —is where he blossoms and makes sense.

But again, New Canaan was the center of an architectural community in the 1950s.

PJ: That's right. You see, I chose New Canaan because Breuer lived there and Johansen lived there and so did Eliot Noyes.

RS: I never think of him as an architect.

PJ: Well, that was my fault. I got him into architecture, the way I did poor Robertson.[6] See, I haven't always been a positive influence.

But you urge people to go into architecture because they want to be urged.

I didn't ever push them, but that was an influential time. And I could teach at Yale and be connected, and New Canaan was sort of the center that, of course, Philadelphia had been and was later to be.

RS: It would really come into focus again under Kahn.

So you had a gathering there of architects, did you not, in the 1950s?

PJ: I had a gathering at the Glass House for Ed Logue[7] when he first came to New York.

RS: I thought there was a gathering when Yamasaki and you . . .

PJ: Oh, that one. No, Yamasaki wasn't there—that was the first time. It was the ancestor really of the dinner at the Century Club. It ended in total disaster. I'm sure I've told you about it, haven't I?

RS: Okay, that was the one. You did talk about that.

PJ: This was a two-day meeting, and I remember a bunch of people had to stay at one of the inns and so on.

RS: Then you had the Logue gathering. It must have been about 1965 or 1966.

PJ: Logue must have been very late. Yes, he had just been appointed here and was looking to hire architects. So I said, "Hang your works in"— Oh, yes, it must have been late 1966, because Foster had already left me.

RS: That was, in my view, one of the more important occasions of the coming of a new generation which, I think, you helped sponsor and were troubled by, both at once. I think your position with regard to Giurgola and Venturi[8] was just as ambivalent as your position about Moore.

PJ: No, I appreciated Venturi because he was an obvious brain. That book,[9] you see, was as much a revelation to me as it was to [Vincent] Scully. He took it a lot more

---

6. Jaquelin T. Robertson, b. 1933, architect and urban planner.

7. Edward Logue, 1921–2000, lawyer, political aide, urban planner, and administrator dedicated to public development projects. He worked primarily in New Haven, Boston, and New York State, serving as president and chief executive officer of New York's Urban Development Corporation from 1968 to 1975.

8. Johnson with architect Paul Damaz, 1917–2008, and Robert Venturi, Philadelphia architect and theorist.

seriously than I did, but it was such a relief that it appeared. Well, for both you and me, don't you think? We were both heavily influenced by that book.

RS: Well, I was heavily influenced also by Bob Venturi's architecture at that stage.

PJ: Mother's House?[10]

RS: Mother's House. I mean, I saw it and that's what made me pursue Venturi. But I can remember you only going so far with respect to his architecture, saying that the plans were interesting.

PJ: I found the plans wonderful of his early house with the green stripe around it, in the ordinary New Jersey coast neighborhood.[11] I found the plan excellent where you came in by the laundry machine, and the big room was on the piano nobile where it should be. Yes, the same plan, in a sense, as the late house in Westchester, Mount Kisco, where you have the bedroom and the utilities on the ground floor and the pleasant room on the second floor.[12]

That and the plan, for instance, of the Yale Math Building,[13] which was a brilliant solution to that very difficult site.

But I don't remember any other individual people who nailed up their stuff at my house.

Were Michael Graves and people like that there?

RS: I can't remember Michael. Certainly Charlie Gwathmey was there and, I think, Giurgola and Venturi.

PJ: Venturi?

RS: I think. But I can't remember. It's not clear in my mind, either. I do remember your having Giurgola there, because the Daytons—and I think this must be before IDS—were shopping for a house architect.

PJ: That's how I got IDS too—the Daytons' suggestion to IDS. That one Dayton[14] was a strong man, and there was nobody else in IDS that—they're all wimps and still are. It's an entirely different company now.

So they didn't know what they were doing, and Dayton said, "I'll take half the building, but you better get a good architect. Why don't you start with Philip Johnson in your search?"

They started with me and they came back to me. But it was all through Dayton. He was looking for a house and I wouldn't do it at the time; I was involved in Seagram's or something. It impressed him that I would refuse that.

RS: Well, it was later than the Seagram's phase. You said you wouldn't do a house, though?

PJ: I said I wouldn't do a house, and then Giurgola built it.[15] Giurgola may have met Dayton in New Canaan. I don't know.

RS: Well, my recollection is—obviously it's not the same as yours, but I was there— that you were squiring Dayton around to introduce him to different architects, and you had Moore scheduled for one point, on a Saturday or a Sunday—

---

9. Robert Venturi, *Complexity and Contradiction in Architecture* (New York: Museum of Modern Art, 1966).

10. Vanna Venturi house, Philadelphia, Pennsylvania. Robert Venturi, 1961–65.

11. Lieb house, Long Beach Island, New Jersey. Venturi and Rauch, 1966–69.

12. Carll Tucker III house, Mount Kisco, New York. Venturi and Rauch, 1975.

13. Unrealized winning competition project by Venturi and Rauch, 1971.

14. Kenneth Dayton, 1922–2000.

15. Kenneth Dayton house, Wayzata, Minnesota. Mitchell/ Giurgola, 1970.

PJ: Oh, that was a different meeting with him, that was with Ed Logue —

RS: I don't want to put words in your mouth because that's not the point of this, but I remember when you finally met Giurgola you couldn't figure him out.

PJ: I still can't. He's got that potatoes-in-the-mouth business that gives me trouble.

Oh, I know why I was trying to push him. It was the Philadelphia influence. That post-Kahnian group was very strong. Venturi's Mother's House and the first Giurgola things were of definite interest.

You could feel a turn in the accepted avant-garde to Philadelphia. I thought this was something to find out about and to recommend.

So, no doubt, I recommended him — I did indeed recommend Giurgola to Dayton.

- -

16. David Salle, b. 1952, American artist.

17. Eric Fischl, b. 1948, American artist.

18. Ironically, Stern replaced Johnson/Burgee in Hines's Boylston Street development in Boston shortly after these interviews.

Albert Speer   *Heidelberg*

MAY 3 1 1979

Dear Philip,

       I have just finished a day's work interviewing Speer, a most interesting experience which gave me much to ponder on ; rather than try and write it all down, I shall recount it to you over lunch when I get back and, if you would like to hearthem, play you some of the tapes. Anyway, Speer talks of you with great affection and respect ; I am directed, so to speak, to send the compliments of the Masterbuilder to the Formgiver. He inscribed a copy of the new book on his architecture to you, and I have it in my suitcase. He asked me to write an essay for his next book, which I shall certainly do, although God knows what the reaction in the better-thinking circles of New York will be ; as the researcher on our film crew remarked, on hearing of this, "First gays, now Nazis — what next ?" He is very curious about AT & T and thought it more in the spirit of his own work than anything he had seen by an American architect since 1945. (I will try not to put this story into circulation, or would you prefer a straight cash arrangement ?)

       I left New York in rather a rush, so I didn't have the chance to tell you that I had lunch with Carleton Smith ; we got on well, although I scarcely had a chance to get a word in between the rolling thunder of names that he kept dropping. If you hadn't told me otherwise, I would have thought he was as mad as a March hare, but I shall go along with him and see what happens.

6900 Heidelberg 1   Schloß-Wolfsbrunnenweg 50   Tel. 26501

19. Letter from art critic Robert Hughes (b. 1938) to Johnson, 1979, on Albert Speer's stationery. Hughes was interviewing Speer in preparation for his eight-part television series, *The Shock of the New* (1980), later published as a book.

When I went to see the finished house, I was less amused.

But since I don't build houses, I didn't have a feel what a house should be looking like in those days. But that's what I did to encourage the whole Philadelphia story.

RS: I think you also, at that meeting that I recall with the Daytons in New Canaan, took them to Johansen's office.

PJ: Oh, Johansen was certainly one of the ones who would be looked at there at that time. I would also do it for Noyes because he was nearby.

RS: In that period, I think, you began what I would call your patronage of other architects. I don't remember whether the Logue thing preceded or came after the Dayton.

PJ: I'm always looking for the next generation. With painters too. I bought a Salle[16] and I'm buying a Fischl,[17] you know, keeping my hand in. It's fun!

But of that generation that I had around me in 1966—that's almost twenty years ago—you're the youngest.

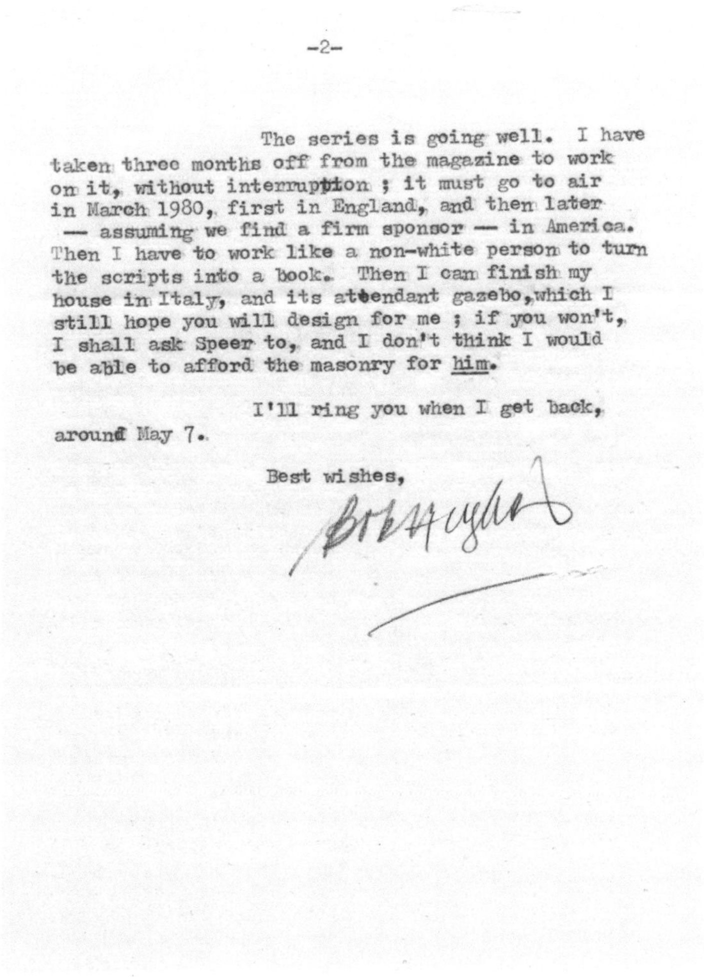

−2−

The series is going well. I have taken three months off from the magazine to work on it, without interruption ; it must go to air in March 1980, first in England, and then later — assuming we find a firm sponsor — in America. Then I have to work like a non-white person to turn the scripts into a book. Then I can finish my house in Italy, and its attendant gazebo, which I still hope you will design for me ; if you won't, I shall ask Speer to, and I don't think I would be able to afford the masonry for him.

I'll ring you when I get back, around May 7.

Best wishes,

Bob Hughes

RS: That's right. Gwathmey and I would be the youngest and Robertson and Eisenman the oldsters.

PJ: Was Robertson there and Eisenman? No, I don't think I knew Eisenman. And at the extreme end would be Noyes.

RS: Well, he's dead. But I think up to Venturi and Moore, that describes a generation.

PJ: New Canaan is where, for instance, Logue met Johansen. That led to his housing on the island [Roosevelt Island]. But you see, recommendations don't always amount to anything. That's why I let them all swim. That was my approach in those days.

Ed Logue had eyes too. So he had fun, and he did pick people from that meeting. I remember Foster coming up, "Well, I'm an architect and local."

I think I was promoting people in the New York area because the jobs at hand were things like Roosevelt Island.

We had lots of fun. In those days I did use the house for that kind of propaganda purpose.

But that's what it was really all about in New Canaan. Discovering younger people and promoting them. Although I wasn't always conscious of making judgments and picking people.

RS: I think you got the aura of having set a style in motion twenty or thirty years before. So you are a tastemaker, Philip.

PJ: Well, I'm in all those books, all right.

RS: So that carries an imprimatur. Besides you're very good at it.

PJ: I must be a good salesman.

RS: Yes. The Ohio boy comes out.

PJ: Ham. My father was the same way. They always said he was a lousy lawyer—his partners. He never did any law work, but boy, he was Mr. Cleveland when he died. That's what he wanted to be. He didn't care about the law. I suppose I'm the same way. We're all more like our parents than we like to think we are.

But I find the whole atmosphere, Bob, has changed enormously among me and the middle-aged architects. As John [Burgee] puts it best, "Instead of colleagues, we're now competitors."

It isn't the same. You can't get around the Century table anymore because everybody's mad at everybody. *Bellum omnium contra omnes,* "the war of all against all." It used to be that Philip would say something nice to Mr. Industrialist down here and maybe I'll get a job. That doesn't work anymore. They've all got jobs and they'd all like to have any jobs that I can get for myself. I can no longer help them.

RS: But you don't gossip anymore. I know at one point you did quite a lot.

PJ: With Kevin [Roche], and I used to with Paul [Rudolph], though I've lost track of Paul. But you see, jealousy can be a very terrible thing. Even Kevin, sweet, nonjealous type that he is, can't help but feel a certain envy toward me.

I had work with both [George] Klein and with Gerry [Hines]. That doesn't endear you to people, when you take the crumbs from their table and then are a competitor. It can't be an easy position to be in. You I don't mind because the generation gap is so big.

RS: That's right. I'm not about to take a job away from you.

---

20. John deButts, 1915–1986; chairman and chief executive officer of AT&T from 1972 to 1979.

21. "What luck for rulers that men do not think."

PJ: You have no problem at all. If you work with Gerry, you're on your own.

RS: I mean, I'd more likely take a job away from Michael Graves.[18]

PJ: But you see, that's what I meant about that younger generation—that middle generation—you are not at loggerheads exactly, but you're competitors.

RS: That's right.

PJ: So why sit around and compare notes? It might lose you the job.

RS: No, but after the fact, do you swap war stories? For example, I do remember your telling me how it was when you interviewed at AT&T,[19] and how the other architects—

PJ: I never talked to them. I didn't even ask them—

RS: Maybe it was John who told me.

PJ: That was a classic story of overkill on everyone's part. There were no patrons there, just a happy-go-lucky man who has since left AT&T.

RS: DeButts?

PJ: No, no. DeButts[20] was a top man, but he was good just because he was a driver. He was no patron of the arts. We got the job because one guy was so pleased that we didn't have any slides. He couldn't believe it. That's how I sold it.

Luck plays a big part in this world.

RS: Absolutely.

PJ: Amazing sometimes, isn't it? It's what Hitler said.[21]

Anyway, it's all developers now. The developer makes the architect,[22] in our world, in New York. I think all over the country developers want to imitate Hines and become the enormous force that is now architectural patronage.

- -

22. Cover of *Time* magazine, January 8, 1979, showing Johnson holding a model of the AT&T Building.

Johnson's Rolodex[1]

Kazys Varnelis

As Robert A. M. Stern describes in his introduction to this volume, the interviews he conducted with Philip Johnson were done in collaboration between two Columbia University institutions: the Temple Hoyne Buell Center for American Architecture and the Oral History Research Office (OHRO). By founding the OHRO in 1948, historian Allan Nevins sought to mitigate the threat of "new media" to the traditional archive. In Nevins's view, as the telephone replaced the letter as the principal medium of informal communication, the contents of the archive were increasingly reduced to rehearsed documents. The new informality of modern life, Nevins feared, would obscure the historical record to the extent that fewer and fewer traces of the past could be captured and preserved. But more than that, Nevins observed that, as individuals lost the habit of letter-writing, they also lost the habit of writing down their thoughts and reflections. With the archive thus doubly impoverished, Nevins concluded, histories of the twentieth century would be immensely poorer.[2]

But Nevins was no Luddite himself, and he sought a solution in the new media of his day, employing sound recordings to capture the memories of Americans who, in his words, had "lived significant lives."[3] "[O]ral history," Nevins explained, "was born of modern invention and technology," and made possible only with the advent of the tape recorder.[4] Transcribed and deposited in an archive, the oral history interview would serve as a raw archival source, recapturing what would otherwise escape both official histories and the diminished paper archive.[5]

Consider, for example, the case of Philip Johnson, and an artifact such as the Rolodex he kept at the Glass House. Each card holds crucial and secret information,[6] but with the loss of the individual who spent a lifetime accumulating, nurturing, and connecting these contacts, Johnson's Rolodex in and of itself has no greater meaning

1. Philip Johnson's Rolodex.

2. Allan Nevins, "Oral History: How and Why it Was Born," *Wilson Library Bulletin* 40 (1966): 600–601.

3. Nevins, *The Gateway to History,* (Boston: Heath and Company, 1938), iv.

4. Nevins, "Oral history," 600–601.

5. Walter J. Ong would call this resurgence of oral culture a "second orality." See Ong, *Orality and Literacy: The Technologizing of the Word* (New York: Routledge, 1982). On Johnson as networker, see my forthcoming essay "Philip Johnson's Empire" in Emmanuel Petit, ed. *Philip Johnson. The Constancy of Change* (New Haven: Yale University Press, 2009).

6. The National Trust for Historic Preservation, which manages the Glass House as a historic site, requested that I remove any personal information from this photograph to protect the confidentiality of the individuals in it.

today. Just what did Johnson do with the information on those cards? What importance did the individuals filed therein hold for him? How was Johnson connected to each of them? Though the nodes in Johnson's network remain, we can hardly deduce a theory of the network from them, let alone reproduce it, without Johnson's own account.

As the most traditional form of the oral history genre, the transcript of the series of interviews published herewith represents a "life-review," to use Nevins's terminology, of a historically significant figure.[7] Although the letters that Johnson wrote into the 1940s offer a crucial glimpse into his thoughts and feelings—we have reproduced some of these in the text—the letters and other surviving documents by no means paint a full picture. Moreover, as Johnson rose to occupy the center of architectural power upon his return to the Museum of Modern Art (MoMA) in New York as director of the Department of Architecture and Design in 1949, he established his weekend salon at the Glass House, and soon supplemented this with his table at the Four Seasons Restaurant in the Seagram building and later the Century Club. With increasing demands on his time and ever more business transacted in private social situations, the chatty letters dwindled and finally ended for good.[8]

In contrast to Hilary Lewis and John O'Connor, who interviewed Johnson between 1992 and 1994 and largely concerned themselves with his career as an architect,[9] Stern approached this oral history project as a comprehensive review of Johnson's life, situating Johnson in the historical context and filling in crucial gaps in the record. If Stern set out to focus on Johnson's professional activities, he wound up inquiring into Johnson's upbringing and education, his political activity of the 1930s and the consequences of that activity, as well as his role as a curator, patron, and promoter in tandem with his architectural practice and works in order to understand Johnson as a whole individual.

Nevertheless, in one respect Stern's oral history of Johnson departs from accepted methodology. Like psychoanalysis, conventional oral history requires a distance between the interviewer and narrator, so that the former can remain "objective" and allow the subject to recount his or her story freely. Sometimes, the voice of the interviewer is even deleted in the process of editing. In this case, however, the interviewer—already an accomplished architect and historian—had been close friends with Johnson for over twenty-five years, and as he acknowledges in the introduction as well as in the interview, owed many of his early professional connections and ultimately his success to Johnson. Stern was by this point commonly seen as one of Johnson's protégés and had provided commentary on the elder architect's official textual record in the 1979 collection of Johnson's texts *Writings*.[10] Thus, when the two sat down to conduct these interviews, Stern was thoroughly familiar with the buildings to which Johnson refers, the individuals he mentions, and the architect's thoughts.

In spite of the closeness between them, or rather because of it, Stern is an incisive interviewer. Sympathetic and informed, he lets Johnson's voice dominate while he guides the story. Moreover, with the remarkable knowledge of history that

----

7. Cf. Paul Thompson's call for the use of oral history to create a "more democratic" history that "allows heroes not just from the leaders, but from the unknown majority of the people." Paul Thompson, *The Voice of the Past* (Oxford, UK: Oxford University Press, 1978), 7, 18.

8. The letters are deposited at the Getty Research Institute.

9. Lewis and O'Connor, *Philip Johnson. The Architect in His Own Words* (New York: Rizzoli, 1994).

10. Philip Johnson, *Writings* (New York: Oxford University Press, 1979).

he repeatedly demonstrates in the course of the interview—often to Johnson's own amazement—Stern is able to draw connections and question statements that a less historically informed interviewer might not.

As a result, the interviews take the form of a *dialogue*, a conversation in which two architects reflect on two subjects that, as Stern suggests, are of most interest to them both: history and gossip. In editing this manuscript, I have tried to capture the sense that Stern and Johnson are sitting and talking together in Johnson's Museum Tower apartment, rendering the conversation as a narrative rather than a verbatim transcript, a reading that Michael Bierut's excellent design underscores. The result gives a sense of the informal side of Johnson that his friends got to know, his sharp, often catty wit, his intelligence, his opinionated attitude, his admiration for some, and his disregard for others. Throughout, we see Johnson as a witness to—and player in—a key century in architectural history.

Deposited with the OHRO, the original transcript remains the document of record for this interview. As editor, I cut material that I judged to be redundant, with the distinct exception of a lengthy excursion on critics of the period that is much less interesting to a general reader today than it would have been twenty years ago. To avoid inevitable ruptures in the narrative flow whenever the two interlocutors digressed to clarify or expand upon a point made earlier in their conversation (as they frequently did), I adopted the approach of incorporating later comments where the first mention of a particular topic was made. Generally, I maintained the organization established by the original themes of the individual interviews, although I occasionally moved or interspersed passages or sections when it seemed appropriate for the sake of the narrative. Throughout, Stern was closely involved in the editing process, helping to flesh out the text or suggesting that particular passages ought to be deleted or reinstated. David Fishman, Jacob Tilove, and Sarah Acheson at Stern's office and Patrick Ciccone at Columbia diligently checked over the facts and identified sources for both the annotations to the text and the thumbnail visual references that run under the text.

Unlike many oral histories, both interviewer and interviewee always intended this document to be published. As Stern mentions in the introduction, it is the second of two sets of recorded interviews in which Johnson recounted his life story. The first, conducted by Peter Eisenman (the only other architect as close to Johnson as Stern), was acquired by Johnson's architect partner John Burgee because he feared that its publication would damage the firm's reputation.[11] To avoid such complications, this oral history was undertaken with the express understanding that it would remain on deposit in a university archive in perpetuity and could only be published after the architect's death, thereby ensuring that Johnson's candid reflections would eventually see the light of day.

Understanding that these interviews would only be published after his death, Johnson felt free to speak about topics that he had previously avoided, most notably the open secrets of his political activities of the 1930s and their impact on his life, as well as his homosexuality, and to give his frank opinion with regard to other people in his life. Undertaken prior to Franz Schulze's biography, these interviews fill out the picture we

---

11. Franz Schulze, *Philip Johnson. Life and Work* (Chicago: University of Chicago Press, 1996), 372–374.

have of Johnson, giving us a better sense of him as an individual, of his psychological and emotional history and the motivations for his actions.

But Burgee was not mistaken in his concern about what Johnson might say. Taped conversations can be dangerous, as Richard Nixon learned in his misguided attempt to document his informal activities as an aid for writing his memoirs. This document, too, is dangerous with respect to the light it sheds on the complicated politics of modern architecture. In his famous introduction to the book *Five Architects* (edited by Eisenman and with a conclusion by Johnson), architectural historian Colin Rowe suggested that in bringing modern architecture to the United States for their 1932 exhibition on the "International Style" at MoMA, Henry-Russell Hitchcock and Philip Johnson stripped it of its ideology. These interviews reveal that the situation was not so clear-cut.[12]

First, as the conversation comprising Chapter 2 reveals, by situating the 1932 exhibition, the research that led up to it, and the subsequent migration of Ludwig Mies van der Rohe and Walter Gropius to the United States, Johnson makes it clear that the European scene was far from homogeneous. In surveying contemporary architecture in Europe, Johnson and Hitchcock turned to figures—most notably Mies, J. J. P. Oud, and Le Corbusier—who shared their interests in *"an architecture still,"* instead of others who were more concerned with mobilizing modern architecture in the service of political causes like affordable social housing.[13] As Johnson points out, that debate raged not only in Europe, but also in the United States—where Lewis Mumford's influence was strong—long after the exhibition had closed.

Second, the interview reveals that Johnson by no means stripped modern architecture of politics, though he did make a decided shift from social issues and international politics to the politics of a particular field of cultural production. Once Johnson turned to architecture as a career, politics for him became first and foremost a matter of establishing personal connections, of creating links between the architectural, artistic, and business elites of his time. Here another comparison with Rowe is apt. Often puzzled by Rowe's apparent fixation on the genealogy of European royalty, guests invited to the frequent dinner parties at his home in Ithaca, New York, in the early 1990s often asked why this brilliant architectural historian focused on what appeared to be parlor trivia. But for Rowe, this wasn't a trivial pursuit. On the contrary, he studied the nature and power of such relationships because he understood that they in fact had shaped nineteenth-century modernity. To focus on political history as a series of battles over ideology or geographical spheres of influence is to ignore the powerful role of personal relationships that have endured through the courtly era into modernity. In this light, Johnson's endless discussion of who he knew, when he knew them, and what connections he was able to make amounts to less of a fixation on biographical trivia than a dangerous history, a narrative diagram of a power network that could not be revealed during his lifetime.

If at various points in these interviews Johnson opines that he was not a very good architect or thinker, never does he question his prowess as a networker. And if almost any conventional interview with such a major figure in the world of architecture would focus on buildings, in these tapes Johnson focuses on his connections, laying bare his network of influence as a construct more formidable than any building he designed.

----

12. Rowe, "Introduction," *Five Architects* (New York: Wittenborn & Company, 1972), 4.

13. From Hitchcock and Johnson, *The International Style*, 106. As well as the section on Hitchcock in Chapter 1.

Even as he talks about his own buildings, Johnson's primary focus is on the patrons who commissioned them.

In the end, this oral history still leaves us with unanswered questions. A period of six years of Johnson's life during the 1930s remains vague and will very likely always remain so. One has the distinct impression that Johnson himself saw the time as wasted, that he considered his political undertakings to have been a needless detour, and also that he utterly lost a certain amount of time during a period of deep depression. Johnson's interest in art is addressed, but not in enough depth to understand how he made his choices or how his interest in art related to his role at MoMA. Crucial questions of his relationship to Stern and Eisenman and his understanding of postmodernism are barely touched upon. And the interview ends before Johnson's last incarnation, the fascinating about-face from postmodernism that constituted his "Deconstructivist Architecture" exhibition at MoMA in 1988.

But this is the document that we have. It is Johnson's own story, expertly coaxed out of him by Robert A. M. Stern. Coming from beyond the grave, it reveals just how critical Johnson really was in shaping not only the fashions of twentieth-century architecture, but the very shape of the field itself.

Index

Page numbers in bold refer to illustrations.

A

Aalto, Alvar 39

Abbe, Charles 128

Abbott, John E. (Dick) 64

Abramovitz, Max 155, **157**

Afrikanischestrasse Municipal Housing 58, **60**

Åhrén, Uno 39

Ahuja, Raj 180

Aldrich, Nelson 49

Aldrich, William T. 49

Alsop, Joseph 64, 101

American Institute of Architects 113

American Mercury, The 66, 71

Amon Carter Museum 167, 168

Amsterdam school of architecture 32

Anderson, Judith **8**, 9

Anderson, Warren 167

Andrews, John 12

anti-Semitism 69, 70

Antonucci, Emil 145

architect-client relationships 104, 119, 120, 125, 126, 143, 144, 146, 157, 167, 172

architects

    camaraderie among 99, 129, 130, 133, 149, 182, 184, 188

    competition between 188, 189

Architects Collaborative, The 88, 89

Architects for Social Responsibility 130

Architectural League of New York 11, 12, 183

architecture

    influences on Johnson 23, 27, 85

    Johnson's early interest in 20, 22, 25, 60, 72

proportion in 52, 57, 169, 173

art

    collecting 50, 187

    Johnson's early interest in 18, 24, 34, 109

    placement in buildings 143, 145, 146, 162, 163, 170

Art and Architecture Building, Yale University 11, **11**

Art Deco 33

Art Nouveau 18

Arts, The 27, **27**

9 Ash Street, Cambridge, Mass. **90**, 91, 94, 103

Asia House 158, **158**, 159

Asplund, Erik Gunnar 39

AT&T Building 164, 170, 178, 189, **189**

Auden, W. H. 34

automobiles

    Johnson's affinity for 25, 64

    Johnson's travels in 28, 29, 30, 33, 72

B

Balanchine, George 152, 161, 162

Barcelona Pavilion 85, 86

Barnes, Edward Larrabee 89, **89**, 125

Barnes, Mary Elizabeth Coss 89

Barr, Alfred H. 28, **28**, 44, 47, 48, 50, 53, 60, 62, 67, **67**, 71, 72, 74, 105, 109, 110, 117, 137, 163, 165, 171

Barr, Margaret Scolari 67

Battery Park 160

Bauer, Catherine 63

Bauhaus

    Building 50, 54, 55, **55**, 58

    Masters Houses **56**

movement 30, 57, 85

Baum, Joseph 144, 145, 146

Bayer, Herbert 55

Bayley, John Barrington 80

Beach Pavilion 82

Beaux-Arts 89, 98

37 Beekman Place, New York City 45, 46

Behrens, Peter 38, 58, 149

Belluschi, Pietro 156, 157, 159

Berlage, Hendrik P. 149

Berlin Building Exposition 58

Berlin, Isaiah 101

Bijvoet, Bernard 32

Blackburn, Alan 63, 63, 64, 69, 72

Blake, Peter 116, 117

Bliss, Mildred Barnes 152

Bofill, Ricardo 171, 172

Bogner, Walter 84, 85, 91

  Bogner house 91

Bogues, Frank Ellis 21

Boissonnas, Sylvie and Eric 125

  Boissonnas house 125, 126

Booth house, Mr. and Mrs. Richard E. 105,
  106, 106, 107, 171

Boston Public Library 175, 179

Bowman, Irving and Monroe 42

Breuer, Marcel 55, 58, 78, 85, 94, 122, 138, 184

  Breuer house 88, 88

Bronfman, Samuel 136, 138, 143, 144

Brooklyn Eagle 33

Buchanan, George 134

Built in U.S.A.: Post-War Architecture
  exhibition 116

Bunshaft, Gordon 10, 154, 157, 157, 158, 159, 178

Burgee, John 12, 14, 64, 176, 176, 177, 178, 179,
  188, 189

C

Cairo 11

Callery, Mary 94, 118, 167

Candela, Rosario 44

Carlhian, Jean-Paul 134

Cartier 38, 60, 61

Castelli, Leo 34

CBS Building 149

Century Association 149, 184, 188

Charlottesville Tapes, The 14

Chartres Cathedral 142

Cheney, Sheldon 47

Church Street Restaurant 81

City Employment Office, Dessau, Germany
  56, 56

Clark, Stephen 72

Clauss, Alfred 32, 46, 47

Clauss & Daub 73

Cleveland, Ohio 16, 18, 63, 71

Cohen, Elaine Lustig 145

color 53, 54

  in architecture 51, 126, 127, 162, 185

Columbia University 14, 162

columns 94, 112, 121, 156, 171

communism 34, 54, 55, 58, 62, 69, 77, 79, 80, 81,
  130, 131

  Johnson's involvement with 62

Congrès International de l'Architecture
  Moderne (CIAM) 86, 87

Congress Street Office Building 82

Cornell University 117, 121, 122

Coughlin, Father Charles Edward 69, 69

craftsmanship 138

  custom 35, 38, 45, 60, 61, 146, 147

Cranbrook school 101

Crandall, Lou R. 138, 143, 144

Cutler, Robert W. 12

D

Dade County Cultural Center, Miami,
  Florida 105

Dahl, Taffy 127

Daily News Building 46, 140

Dalton, John 13

Damaz, Paul 184

Danes, Gibson 183

Dartmouth College 156

Daub, George 46, 47

Dayton, Kenneth 185, 186, 187

Dearstyne, Howard 55

deButts, John 189

de Klerk, Michel 32

de Mandrot House 37, 105, 171

DeMars, Betty Bates 90

DeMars, Vernon **90**

de Menil, Christophe 120

de Menil, Dominique Schlumberger 118, 119, 125, 168

de Menil house 118, 120, **120**, 121, 124

de Menil, John 118, 167, 168

de Menil Museum 119

Demos, Raphael 23, 26

Dempsey, John 50, **63**

Dennis, Lawrence 66, **67**, 69, 71, 76, 96, 97

Depression (era) 41, 50, 62, 66, 72

Der Querschnitt 34

Deskey, Donald 32

Dessau Employment Office (Arbeitsamt) 56

Dessau Törten 56

de Stijl 42

Dewey, John **61**

d'Harnoncourt, René 165, 166

Das Neue Frankfurt 57

Dobbs Ferry Tower 40, **40**, 46

Dodge House 42

Dow, Alden 104

Drexler, Arthur 12, 38, 116, 117, **118**, 123, 130

Dudley, George 167

Dudok, Willem 32

Duiker, Johannes 32

Dumbarton Oaks Research Library 152, **153**

Dutch modern architecture
see Amsterdam School

Dyer, J. Milton 18

Dymaxion House 43

E

Eames, Charles 100

Earhart, Amelia 60, **61**

education
Johnson's academic progress 19, 21, 24, 26, 28, 37, 76, 77, 79, 92

Eight Automobiles: An Exhibition Concerned with the Esthetics of Motorcar Design (MoMA Exhibition #488) 117, **117**

Eisenman, Peter D. **13**, 14, 70, 131, 188

Elmer Holmes Bobst Library and Study Center 171, 172, **173**, 174

entryways 52, 53, 120, 141, 142, 143, 149, 174, 185

Eriksson, Nils Einar 39

F

facades 154, 158, 172, 176

Fallingwater 11

Farney house, Mr. and Mrs. Eugene 103, **103**, 104, 118

Farnsworth, Dr. Edith 94

fascism 69, 96, 97

Fathy, Hassan 11

Federal Bureau of Investigation 76

Ferriss, Hugh 47

Fifty-by-Fifty House 121

242 East Fifty-second Street, New York City **124**, 125, 133, 139

424 East Fifty-second Street, New York City 44, **44**

15 West Fifty-third Street, New York City 14, **14**

Fischl, Eric 187

Flechtheim, Alfred 34

241 East Forty-ninth Street, New York City 46, **46**, 67

Foster, Richard 12, 64, 122, 128, 147, 171, 172, 175, 179, 184, 188

fountains 141, 145, 146, 181

Frank, Josef 39

Franzen, Ulrich J. 93, 94

Frost, Henry Atherton 84, **84**, 85

Fry, Varian 62, **62**

Fuller Company 138

Fuller, Richard Buckminster 43

functionalism 51, 53, 57, 62, 80, 92, 99, 142

furniture and furniture design 45, 52, 53, 58

Dymaxion House 43

G

gatehouses 52, 53

Gatje, Robert 122

Gehry, Frank **13**

General Foods headquarters 138

General Motors 100

geometry 169

George Howe: Toward a Modern American Architecture 8, 28

German language 25, 51, 96

German Workers Party 33

Germany 87

    Johnson's architectural influences from 29, 34, 36, 57, 58, 99, 117

    Johnson's extended travels in 25, 34, 35, 37, 50, 57, 69, 72, 73, 76, 77

    Johnson's perceived allegiance to 96, 123

    Johnson's political influences from 62

Gilpatric, Roswell 103

Giurgola, Romaldo 122, 184, 185, 186

glass 158, 166, 177

Glass House 8, **13**, 105, 116, 118, **119**, 137, 142, 149, 182

    architectural gatherings 9, 10, 12, 182, 183, 184, 185, 188

    structures on 114, 118, **132**, 133, 140, 149, **182**, **183**

Goldberg, Bertrand 55

Goodwin, Philip L. 67, 68, 72, 74, 129, 130

Goodyear, A. Conger 64

Gores, Landis 123

Göring, Hermann 73

Graves, Michael **13**, 185, 189

Greenberg, Allan 57

Gropius house 85, **85**, 88

Gropius, Ise Frank 86

Gropius, Walter 10, 30, 50, 54, 55, 56, 57, 58, 78, 80, 85, 86, 87, **87**, 91, 92, 94, 95, 102, 169

Gwathmey, Charles **13**, 127, **134**, 185, 188

H

Hackley School 21, 22

Haesler, Otto 57, 71

Hagmann, John 9

Hale, Peter P. 89

Hamilton, Edward A. 10

Hanfstaengl, Ernst Putzi 33

Harkness, John "Chip" 89

Harkness, Sarah Pillsbury 89

Harris, Cyril 162

Harrison & Abramovitz 154

Harrison, Wallace K. **47**, 48, 110, 124, 154, 156, **157**, 160, 163, 167

Harvard University 22–27, 28, 33, 37, 43, 44, 46, 65, 74, 76–94, 98, 104, 123, 152

Heckscher Building 44

Heimatstil 72

Henry Ford II house 105, **105**

Hester, James 171

Hidden House

    see 751 Third Avenue

Hillside Home School 41, **41**

Hilversum, Amsterdam 32

Hines, Gerald D. 138, 139, 147, 172, 180, **180**, 181, 188, 189

historicism 151

Hitchcock, Henry-Russell 8, 9, 27, **27**, 28, 29, 30, 32, 34, 37, 39, 40, 42, 50, 51, 53, 54, 57, 58, 68, 72, 80, 109, 110, 115, 123, 124, 156

Hitler, Adolf 33, 35, 72, 87, 131, 189

Hoffmann, Josef 39

Hohnsbeen, John 133

Holabird, John A. 72, 74

Hollander, Michael **134**

Hollein, Hans 12

homosexuality 9, 21, 23, 24, 25, 34, 50, 89, 99, 110

Hood, Raymond 40, 41, 46, **47**, 178

Hook of Holland 27, 32, **32**

House in Lincoln, Massachusetts **82**

House on the Mesa **42**

House, student project **83**

Houston, Texas 118, 120

Howe, George 9, 29, 38, 47, 48, 61, 89, 91, 96, 99, 128, **128**, 130, 131, 132, 133

Howe house 131, **131**

Howe & Lescaze 48

Hudnut, Joseph "Vi" 78, **78**, 86, 87, 89, 91, 92, 102

Hughes, Robert 186

Huxtable, Ada Louise 145, 160

Huxtable, L. Garth 145

I

IDS Center 176, **177**, 185
Illinois Building, "Mile-High" 138
Illinois Institute of Technology chapel 135
independent wealth 28, 34, 41, 48, 50, 54, 64,
   107, 108, 109, 119
International Style 28, 39, 42, 50, 73, 80, 84,
   104, 105, 110
   Johnson's enthusiasm for 50
*International Style: Architecture Since 1922,
   The* 8, 27, 28, 29, 37, 41, 73, 77, 84
In the Nature of Materials 72
Isherwood, Christopher 34, 50

J

Jacobs, Robert Allan 12, 139
Jadwin, Edgar 20
Jarrett, James 169, 180
Jeanneret, Pierre 52
Jefferson National Expansion Memorial
   Gateway Arch 170
Johansen, John M. 84, 90, 94, 126, 184, 187, 188
Johns, Jasper 105, 163, 171
Johnson, Homer Hosea 16, 17, **17**, 18, **18**, 20, 21,
   23, 31, 98, 107, 108, 148, 188
Johnson, Jeannette 16, **16**, **18**, 25, 35, **63**
Johnson, Louise Pope 16, 17, 18, **18**, 21, 23, 25,
   28, 31, 32, 34, 35, 108, 109
Johnson, Ruth Carter 167, 170
Johnson, Samuel 22
Johnson, Theodate 16, **18**, 20, 25, 35, 46, **63**, 65,
   66, 70, 97, 108, 110
juries (architectural) 90

K

Kahn, Ely Jacques 32, 139, 140
Kahn & Jacobs 12, 139, 141, 147
Kahn, Louis I. 9, 84, 129, 130, **130**
Kamiya, Takeo **12**
Kandinsky, Wassily 54, 55
Kaufman, Donald 127
Kaufmann Jr., Edward 49

Kelly, Richard 140, 144, 146
Kiesler, Frederick 86
Kings Road House 42
Kirstein, Lincoln 23, 24, **24**, 46, 58, 62, 68, 69,
   70, 97, 98, 110, 112, 132, 133, 152, 153, 159, 161,
   162
Kirstein Tower **132**, 133
Klee, Paul 50, 54, 55
Kleihues, Josef Paul 58
Klein, George 188
Kneses Tifereth Israel synagogue 125, 126,
   126, 140, 147

L

Lambert, Phyllis 10, 136, **136**, 138, 141, 143, 144,
   145, 148, 149, 153
Lapidus, Morris 88
League of Nations 20
League to Enforce Peace 20
Le Corbusier 29, 30, 40, 41, 53, 92, 110, 121,
   122, 149, 169, 170, 171, 172
Leighton, Constance Crocker 94
Lemke house 58, **59**
Lemke, Karl 58
Lerski, Helmar 34
Les Barrières, Paris 20
Lescaze, William 47, 48
Lewerentz, Sigurd 39
licensing 106, 112, 113, 115, 134, 135, 140
Lieb house 185
Liebknecht, Karl 58
lighting 115, 119, 140, 146, 162
   considered unsuccessful 38
Lincoln Center 151–164, **154**, **155**, **157**, **163**,
   165, 167, 176
   Damrosch Park 160
   Daniel and Florence Guggenheim Band
   Shell 160
   Juilliard School 155, 159
   Metropolitan Opera 155, 156
   plaza 156, 157
   Vivian Beaumont Theater **156**, 157
Lipchitz, Jacques 170
Lippold, Richard 146

Lipstick Building
  see 885 Third Avenue
Loeb house **108**, 109
Logue, Edward 184, 186, 187, 188
Long, Huey 62, 63, **63**, 64, 65, 69
Louchheim, Joseph H. 100
Louis Sullivan, Prophet of Modern
  Architecture 29
Lovell Beach House 42, **43**
Lovell House 42
Luckman, Charles 136
Lustig, Alvin 145
Lutyens, Sir Edwin Landseer 125
Luxemburg, Rosa 58

M

Machine Art (MoMA Exhibition #34)
  59, 60, **61**
Manley, John 147, 179
Manny, Carter 84, 89, 176
Manufacturers Trust Company 158
marble 86, 172
Markelius, Sven 154, 160
Massachusetts Institute of Technology 92
Mathews, Edward J. **157**
May, Ernst 57
McAndrew, John 49, 50, **50**, 67, 72
McGraw-Hill Building 40
Mellor, Meigs and Howe 129, 131
Mencken, H. L. 66
Mendelsohn, Eric 100
Merrick, Dick **84**
Meyer, André 174
Meyer, Hannes 50, **50**, 54, 55, 58, 80
Mielziner, Jo 156, **157**, 161
Mies van der Rohe, Ludwig 8, 29, 30, 37, 38, 41,
  44, 45, 51, 54, 55, 57, 58, 59, 67, 72, 73, 74, 78, 84, 85,
  86, 87, 92, 94, 95, 99, 102, 105, 107, 109, 110, 111,
  112, **112**, 116, 120, 121, 122, 123, 124, 125, 132, 134,
  135, **136**, 137, 138, 139, **140**, 141, 143, 144, 147, 148,
  163, 169, 170, 173, 176, 177
Mies van der Rohe (exhibition) 111, **112**
military service 94–101
models 41, 42, 84, 86, 115, 157

Modern Architecture—International Exhibition
  27, 41, 59
Modern Architecture: Romanticism and
  Reintegration 28, 29
modernism 12, 28, 29, 30, 42, 101, 103, 107, 123, 131,
  166, 175
Moholy-Nagy, László **30**, 55
monumentalism 80, 81
Monument to the November Revolution,
  Berlin-Lichtenberg, Germany 58, **59**
Moore, Charles W. 12, **13**, 183, 184, 185, 188
Moore, Henry 156
Morgenthau, Henry 20
Morrison, Hugh 29
Morris, William 29
Mosely, Oswald 75
Moser, Werner 59
Moses, Robert 153, 160, 166, 167
Mother's House 185, 186
Mumford, Lewis 63, 148
Munson-Williams-Proctor Arts Institute 167,
  168, **168**
Museum of Modern Art 8, 12, 28, 36, 43, 47, **48**,
  59, 64, 67, **68**, 71, 74, 85, 89, 105, 107, 109, 111, 123,
  130, 144, 152, **165**, 166, 167
  Abby Aldrich Rockefeller Sculpture Garden
    165, **165**, 166
  architecture department of 48, 49, 116, 137
  design of 67, 68, 72, 74
  Grace Rainey Rogers Memorial 117, 118, **118**,
    123, 175
  Johnson as curator 59
Museum Tower
  see 15 West Fifty-third Street
music
  Johnson's proficiency in 21, 22, 44, 71
Muthesius, Hermann 29

N

Nabokov, Vladimir 101
Nadelman, Elie 162
Nathan, George Jean 67
Nazi Party
  architecture of 73

political group 72, 87

Nelson, George 117

Neuhaus Jr., Hugo V. **78**, 79

Neuhaus residence 79, **79**

Neutra, Richard J. 10, 42

Newbold Estate, Arthur E. **131**

Newburgh, New York 121

New Canaan, Conn.

    architectural community 183, 184, 185,
      187, 188

    Glass House estate

    see Glass House

    Johnson's architectural practice in 113,
      114, **114**, 115

New Harmony, Indiana 168

New London, Ohio 69, 98, 99

New York

    Johnson's architectural practice in 102,
      104, 105, 115, 128, 140

New York Herald Tribune 64, **65**

New Yorker 148

New York State Theater 147, 151, **152**, **155**,
    161, 164, **164**, 170

New York Times 42, 58, 64, 145, 178

New York University 174, **174**

    see also Elmer Holmes Bobst Library
      and Study Center

New York World's Fair 154, 166, **166**, 167

Niagara Falls Convention Center 167

Nichols, Marie 146

Noguchi, Isamu 159

Noyes, Eliot 114, 184, 187, 188

O

Objects 1900 and Today (MoMA Exhibition
    #27) 60, **61**

Old People's Home for the Henry and
    Emma Budge Foundation, Frankfurt am
    Main, Germany 58, **59**

Oneto House, Mr. and Mrs. George J. 80, **80**

Ordensburgen 73

ornament

    in architecture 40, 46, 92

Östberg, Ragnar 39

Oud, Jacobus Johannes Pieter 27, 30, **30**, 51,
    71, 75

Owen, Jane Blaffer 168, 170

P

Pacelle, Mitchell 13

Pahlmann, William 145

Palais Garnier 164

Paley, William S. 165, 166

Palladio 33

Parc des Buttes Chaumont, Paris 20

patrons and patronage 48, 125, 129, 158, 165,
    167, 168, 169, 170, 175, 181, 187, 188, 189

Pei, Ieoh Ming 92, 93, 137, 148, 149

Pelli, Cesar **13**, 125

Perkins, G. Holmes 84, 92

Persius, Friedrich Ludwig 34, 35, **36**, 58

Peter, John 10

Pevsner, Nikolaus 87

Philadelphia Saving Fund Society Building
    38, 47, 61

pillars and pilotis 51, 52, 73

Pinehurst, North Carolina 18, 31, **31**, 32

placement in buildings 143

Poelzig, Hans 58

politics

    Johnson's political aspirations 69

    Johnson's alleged right-wing affiliations
      33, 48, 66, 67, 69, 70, 71, 72, 75, 76, 81, 110,
      123, 125, 130

Pratt Institute 122, 128

R

Radiator Building 46

RCA building 140, 152

Read, Helen Appleton 33, **33**

Reagan, Ronald 66

Reed, Henry Hope 80

Reich, Lilly 38, **38**, 44, 58, 74

Reminiscences of Philip Cortelyou Johnson:
    Oral History, 1985 15

Republican Party 19, 20

Republic National Bank 174, 181

Resor, Stanley 120

Reynolds Metals Company 11

Rhode Island School of Design 10

ribbon windows 42, 54, 166

Richards, Charles R. 61

Riddle, Alfred 17

Riddle, Theodate Pope 17

Robertson, Jaquelin T. 14, 104, 100

Roche, Kevin 168, 188

Rockefeller, Abby Aldrich 28, 47, 49, 67

Rockefeller Center 152, 153

Rockefeller Guest House
    see 242 East Fifty-second Street

Rockefeller, John D. 3rd 153, 157, **157**, 158,
    159, 167

Rockefeller, Mrs. John D. 3rd 48, 124, 144,
    159, 170

Rockefeller, Nelson A. 48, 110, 124, 151, 152,
    153, 159, 160, 161, 163, 164, 165, 166, 167

Rodgers, Richard 161

Römerstadt, der 57

Roofless Church 168, 169, **169**, 170

roof styles 73, 74

Roosevelt, Franklin Delano 63, 66

Rorimer, Louis 18

Rosenquist, James 146

Rowe, Colin 183

Row houses, Johnson's student project
    83

Rudolph, Paul 9, 11, **12**, 92, 93, 99, 100, 122,
    127, **134**, 147, 148, 168, 188

Ruskin, John 29

S

Saarinen, Aline Bernstein Louchheim
    100

Saarinen, Eero 10, 86, 99, 100, 137, 138, 148,
    154, 156, 157, **157**, 159, 168, 170

Saarinen, Eliel 101, 157

Saarinen, Lillian Louisa Swann 100

Salle, David 187

Sanssouci Gardens, Potsdam 34

Schindler, Rudolph 42, 43

Schinkel, Karl Friedrich 34, 58, 74, 169

Schinkelschüler 34

Schlesinger, Jr., Arthur M. 81

Scully, Vincent 8, 9, 32, **134**, 184

Seagram Building 8, 10, 125, 136–150, **137**,
    140, **142**, **148**, 154, 185
    critical reception of 148
    Four Seasons Restaurant 139, 141, 142,
        142, 143, 144, 145, 146
    interior and exterior details 140, 141,
        143, **143**, 145, **145**, 146, **146**

Sheldon Memorial Art Gallery 174, 175, **175**

Sheldon, Olga Nielsen 175

Shell Building **74**, 75

Shirer, William 70, 72, 78, 87, 95, 123

Silsbee, Joseph Lyman 41

Skidmore, Owings & Merrill 12, 156, 157

Soby house, James Thrall **123**, 124

Social Justice 69, 70, **70**

Spaces of Abraxas 171

Speer, Albert 72, 73, 186

staircases 53, 57, 58, 133, 142, 143, 159, 164,
    173, 175

Stam, Mart 57, 58, 59

Standard Oil Company Filling Station,
    Cleveland, Ohio 73, **73**

Stein, Michael 53

Stevenson, John R. 167

Stirling, James 122, 183

Stockholm Exhibition 39, **39**

Stockholm Public Library 39, **39**

Stockholm Town Hall 39, **39**

stone 131, 140, 172, 175

Stone, Edward Durell 67, 68, 72

Stonorov, Oskar 133

Stotesbury, Mrs. Edward T. 129

Stubbins, Hugh 85, 92, **92**

Sullivan, Louis 29

Sullivan, Mrs. Cornelius J. 47

Swanson, J. Robert 100

T

Tageblatt 33

Taliesin East 41

Tange, Kenzo **12**

Taut, Bruno 30

teaching 121, 122, 128

technology 169

Tessenow, Heinrich 73

751 Third Avenue, New York City 65, **66**, 77

885 Third Avenue, New York City 178, 180

Tigerman, Stanley **13**

Times Square 181

Todd, John 152, 153

Townsend Farm barn 98, **98**

Transco Tower 181

travels (Johnson's)

    Chicago, Illinois 29

    Czechoslovakia 39, 50

    Egypt 23

    England 22

    Geneva, Switzerland 20

    Germany 25, 50, 54

    Grand Canyon **22**

    Greece 23

    Italy 23

    London, England 75

    Montana 22

    Netherlands 23, 30

    Paris, France 20, 51

    Siena, Italy 20

    Stockholm, Sweden 39

    Switzerland 70

    Vienna, Austria 39, 57

    Washington, DC 65

Tucker house, Carll III 185

Tudor-style architecture 18

Tugendhat family 37, 38

Tugendhat house 37, **37**, 54

Tunnard, Christopher 79, 80, **80**

Tycon Towers 147

U

United Center Bank Tower 179, 180

United Nations 110, 154

V

van Beuren, Michael 55

Van Nelle Factory, Amsterdam 32

Venturi, Robert 12, **134**, 184, **184**, 185, 186, 188

Versailles, Treaty of 20

Vers une architecture 30

Villa at Mathes 37

Villa Savoye **42**, 51, **51**, **52**, 53, 54

Villa Stein **52**, 53, **53**

Völkischer Beobachter 33

Voorhees, Walker, Foley & Smith 139

W

Walker, John 172

Walker, Ralph T. 138

Warburg apartment

    see **37** Beekman Place

Warburg, Edward M. M. 24, **24**, 45, 62, 69

Warburg, Felix 45

Warhol, Andy **13**, 171

Washington, D.C. 99, 102, 133

Water Gardens, Fort Worth, Texas 170

Weese, Harry 100

Weissenhofsiedlung, Stuttgart, Germany 57, 172

Wellesley College 28

Wesleyan University 28

Wharton, Edith 25

Whitehead, Alfred North **26**, 27, 71

Whitehead, Mrs. Alfred North 27

Whitney, David 10, **10**, **13**, 125, 133, 161, 163, 171

Whitney Museum of American Art 33

Wiley Development Company house 111, **111**

Wiley, John 101, 149

Wiley, Robert C. 110, 111, 125

Wiley house, Robert C. 125, **127**

Wilson, Woodrow 20

Wittgenstein house **57**

Wittgenstein, Ludwig 57

Wolf house, Benjamin V. 121, **121**

World War I 25

World War II 25, 30, 66, 68, 69, 75, 76, 81, 103, 107, 110, 123, 133

Wright, Frank Lloyd 11, 31, 40, 41, 46, 54, 72, 104, 107, 109, 120, 122, 123, **123**, 137, 138, 172

Wrightsman, Charles 172

Wurster, William Wilson 89, **90**

Wyman, Jeffries 86

Y

Yale Mathematics Building 185

Yale School of Architecture 8, 9, 10, 11, 79

Yale University 117, 122, 129, 130, 132, 133,
    134, 158, 183, 184

Yale University Art Gallery 129, **129**

Young, Edgar 159

Z

Zonnestraal, Amsterdam 32